D0142882

BABIES MADE US MODERN

Placing babies' lives at the center of her narrative, historian Janet Golden analyzes the dramatic transformations in the lives of American babies during the twentieth century. She examines how babies shaped American society and culture and led their families into the modern world to become more accepting of scientific medicine, active consumers, open to new theories of human psychological development, and welcoming of government advice and programs. Significantly, Golden also connects the reduction in infant mortality to the increasing privatization of American lives. She also examines the influence of cultural traditions and religious practices upon the diversity of infant lives, exploring the ways class, race, region, gender, and community shaped life in the nursery and the household.

Janet Golden is a professor of history at Rutgers University – Camden. She is the author of several articles and books, including *Message in a Bottle: The Making of Fetal Alcohol Syndrome*. She is coeditor of the Critical Issues in Health and Medicine Series at Rutgers University Press.

BABIES MADE US
MODERN

How Infants Brought America into the Twentieth Century

JANET GOLDEN
Rutgers University – Camden

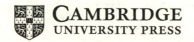
CAMBRIDGE
UNIVERSITY PRESS

CAMBRIDGE
UNIVERSITY PRESS

University Printing House, Cambridge CB2 8BS, United Kingdom

One Liberty Plaza, 20th Floor, New York, NY 10006, USA

477 Williamstown Road, Port Melbourne, VIC 3207, Australia

314–321, 3rd Floor, Plot 3, Splendor Forum, Jasola District Centre,
New Delhi – 110025, India

79 Anson Road, #06–04/06, Singapore 079906

Cambridge University Press is part of the University of Cambridge.

It furthers the University's mission by disseminating knowledge in the pursuit of
education, learning, and research at the highest international levels of excellence.

www.cambridge.org
Information on this title: www.cambridge.org/9781108415002
DOI: 10.1017/9781108227308

© Janet Golden 2018

This publication is in copyright. Subject to statutory exception
and to the provisions of relevant collective licensing agreements,
no reproduction of any part may take place without the written
permission of Cambridge University Press.

First published 2018

Printed in the United States of America by Sheridan Books, Inc.

A catalogue record for this publication is available from the British Library.

Library of Congress Cataloging-in-Publication Data
Names: Golden, Janet, 1951– author.
Title: Babies made us modern : how infants brought America
into the twentieth century / Janet Golden.
Description: New York, NY: Cambridge University Press, [2018] |
Includes bibliographical references and index.
Identifiers: LCCN 2017054703 | ISBN 9781108415002 (hardback) |
Subjects: | MESH: Child Rearing – history | Parent – Child Relations |
Infant Welfare – history | History, 19th Century |
History, 20th Century | United States
Classification: LCC HQ769 | NLM WS 11.AA1 | DDC 649/.1–dc23
LC record available at https://lccn.loc.gov/2017054703

ISBN 978-1-108-41500-2 Hardback

Cambridge University Press has no responsibility for the persistence or accuracy of URLs
for external or third-party internet websites referred to in this publication and does not
guarantee that any content on such websites is, or will remain, accurate or appropriate.

FOR ERIC

CONTENTS

ILLUSTRATIONS

ACKNOWLEDGMENTS

WHEN YOU WORK ON A BOOK for a very long time, you have a very long list of people to thank, and a deep fear of forgetting someone. Let me begin at the beginning. Credit for the idea for this book belongs to Lynn Weiner. We intended to write it together and wrote one article before she bowed out because she was so busy being a dean. And the writing took so long that she became a grandmother before I finished. Lynn and her research assistants provided valuable support, and Lynn read the entire manuscript and offered enormously helpful comments and a few chapter titles. Other wonderful friends read the entire manuscript and gave vital feedback. Laurie Bernstein, Arleen Tuchman, Richard Meckel, Cynthia Connolly, and Benjamin Schneider – I cannot thank you enough. Others who read portions of this work and gave excellent advice include Heather Munro Prescott, Beth Linker, Ben Harris, Jonathan Sadowsky, Patricia D'Antonio, and Christian Warren.

I had the opportunity to give papers based on this work to many audiences, and their questions helped me develop this work. I thank Paula Michaels and the participants in the History Department Seminar at Monash University; Warwick Anderson and the participants in the History on Monday Seminar at the University of Sydney; George Weisz and the participants in the Social Studies of Medicine Departmental Seminar at McGill University; Elizabeth Toon and the participants in the seminar at the Centre for the History of Science, Technology, and Medicine at the University of Manchester; Ellie Lee and the participants in the Centre for Parenting Culture Studies Conference at the University of Kent; and attendees at the Lees Seminar in History at Rutgers University–Camden and the Psychology Department Seminar at Rutgers University–Camden.

ACKNOWLEDGMENTS

I was able to undertake the research for this book and to find the time to write it thanks to a Fellowship for College Teachers from the National Endowment for the Humanities, sabbatical support from Rutgers University – Camden, funding from the Rutgers Research Council, a research support grant from the Radcliffe Institute for Advanced Study at Harvard University, a Charles Donald O'Malley Short Term Research Fellowship in the History and Special Collections for the Sciences at the David Geffen School of Medicine at UCLA, and a Hartman Center Travel Grant from the Duke University Libraries.

A vital form of research support came to me from Emily Abel, who shared all of her detailed notes from the Community Service Society records at the Columbia University Archives and of the Field Nurses Monthly Reports from the Department of the Interior Bureau of Indian Affairs Records at the National Archives. Others who assisted me with information and sent me materials include Jacqueline Wolf, Alexandra Minna Stern, Susan Miller, Cheryl Lemus, Lynn Weiner, and Gabe Rosenberg. Joe Shapiro, Sally Griffith, and Susan Walton shared family baby books with me. I also want to thank my many hosts who kept me going on research trips: Bopper Deyton and Jeffrey Levi, Lynn Weiner and Tom Moher, Margaret Humphreys and Ted Kerin, Ruth Horowitz, Susan Porter, and Eric Luft and Diane Davis Luft.

While working on this project I often told people that I had my own private archivist: Russell Johnson. As curator for history and special collections for the sciences at the UCLA Louise M. Darling Biomedical Library, he collected the baby books and related material that are at the core of my research. I would also like to thank Arlene Shaner, Historical Collections Librarian at the New York Academy of Medicine; Stephen Novak, Head of Archives and Special Collections at the Columbia Health Sciences Library; and Daniel M. May, archivist at the Metropolitan Life Insurance Company, who provided me with extensive help, as well as the staffs and archivists of all the other institutions that opened their doors to me. Archivists and librarians make it possible for us to be historians.

This book could not have been written without my family. My son Ben Schneider brought his editorial skills to this work, and my son Alex Schneider and his partner, Hanna Schwing, visited often and took me to many great meals when I visited Washington, DC, for research. My mother, a proud UCLA alumna, was especially pleased to see me after my long days working in the UCLA archives. My beloved husband, partner, and fellow historian, Eric Schneider, read each draft of this book far more often than anyone can imagine. He died shortly before the manuscript went to press. I dedicate this book to him.

ABBREVIATIONS

AAA	Archives of American Art, Smithsonian Institution, Washington, DC
CHM	Chicago History Museum Research Center, Chicago, Illinois
CHSL	Archives and Special Collections, Augustus C. Long Health Sciences Library, Columbia University, New York, New York
CUA	Rare Book and Manuscript Collections, Columbia University Archives, New York, New York
CYUCLA	Charles E. Young Research Library, UCLA, Los Angeles, California
DURL	David M. Rubenstein Rare Book and Manuscript Library, Duke University, Durham, North Carolina
GPO	Government Printing Office
HART	Hartman Center for Sales, Advertising, and Marketing History, David M. Rubenstein Rare Book and Manuscript Library, Duke University, Durham, North Carolina
HLHU	Houghton Library, Harvard University, Cambridge, Massachusetts
JKFL	John F. Kennedy Library, Boston, Massachusetts
LCK	Logan Clendening History of Medicine Library, University of Kansas Medical Center, Kansas City, Kansas
LOC	Manuscript Division, Library of Congress, Washington, DC
LOV	Library of Virginia, Richmond, Virginia
MANYPL	Manuscripts and Archives Division, New York Public Library, New York, New York

MLIC	Metropolitan Life Insurance Company Archives, New York, New York
NARA	National Archives, Washington, DC
NARA II	National Archives at College Park, Maryland
NLC	Newberry Library, Chicago, Illinois
NMAH	National Museum of American History Archives Center, Smithsonian Institution, Washington, DC
NYAM	The Drs. Barry and Bobbi Collier Rare Book Reading Room, New York Academy of Medicine Library, New York City, New York
NYPL	New York Public Library, New York City, New York
SCRBC	Schomburg Center for Research in Black Culture, New York Public Library, New York, New York
SCRC	Special Collections Research Center, University of Chicago Library, Chicago, Illinois
SLRI	Schlesinger Library, Radcliffe Institute, Harvard University, Cambridge, Massachusetts
SYR	Syracuse University Library Archives, Syracuse, New York
UCLA	Louise M. Darling Biomedical Library, UCLA Biomedical Library, Los Angeles, California

INTRODUCTION
Did Babies Make Us Modern?

D ID BABIES REALLY MAKE US MODERN? Of course not. No single group or event or discovery made America into a modern nation. And what exactly is modern and when did modernity begin? Any effort to construct an answer is to wade into a vast ocean of big ideas and big changes – among them American empire building, expanding suffrage, urbanization, industrialization – and to confront a tsunami of technological developments that reshaped daily life – automobiles, radios, airplanes, telephones, motion pictures. One is more likely to drown than to make sense of how modern beliefs and practices overlaid ones that came to be seen as traditional. This book does not dive into the deep or take the long view of modernization; it looks at small tributaries, examining social life in the twentieth-century United States through the changes in infants' lives. It does not argue that babies transformed the nation from a rural, traditional society into an urban, industrial, fast-paced, and rapidly growing one in which elite citizens developed a new set of cultural norms. Babies didn't develop new ideas, invent new products, alter established political structures, or capsize traditional customs.[1]

How, then, did babies help usher in the modern? The answer is that babies played a critical role in joining ordinary Americans to the modern revolutions of the twentieth century – revolutions in scientific medicine, in consumer culture, in the rise of the social welfare state, and in the understanding of human development and potential. Another way of explaining that is to point to a parallel development. Adolescence was a twentieth-century idea – a concept and a demarcated place in the life course in which people in their teenage years came to be seen as "emerging adults" entering a period of transition from childhood marked by

1

formal education rather than work, by emotional upheavals, and by a strong peer culture. So too was "modern babyhood" defined and created in the twentieth century. It was a life stage in which the individual vulnerability of babies produced a new kind of shared public and private responsibility for protecting and enhancing their welfare.[2]

Modern babies pushed their families and the state to accommodate their needs and to change their practices. To offer an example, recognition of cod liver oil as a preventative for rickets led government agencies to give it away, parents of limited means to buy it, and cod liver oil producers to advertise it widely. An understanding of new biomedical ideas – that rickets and perhaps other ailments could be prevented – spurred both health consumerism and the belief that government agencies should provide help in the form of information and funding for direct services. Both ideas trickled into public consciousness. These were microrevolutions, but revolutions nonetheless. The new ways of living provoked resistance and backlash as well as support. In these instances, babies played a role in maintaining traditional practices. With their frequent illnesses they kept families reliant on local healers and on prayer as well as medicine.

Frequently historians of childhood embrace the concept of agency, arguing that children, once viewed as mastered by adults, need to be understood, at least in part, as creators of their own lives. Babies did not and do not have this kind of agency, but neither were they or are they powerless. Their actions – dying, living, ailing, growing, eating, sleeping, emptying their bowels and bladders, acquiring motor skills – do not change over time, but responses to them and understandings of their meaning do change and in ways that shape and reflect broader structural transformations. In the early decades of the twentieth century infant mortality began to be understood as both a social and a political problem. In the opening decades of the twenty-first century infant deaths are still spoken of, but in ways that reflect knowledge of and concern with the disparities among racial and ethnic groups and awareness of demographic data from other developed nations. Similarly, while some see babies as having agency through the demands they make – to be fed, changed, rocked, or cuddled – it is important to note that not all cultures view babies as having the same demands or even claims to adult attention. The belief that answering the cry of a hungry baby or comforting an infant who wakes in the night is the proper decision changed over time and reflects local circumstances and cultural norms.[3]

A rich lode of historical literature presents information about infant lives, but it often does so without probing babies' actual experiences. Historians of childhood offer overarching accounts of the changing features of children's lives as well as portraits of particular groups of youngsters, establishing models for studying the young. However, these scholars often neglect to fully investigate how the social, economic, and cultural shifts they study shaped the lives of babies. Other scholars engage in close readings of infant care advice literature, making evident what experts wished infants' lives to be, but they give little insight into babies' actual experiences. Yet another strand of historical research follows changing ideas about the responsibilities of parents as new childcare authorities emerged over the course of the twentieth century. All of this work can be mined in order to understand the new theories about infant development and infant care taught to generations of parents. It can also be combined with other sources to illuminate the contrast between ideal practices and lived experiences. Additional useful accounts of babies can be found in writings on the history of motherhood and on the history of parenting with its attendant and shifting priorities and anxieties. It is important too to acknowledge that the interests of mothers and infants can be and have been in conflict, as was the case in the debate over maternity benefits. Keeping new mothers out of the paid labor force allows their infants to receive more attention and care than might otherwise be the case. It also has the effect of limiting mothers' lifetime work opportunities and earnings. As this illustrates, the histories that serve as the foundation of this book can help expose and conceal the ways infants influenced Americans' lives.[4]

Writing the history of babies presents numerous challenges, not the least of which is that infants, which I define as those under one year of age, are inarticulate historical actors. Their lives must be studied, for the most part, by examining the actions and writings of the people who do have agency. We inevitably end up asking what grownups and siblings had to say about babies. And then we question what adults did to shape infants' lives and why they took those steps. What material conditions, cultural values, and secular and religious beliefs influenced adults' actions? But we can in turn ask what role the babies' actions played in determining adults' beliefs and in organizing their social world. By moving back and forth from accounts of individual babies' lives and collective actions on their behalf we can begin to write babies back into American history.

Perhaps the most difficult problem in writing the history of babies is one that scholars preparing synthetic histories of the United States confront: how can you draw useful conclusions about millions of subjects? Approximately 330 million babies were born between 1900 and 2000 (a period for which scholars have relatively good data). The infants that I write about were born between the late 1890s – the dawn of the twentieth century – and the mid-1960s – the end of the baby boom. In describing them, I use the term *baby citizens* when discussing the lives of infants in their families and communities and the term *citizen babies* in reference to the way government agencies conceived of and responded to the very young.

No wars, elections, or demographic transformations provide a neat periodization for the history of modern babies. It is hard to date precisely when infants attached their families to particular new ideas, processes, and products. Did the consumer revolution fully transform the nursery when the majority of babies dressed in purchased rather than homemade infant clothes? Or did consumer culture arrive slowly, reflecting changes in the economy and the growth of advertising that led increasing numbers of families to buy infant formulas or tinned baby food?

Unable to develop a precise chronology of emerging modern babyhood, we must instead view the history of infants' lives as something like a crazy quilt – there are many pieces and much overlaid stitching, but patches of the same material can be seen again and again. The pieces that appear most often include measures of a decline in infant mortality, evidence of a growing reliance on so-called scientific methods of infant care, the expanding production of goods for babies, the arrival of new immigrant groups, the movement of internal migrants from rural areas to cities that challenged and changed beliefs about babies and their care, and the appearance of new ideas about infants' cognitive and emotional development. The crazy quilt analogy makes clear that change is neither orderly nor consistent. So, to the extent the sources make possible, I have chosen to emphasize the variations among babies rather than to smooth out the many textures of their lives. Like all Americans, babies were a diverse group – marked by racial, ethnic, regional, and gender identities, abled and disabled bodies, and most profoundly by the economic circumstances in which they lived. Nevertheless, the microrevolutions named earlier affected them all.[5]

To find the lives of babies I probed diaries, letters, oral histories, newspapers, welfare agency case records, magazines, books, radio scripts, and, most importantly, more than 1,500 baby books. Kept by mothers and recording the lives of individual infants, baby books provide a critical window into nursery life, health practices, material culture, and popular expectations. They are not a representative sample by any means as the majority come from Euro-American families. And they have to be read skeptically. Consider Charlie Flood, born in Red Bud, Illinois, in 1914. According to his baby book, at the age of four months, he burned his face with quicklime. Three months later, he pulled off part of his tongue with a buttonhook. (Toddlerhood wasn't any easier for him; he once got a nail in his foot and on another occasion fell while holding a bottle, leaving glass in his hand.) Charlie's mother carefully recorded each accident in his baby book and he was hardly the only infant to have his calamities written down. Babies fell down stairs, off porches, and out of high chairs and cribs. Some baby books even had places designated for writing down "first tumble." Jeannette Palache's baby book records details of her life following her birth in August 1900 in Cambridge, Massachusetts, including an entry for the following January: "She fell all the way down stairs and did not hurt herself." After World War II, accounts of accidents largely vanished from baby books, although one mother diligently recorded her son's two falls off the bed in 1948. Had baby-proofing improved? Was parenting more vigilant? Were infants less curious and accident-prone? Had home safety programs made a difference? Not likely. It appears that mothers learned not to record the common accidents of babyhood because expectations about parenting and infant life changed. Emergency room records would tell a different story.[6]

Accounts of accidents and their disappearance tell us something about actual babies' lives and about expectations regarding how to care for babies. The same is true of records of physical discipline. They too largely disappeared from baby books after World War II. Most mothers stopped recording the spankings they gave to infants and baby books, which once offered places for recording "first discipline," eliminated this entry. Certainly babies did not cease being punished and, in some instances, parents made notes without the prompts in baby books. One woman wrote in a baby book about spanking her baby's hands for "pulling the davenport fringe." Moreover, individual households and communities may have viewed physical discipline as more or less useful and important and the variations and beliefs and customs do not always appear in baby books.

Reading large numbers of baby books written over many decades, however, can be revealing. They show changes in infant care practices occurring slowly and unevenly and the reasons families jettisoned or adopted them must be inferred from the context. Perhaps spankings ceased or became a marginal practice in the second half of the twentieth century, but we have no reason to assume that they did and a lot of reasons to believe that baby books reflected what mothers wanted to do or were advised to do. Modernization, in this instance, appeared as an intellectual shift. It produced new ideas about what babies ought to experience and what parents ought to be doing or recording as they raised babies.[7]

As disingenuous as baby book entries can be, they can be equally forthcoming about nursery practices that experts saw as valuable or dangerous. The voluminous infant care advice found in print – women's magazines, baby-rearing manuals, health department pamphlets, and radio scripts – makes clear what professionals including doctors, developmental psychologists, and social workers believed. They preached loudly and clearly, but the congregation sometimes ignored their exhortations. In the first half of the twentieth century knowledgeable experts told mothers not to play with their babies. Baby books reveal their advice was not infrequently disregarded. The delights of peek-a-boo and the joy in teaching an infant to wave bye-bye overcame admonishments against overstimulation. More critically, professional dictates about infants' diet and health often could not be followed simply because a family lacked resources. If anything overdetermined the lives of babies, it was the economic conditions of their families, a situation that remains true to this day.

Baby books provide indirect evidence about social class and social capital. Like colonial historians who read inventories of estates to discern a family's wealth, gift lists in baby books offer important clues. Some babies received a cornucopia of toys, blankets, clothes, and dollars; other infants acquired only a few practical items or none at all. The extensive family visiting described in some baby books suggests that many infants had a rich supply of social capital even if their families lacked a decent standard of living. Details of births point to the families' connection to medical institutions and providers, while entries about deaths suggest why families needed the solace provided by religious practice. A baby book begun in 1936 contained a collection of sympathy cards and an account of a funeral for the then three-year-old who died of influenza. Another from 1943 hinted in a mere ten words at an earlier loss: "My second name is in memory of my big brother." Letters to the US Children's Bureau also supply, indirectly, information about the social world of individual infants, while community studies conducted by the Children's Bureau and by social scientists offer more evidence about the effects of poverty and isolation on health and family practices.[8]

Over the course of the twentieth century, babies helped introduce ordinary families to the principles of modern hygiene and to acceptance of medical authority. Much of the professional advice given to mothers – to kill germs, to weigh and measure babies regularly, to feed them at proper times – received a boost from advertisers who promoted the products needed to transform the nursery into a fortress against germs. Manufacturers of consumer goods and advocates for biomedical science formed an uneasy alliance that benefited from the belief that each had something to contribute to the saving of infant lives. At times, however, their partnership broke down, as when doctors wanted their well-to-do patients to visit them for written prescriptions for mixing infant formulas, while formula companies urged patients to buy their premade products. Likewise, doctors wanted the revenue from treating babies suffering from teething or colic; so too did patent medicine sellers.

As infant mortality rates fell, families invested in their infants' futures by saving money and by learning not just what to do to protect their babies' physical health, but to nurture their emotional growth. Modern psychology and new understandings of the self entered households by way of the nursery. Babies became ambassadors of the modern as experts began urging parents to their monitor infants' intellectual growth. Not unexpectedly, middle- and upper-class families with access to medical advice and infant care manuals were first to adopt the protocols of infant monitoring. Baby books and other sources suggest that the habit of psychological and emotional oversight came later to working-class families as their access to health professionals grew and as published materials and radio shows featuring experts taught them about the inner lives of babies.

If twentieth-century babies can be seen as integral to the growing cultural authority of scientific medicine, the robust expansion of the consumer economy, and the rise of new theories of self and society, they can also be seen as critical to the shifts in the relationship of the state to the family. Deemed vulnerable future citizens, babies sparked new government programs, but the growing collective interest in their health and well-being never overcame the belief that their families were ultimately responsible for their lives. Federal government support for babies included both short-lived programs such as the Sheppard-Towner Act, which provided funds for maternity and childcare programs from 1921 to 1929, and the Emergency Maternity and Infant Care Act, which provided assistance to servicemen's wives during World War II. A regular funding stream to the states for maternal and child welfare under Title V of the Social Security Act of 1935 led to more sustained federal involvement with infants. After the baby boom years still other federal and state programs began to assist some infants.

The creation of limited, means-tested efforts nodded to the great irony of twentieth-century babyhood – as collective concern for "our babies" ebbed, with each successful effort to save their lives, private interest in "my baby" grew into an even stronger cultural ideal and federal programs narrowed. The incomplete public commitment to ensuring the welfare of all babies today is not the subject of this book, but it informs every chapter. Babies before and after the twentieth century were economic actors; they have needs that must be met by individuals – parents or other caretakers – and needs that can only be addressed by the broader community and by civil society.

This book ends at the conclusion of the baby boom in 1964. The lives of the babies born after that can be discovered in numerous social science studies, observed from afar in demographic data, unearthed in biographies, revealed in newspaper and magazine articles, and found in institutional records. But many of their experiences are still recounted only in baby books, which have recently migrated to the online world. When the late twentieth-century and twenty-first-century babies grow up to become historians, as some surely will, they can access the baby books electronically and find other material about infants' lives on social media. And they can then look back and discover how infants shaped the postmodern world.

Many babies' lives are recounted in this book. I have changed all of their names when I used their baby books and other family records. However, if those babies grew up and deposited their papers in archives without asking for restrictions, I identified them by name. I also quote from the baby books given to me by friends and, with their permission, use their names. Because the overwhelming majority of baby books and other records come from Euro-American infants, I do not designate their racial or ethnic identification unless it differs from this prevailing one. My hope is that others will explore the materials I used and further explore the lives of babies. For that reason, in the case of the more than 1,600 baby books housed in the collection of the UCLA biomedical library, I have provided a call number, since there are numerous editions of each book.

1

INFANT LIVES AND DEATHS
Incubators, Demographics, Photographs

VISITORS STROLLING THE GROUNDS AT THE Trans-Mississippi Exposition in Omaha, Nebraska, in 1898 might have been tempted to enter the small white building with the words "Infant Incubators with Living Infants" painted over the entryway. Nearing the building, they would have seen other words designed to entice them, including ones boasting that the incubator display mounted in London the previous year (for the celebration of Queen Victoria's Diamond Jubilee) drew 207,000 viewers. The incubator show differed from traditional fairground baby shows and baby parades featuring cute little ones in fancifully decorated strollers because it presented Omaha spectators with the chance to see a struggle against death.[1]

As the nineteenth century came to a close, new efforts got under way to save babies via charity work and government programs. Proponents of baby saving argued that citizens bore a collective responsibility for assisting the nation's most vulnerable members; their opponents believed that parents alone bore responsibility for an infant's survival. People were free to pay admission and gaze at premature babies in incubators, knowing their fees supported the babies' care. But should these spectators be forced to underwrite baby-saving initiatives in their communities, in their states, and across the nation? Collectively and individually, babies placed this question before the American body politic. What was a private matter and what was a public concern? The answer would be debated, sometimes loudly, sometimes not, over the course of the twentieth century. The debate continues to this day. Although babies no longer play the most prominent role in the argument, they ushered it onto the stage, and discussions of their lives and their futures continue to be part of the script.

To think about the collective needs of babies requires seeing them as individuals and as valuable. The plight of thousands of infants and the plight of a few needed to be united in the public consciousness. Visitors to the Trans-Mississippi Exposition had the opportunity to make the connection in several places on the grounds. If they left the main part of the Exposition and explored the adjacent Indian Congress, they could view a hopeful display: Little Spotted Back (his name until his christening), a newborn member of the Omaha Nation. He went on view a mere eight hours after his birth. Unlike the incubator babies, he was not premature, but like them, he was a novelty. His arrival made the front page of the local paper, the *Omaha Daily Bee*, and Frank A. Rinehart, the official Exposition photographer who later became famous for his portraits of Native Americans, took several pictures of him cradled in his mother's arms.[2]

Little Spotted Back represented a Native American population in decline. He and his family, along with the others at the Indian Congress, offered two messages to viewers: a nostalgic and entirely mythic representation of the time when proud Native Americans ruled the land, and a staged presentation of presumed primitive people living outside the modern world of art, science, and culture, as one observer reported. Decimated by disease, war, and forced assimilation, Native Americans shrank in number while mandated relocations confined them to reservations. The population reached its nadir around the time of the Trans-Mississippi Exposition, falling to about a quarter of a million. Little Spotted Back's family lived among approximately 500 Native Americans from different tribes encamped at the thirty-acre Indian Congress – a human display supported by federal funds. Photographs taken there include several of Native American babies in cradles or in the arms of their mothers. What is unclear is whether fairgoers paid to see the newborn Little Spotted Back simply because of the rarity of Native American babies or because they believed, as Social Darwinists proclaimed, that Native Americans were on their way to extinction as higher races surpassed them in a biological struggle to survive.[3]

Designed to highlight development west of the Mississippi River, the Trans-Mississippi Exposition attracted approximately 2.6 million people, nowhere near the 25 million mark reached at the Chicago World

Figure 1.1 Omaha brave – age eight hours, Indian Congress, Omaha,
Nebraska, 1898
Trans-Mississippi and International Exposition
Photographer: Frank Rinehart
Credit: Omaha Public Library

Columbian Exhibition five years earlier. But Omaha was a much smaller
city, of about 100,000 inhabitants in 1900 (as compared to Chicago's
1.6 million that year), and the nation was coming to the end of a five-year
depression. Like other grand expositions, the one in Omaha featured
the human displays loved by crowds, from so-called freak shows on the
midway to special encampments of "primitive peoples" from around the
globe that are now understood as expressions of racism, colonialism,
and rejection of the disabled. Other areas at the Exposition showcased
the modern in the form of new inventions. Futuristic technologies
enchanted visitors who toured the Electrical and Machinery Hall and
paid a dime to gaze at the Roentgen's Wonderful Ray of Light (X-ray)
exhibit. To see the incubator babies or Little Spotted Back, viewers
paid a premium: twenty-five cents. Although the entrance fees were the
same, the messages diverged. Little Spotted Back represented a natural, primitive world ceding ground to a mechanized and modernized

one; incubator babies represented the promise of the modern as new technologies saved lives.[4]

Modern psychologists speak of the "vividness effect" – the compelling personal encounters and stories that can substitute for or even displace scientifically verified evidence. Information that resonates on an emotional level is easily recalled and can shape beliefs about social or political issues in ways that numeric data cannot. Undoubtedly, the accounts of visitors to incubator shows and the stories and pictures of tiny babies in incubators that ran in local newspapers helped propel an interest in infant life at the turn of the century, as did the exhibits of Native American infants. But these were just some of the many presentations of babies as both vulnerable and salvageable that contributed to the rising chorus of concern about infant lives. Moreover, the stories about vulnerable babies proved emotionally powerful precisely because few Americans failed to understand them – infant mortality was a plague on many houses.

The drama of incubator shows – a struggle for life presented in small glass boxes – gave them an outsized cultural presence. The tiny babies captured the imagination of viewers who lined up to see them in Omaha and in the exhibitions that followed. The incubators themselves provided little excitement. As physical structures they consisted of metal boxes with glass sides. The bottom part, beneath the infant's mattress, held a warm-water heating system and the top contained a ventilation system providing fresh air. At a time when the majority of Americans lived in rural areas, familiarity with incubators used to hatch poultry meant that most fairgoers understood how the devices worked, even if they held babies that had already "hatched." The idea that incubators could be used for helping premature infants must have seemed sensible; most efforts to preserve newborns, especially premature ones, involved keeping them warm, a necessity because they had little fat to protect them.[5]

Operating human incubators presented challenges, as did the care of the infants they contained. At the Omaha fair the tiny patients received careful attention from a cadre of nurses supervised by Dr. Martin Couney. As incubator overseer, Couney functioned as both physician and seasoned showman. By the time he arrived in Omaha, he had directed incubator exhibits in Germany, France, and Great Britain. He would subsequently host American baby displays until the eve of America's entry into World War II. Within the incubator buildings trained nurses did the hard work of maintaining the devices and overseeing their hygiene. The babies were often too weak to take milk from the breast or a bottle, and received their nourishment from nurses who fed them through a nasogastric tube or a dropper. Once the infants reached a sufficient weight and appeared to be in good health, they went home.[6]

Infant incubator shows became regular features at expositions and fairgrounds in North America, Europe, and South America in the twentieth century. Following their introduction in Omaha, incubators appeared at the 1901 Pan-American Exposition in Buffalo, New York, in an exhibit that featured, according to the *Buffalo News*, the premature offspring of Apache Indian Princess Ikishupaw and Chief Many Tales. Both the world's fairs and the incubator exhibits they contained received attention from the local press and national magazines. An article about the Buffalo fair in *Cosmopolitan* advised tourists to see the incubator exhibit and described the "little human dynamos" in their "hot-air boxes." The incubator exhibit at the 1904 Louisiana Purchase Exposition in St. Louis, Missouri, served as both a fairgrounds showpiece and a medical research site for pediatrician Dr. John Zahorsky, who published several articles on the care of premature babies in incubators. The cost of saving lives this way, he concluded, made it "questionable whether any hospital or asylum could undertake this work unless the State would give liberal support."[7]

Complicated economics kept infant incubators out of hospitals and on fairgrounds. The incubators cost money, the babies residing in them required intensive nursing care, and with most births taking place at home, transporting fragile premature infants to the hospital (or fairgrounds) presented an additional challenge. Incubator shows attracted paying customers who underwrote the costs involved in saving babies. At the 1915 Panama-Pacific International Exposition in San Francisco, California, the incubator display took in $72,000, nearly $1.7 million in today's dollars. The popularity and profitability of incubator shows inspired a few entrepreneurs to establish permanent exhibitions. From 1905 to 1912 the Wonderland Amusement Park in Minneapolis, Minnesota, contained an "Infantorium," ostensibly a

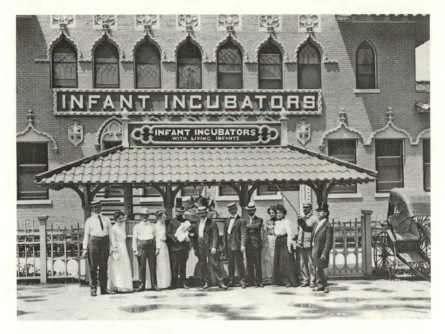

Figure 1.2 The Infant Incubator Building, Pan-American Exposition,
Buffalo, New York, 1901
Photographer: C. D. Arnold
Credit: C. D. Arnold. The Pan-American Exposition
Illustrated (Buffalo, NY: C. D. Arnold, 1901)

scientific exhibit rather than entertainment, and the boardwalks of
Coney Island, New York, and Atlantic City, New Jersey, both hosted long-
surviving incubator shows.[8]

The idea of the incubator as a technological triumph proved somewhat
illusory. Prematurity caused a substantial number of infant deaths in the
late nineteenth and early twentieth centuries and is the single greatest
cause of infant mortality today. Incubator shows served and saved only
a tiny portion of what were then called weakling babies. The exhibits
proved better at attracting paying crowds than at arousing attention
from physicians, and they remained inaccessible to the vast majority
of infants who might have benefited from them. It would take several
decades for incubators to become standard equipment in hospital nurseries. But the principles on which incubators operated, whether for
poultry or humans, would be widely applied, with improvised incubators

being built as needed. Physicians and families faced with caring for premature newborns sometimes constructed their own devices. Instructions for making an incubator appeared in an 1892 medical journal. Well after that, in 1935, a premature baby born in a Liberty, Missouri, "sporting house" survived in a crude replica of an incubator – a box by the stove – while being fed by a dropper.[9]

While the vast majority of babies continued to be born at home, other medical care began moving into hospitals in the early twentieth century. However, many facilities closed their doors to babies because of the deadly diseases that passed so easily from crib to crib. A history of the Welfare Society of Chicago opened with an account from 1902 of an infant dying of diphtheria in his father's arms on the streets. The man took the baby from hospital to hospital seeking help, but there were only sixty-four beds in the city for children with contagious diseases. After the development of the germ theory showing that particular microorganisms caused specific diseases, hospitals slowly transformed from death houses to temples of healing. Measures taken to kill pathogens (antisepsis) and to prevent contamination (asepsis) made surgery and eventually childbirth safer, and this in turn enhanced the status of medical professionals and institutions. As a result, hospitals grew in number, as did the number of hospital beds.[10]

Propelled by advances in scientific medicine, the specialty of pediatrics grew in tandem with the growth of hospitals and children's hospitals in particular. By the opening decades of the twentieth century, a small number of doctors who once made a living caring for patients of all ages found they could maintain a private practice limited to the care of the young. Pediatricians formed professional organizations, created professional journals, found a place in medical school faculties, and established clinical sites of practice in general hospitals, infant health clinics, and children's hospitals. Faced with serving the most vulnerable of patients and recognizing that the survival of infants and children depended on their home environments and their families' resources, pediatricians as a specialty group would form alliances with social reformers, setting them apart from and at times in opposition to their medical brethren.[11]

When world's fairs ended, nearby hospitals sometimes purchased or received as donations the no-longer-needed incubators. At the conclusion of the Pan-American Exhibition, the Buffalo Children's Hospital bought the leftover devices. But it is not clear if hospitals, even if they had one or more incubators, actually made use of them, as some physicians remained skeptical of their value. Obstetrician Joseph B. De Lee established an incubator station in Chicago's Lying-In Hospital at the turn of the century, but the personnel required to maintain the apparatuses and the numerous requests for admission that could not be met led the hospital to first limit the size of the incubator area and then to shut the unit in 1908. Another Chicago physician, pediatrician Julius Hess, opened an incubator station at Chicago's Michael Reese Hospital in 1914. Hess became an ally and supporter of Couney, working with him during the Chicago Century of Progress International Exposition in 1933–1934. The incubator exhibit attracted more than a million patrons, and employed the nursing staff and equipment from the Michael Reese Hospital's Premature Infant Station, which had opened in 1922.[12]

With the expansion of hospital births and hospital nurseries, incubators eventually became standard equipment and physicians learned how to better care for the premature. The effort advanced slowly. Only in 1939, for example, did the New York Hospital inaugurate the first training program in the care of premature babies on the East Coast. In some cases private philanthropy underwrote hospitals' incubator purchases, especially during the Great Depression.

Hospital incubator protocols differed little from the routines used at fairground shows. David Shedd Bradley, born in Evanston Hospital in Illinois in 1920 and weighing only three pounds, ten ounces, remained in an incubator for nineteen days, receiving milk sent from his mother and being kept away from her in the incubator ward. In her diary, David's mother lamented his absence as well as expressed her appreciation for the new technology: "Wish I could see him, but he is being kept in a warm spot." (Bradley survived to become a movie producer.) Mrs. Bradley made no mention of the cost of his care, something that likely limited access to incubators. Unlike the fairground exhibits, which provided free services underwritten by admission fees, hospitals had to find ways of covering their costs and billed patients. But geographic distance from hospitals and hospitals' reluctance to invest in incubators likely remained the most significant barriers to their use.[13]

Americans engaged in the fight for infant survival built on the work of earlier reformers who constructed child-saving institutions such as infant asylums. Their efforts to lower infant death rates also benefited enormously from the development of a public health infrastructure constructed to make cities sanitary and to control epidemics. The provision of clean water, the removal of solid waste through sewer systems, arrangements for publicly supported garbage disposal, and efforts at pest control helped to reduce significantly the infant mortality rate. But not enough. Infant deaths remained frequent and visible. The aggregate data made this clear; the vivid images of incubator babies and other infants made this palpable.

In the early part of the twentieth century, the United States was a young nation in terms of population age and a less diverse one than it would become in later decades. In 1900, the population stood at 76 million and there were more than 2 million births. Households were large, with the most common size being those with seven or more individuals. This was the big picture. Each household and every neighborhood contained a smaller picture that highlighted the vulnerability of the very young. As a scholarly study of Buffalo, New York's Italian community at the turn of the century explained, 60–89 percent of women over thirty had lost at least one child, and among Polish women in the city the rate was nearly as high.[14]

Aware of the high but declining infant death rate and of the ability of both large-scale public health projects and local community-based programs to bring down the death toll, the public gave increasing support to programs designed to save the young. The twentieth-century efforts drew from long-standing traditions of compassion and philanthropy and from the commitment of social activists. The vividness effect – from incubator shows to stories of charitable endeavors that succeeded – helped make an enormous problem seem solvable. Infant deaths in one's own family or among acquaintances and neighbors reinforced the concern, making the infant mortality problem tangible and urgent. Even if infants' actual vulnerability varied according to their family income, the risks of dying were well known to all. And there were always new babies to worry about.

With the development of the germ theory that made the laboratory central to what some called the new public health, the focus of reformers narrowed from cleaning the environment to preventing deadly infections. At the same time, it expanded to emphasize social medicine, an effort that connected the prevention of disease with knowledge of how people lived. Health and welfare advocates turned much of their attention to instructing poor, immigrant mothers in the modern principles of infant care and reaching out to families living in isolated communities. Reformers and health professionals together delivered advice about the rigorous application of household hygiene, especially in the nursery. They achieved significant success, as evidenced by a dramatic drop in infant mortality and morbidity rates. But again – it was not enough.[15]

Combating infant mortality began with asking simple questions: How many babies were born? How many of them died? At what ages did they die? Without national birth and death registration – something that would come later in the twentieth century – the answers remained elusive. The existing data make clear that fertility rates declined after the mid-nineteenth century, but even in the 1900s and 1910s the number of births remained high when compared to later decades. The infant mortality rate, defined as the number of deaths before one year of age per 1,000 live births, fell from its peak but remained distressingly high. In Omaha, Nebraska, host city to the Trans-Mississippi Exposition, the infant mortality rate stood at 140 per 1,000 in 1910. National data from that decade showed clear racial differences with an estimated death rate of 110 per 1,000 for white infants and 170 per 1,000 for African American infants. Reformers, hopeful that interventions would lead to further reductions, focused on infant deaths overall. Concern about racial as well as regional and economic disparities, and programs to address them, would come later and often haltingly.[16]

Viewed against a backdrop of high infant mortality rates and millions of births, media accounts of the lives saved at incubator shows appeared as expressions of hope. The Omaha newspaper, for example, reported that 85 percent of the tiny babies brought to the Trans-Mississippi Exposition incubators survived. Probably the weakest ones died in transit, helping to boost the figure reported by the press. Other incubator shows rejected the smallest babies who were least likely to live, or began collecting data after the infants remained alive for a few days, signaling their vitality and likely survival. Both tactics bolstered the claims about the effectiveness of incubator care. Survival, however, was far from assured. Like the babies they housed, the machines required careful tending. An epidemic of infectious diarrhea led to the deaths of half of the premature babies housed in the Incubator Institute at the Louisiana Purchase Exposition in 1904. When pediatrician John Zahorsky stepped in to run the show, he introduced new health routines, including improved sanitation through frequent disinfection of the incubators and the other medical devices in the exhibition, as well as better infant nutrition and individualized and improved temperature controls.[17]

Despite their limited impact on infant death rates, incubator shows remained crowd pleasers and endured well into the period when incubators became standard equipment in hospital nurseries. Dr. Couney oversaw an incubator exhibit at Luna Park in Brooklyn's Coney Island every summer for nearly forty years, beginning in 1903. It attracted a regular following, including childless women who returned regularly to view the progress of their favorite babies. Couney's daughter Hildegard, a trained nurse, helped organize and run a summer incubator exhibit that ran for years on the Atlantic City, New Jersey, boardwalk. (It would be depicted, decades later, in the television show *Boardwalk Empire*.) Ironically, Hildegard had herself been a premature baby, weighing only three pounds at birth but tipping the scales at 135 pounds as an adult, according to a Utica, New York, newspaper. An incubator saved her life.[18]

Newspaper stories about incubator babies continued to be regular features because they provided reporters and readers the opportunity to share and enjoy some good news. Many of the articles featured reunions of incubator graduates. In August 1904, forty alumni of the incubator shows at Coney Island, New York, Atlantic City, New Jersey, and the Buffalo Pan American Exposition of 1901 met up and had their pictures taken for the newspaper. The *New York Times* reporter covering the event gave special attention to some current incubator denizens and, like other writers, featured surviving multiples, including the Cohen triplets – Rebecca, Rosie, and Rachel – born in 1901 and taken to the Buffalo exhibit, and the wonderfully named Rosofsky triplets – Theodore Roosevelt Rosofsky and his two brothers, William McKinley Rosofsky and

Benjamin Harrison Rosofsky – both of whom still resided in incubators at the time of the gathering.[19]

Decades later, a homecoming of incubator babies from the Chicago Century of Progress Exposition brought together forty-one of the "tiny tots," among them Raymond Bush, who arrived weighing one pound, ten ounces; Claude Chapman, who at birth weighed in at one pound, fourteen ounces; and Judith Hackelman, who at birth tipped the scales at one pound, fifteen ounces. Pediatrician Julius Hess, who worked with Couney at the Chicago Exposition, credited incubator shows for exciting public interest in the prematurely born and for underwriting their care. The "thousands upon thousands" who visited the shows, he wrote, did not realize they were supporting the care of the babies when they bought their tickets.[20]

In 1906 prolific novelist and poet Ellis Parker Butler published the novel *The Incubator Baby* following its serialization in *Good Housekeeping* magazine. Butler imagined the experiences of a tiny incubator inhabitant, a sweet-natured baby named Marjorie. He described Marjorie looking out at the faces of visitors and their reactions to her: "Some expressed the most violent curiosity, some were softened by kindly pity, some wore expressions of disappointment as if the show was not as interesting as they had expected, and some showed a certain weak disgust." When Marjorie graduated from the incubator and returned in good health to her mother, Butler wrote, she missed the incubator and the smiles of fairgoers and lamented that her mother's attention focused on recording her height, weight, and surroundings, rather than on her. Butler's book suggested he regretted the ways in which the science of infant care, exemplified by Marjorie's mother's careful notations of growth and weight, displaced older methods that relied on affection rather than accounting. But it was precisely this science of nursery management based on record keeping and hygiene that had, presumably, led to Marjorie's survival. And it was this science that would subsequently be taught to rich mothers and to poor ones.[21]

The widely acknowledged vulnerability of infants helped make baby saving a national project in the twentieth century, but awareness of the shared risks babies faced did not build bridges between social classes. Nor did the slow accumulation of data linking deaths and income lead to a public commitment to address the structural and economic problems many families confronted. Instead, poor mothering came to be seen as causing the deaths of poor babies and the solution to lowering mortality rates came to be regarded as best achieved by improving the instruction of the poor. Entrenched segregation and racial discrimination, severe chronic poverty, rural isolation, urban crowding, a rickety public health infrastructure, an inability to access care – all of these things mattered, all of them were visible, and few were acted upon. Progressive reformers and public health advocates would push infant mortality to the forefront of the public agenda, but they never had the means or perhaps the determination to attack the root of the problem: poverty.

Perhaps that mission was impossible. A deep cultural divide often separated individuals concerned with saving their own babies' lives from others who shared the same worries. Ideas about responsibility rooted in social class explained much of the gap. The experience of one visitor to the Trans-Mississippi Exposition, Josephine Knowland Laflin, offers a powerful illustration of that point. Knowland, a wealthy Chicago woman, saw the Omaha Exposition in 1898 along with her husband. Perhaps the Laflins saw the incubator babies or Little Spotted Back, but Mrs. Laflin's diary made no mention of either attraction. Her diary does record that upon returning home, the couple found their seven-month-old son, Louis Ellsworth, ailing. As they watched, he grew sicker until he was screaming in pain. A doctor came to house and diagnosed "bladder and bowel colic due to over acidity of the blood." Mrs. Laflin stayed by her infant's side as he recovered, leaving him with the servants only to go to church or to dine with friends. Hovering over Louis, she must have remembered the death of her daughter a few years earlier, shortly after her birth. Fortunately, the outcome was better in this instance. Louis Ellsworth Laflin Jr. survived his colic and other bouts of illness; he grew up to become a playwright.[22]

Despite her intimate knowledge of infant illness and death, Mrs. Laflin evinced no sympathy for or understanding of families who could not afford to summon doctors or whose methods of baby care differed from her own. She wrote in her diary about the death of a four-month-old baby, blaming the "young inexperienced mother" who was "taking every old woman's advice instead of consulting a good doctor." Mrs. Laflin may have understood the shared vulnerability of infants at the turn of the century, but her empathy stretched only so far. A personal reaction to seeing others suffer – the vividness response – might easily be trumped by other kinds of psychological mechanisms – distancing from those who seemed different, or simply a sense of superiority and entitlement. Mrs. Laflin's response to the death of the young baby with the inexperienced mother echoed the reaction of others at the turn of the century and later. Some people argued that all babies merited public investment in their welfare; others perceived babies as deserving of what their parents provided for them.

Over the course of the twentieth century, many stories would be told about babies; some inspired action, others made hardly a ripple in public consciousness. New visible technologies, like incubators, impressed viewers and helped bring donations to charitable groups assisting women and children. The far greater impact on mortality rates made by the provision of clean water and the removal of sewage did not inspire calls for increased public taxation and spending, although the nation's public health infrastructure did grow. And, as infant death rates fell over the course of the twentieth century, public imagination and political will would shift from lamenting the losses to countering the threats.

To understand the transformations in the lives of American babies, it is necessary both to see their individual differences and to chart the waxing and waning of programs initiated on their behalf. A time-lapse view reveals that advances in medicine, infrastructure improvements, and the growth of the American economy, along with new government programs, improved babies' life chances. Applying a close-up lens shows that, in many cases, the changes came very slowly. Poor infants continued to confront significant obstacles to their survival. Their death rates remained relatively high, the growing wealth of the nation did not change the material conditions of their households very quickly, if at all, and their access to biomedical advances remained inadequate. Contrasting pictures laid side by side would show, for the early decades of the century, Americans experiencing depressions, recessions, and panics, including grim scenes of hungry men and women. They would show the infant deaths taking places in crowded urban tenements, rural farmsteads, sharecropper shacks, and desolate reservations. Other, happier snapshots

Figure 1.3 Baby in casket in Keene, New Hampshire, ca. 1900–1920
Photographer: Bion Whitehouse
Credit: Keene Public Library and the Historical Society of Cheshire County

would offer scenes with images of world's fairs, panoramas of growing cities, and delightful pictures of healthy, well-cared-for infants.

Turning from metaphorical pictures to actual ones makes the point that things slowly got better. In 1898, as Frank A. Rinehart took pictures of Native American babies at the Trans-Mississippi Exposition, many other photographers worked in studios and funeral parlors making postmortem images of infants. Families viewed the creation of these keepsakes as a moral obligation. The images showed the babies with eyes opened, as if, one scholar explained, "to simulate life." Yet, on the cusp of the new century, other customs that celebrated babies began to develop as infant mortality rates declined.

The postmortem photograph died a slow death. Photographs of living infants took their place. Signaling this trend, *American Agriculturalist* magazine sponsored a baby photography contest in 1897 that brought in hundreds of entries from its small-town and rural subscribers, with most of the images presumably produced by photography studios. Baby pictures appeared as well in fund-raising materials printed by philan-thropic organizations and in private family baby books. By the time New Jersey inventor Thomas Edison made a motion picture of the Baby Parade on the boardwalk in Asbury Park, New Jersey, in 1904, the pic-ture of infant lives had slowly begun to change. Americans wanted babies to survive, they saw that more babies could survive, and they wanted to make sure more babies did survive.[23]

2

VALUING BABIES
Economics, Social Welfare, Progressives

I N MAY 1910, A MRS. TILTON reached out to New York City's Charity Organization Society (COS) for help. Deserted by her husband, she confronted a difficult situation: her sick baby kept her from her job as a janitress, and if she did not earn a living, her family might go hungry or lose its home. Told by the COS agent to hospitalize her baby, Mrs. Tilton refused. She feared hospitalization would kill her baby and so she took the infant to the hospital dispensary for outpatient care. Although she ignored the recommendation of the charity worker in this instance, Mrs. Tilton accepted help in other situations. From the COS worker she received tickets enabling her to obtain free milk for her children and the COS agent arranged for the Tilton family to receive assistance from a visiting nurse. When Mrs. Tilton returned to work after her baby recovered, she arranged for an older neighbor to care for the infant and an older child.[1]

Some months later, the Tilton baby became sick once again. Fearing the infant had "summer complaint," an acute and deadly diarrhea caused by bacterial contamination of food or milk that often developed as the temperature rose, Mrs. Tilton turned to a Board of Health physician for help. The record does not make clear what happened. However, some time after that Mrs. Tilton permitted her baby to be hospitalized briefly for an operation. The baby was later discharged and taken home. A nurse reported that he looked dreadful and a doctor at a dispensary confirmed this, predicting the infant would not get better. A week after that, the baby died.

Cultural conflicts and communication difficulties spoiled many encounters between patients and providers. In 1915, the infant daughter of an immigrant Hungarian family, the Toths, became ill and entered the hospital. When Mrs. Toth went to the hospital she found her daughter lying face-down on the bed, something she viewed as dangerous, but she lacked a sufficient command of English to relay her concern to the nurse. Even more distressing to Mrs. Toth, the hospital sent her baby up to the roof for fresh air where, Mrs. Toth feared, she would catch cold. The doctor insisted on the treatment and ignored her complaint. The case records note that some time after the hospital admission, a policeman took the baby's parents to the hospital, where they found their infant daughter dying of pneumonia. She hung on only for a few days.[2]

The Tilton and Toth families' experiences reveal the intersection of poverty and infant mortality and expose the deep skepticism poor families held regarding the value of inpatient hospital care. Mrs. Tilton, like many other mothers aided by the COS, rejected institutionalization, viewing hospitals as conduits to the burial grounds and the advice of charity agents as suspect. Institutional care made sense to social welfare workers as an obvious response to a serious illness, but it involved a complex calculus for parents. They assessed its value not simply in terms of whether it would hasten or prevent death, but they also considered the financial and emotional costs. COS case records make this clear. An account from 1904 described a recently widowed woman who hesitated to permit her sick infant suffering from bronchitis to enter the hospital. She wanted to wait a day or two to see if he improved. Another mother explained to the COS agent that she removed her baby from the hospital because "the carfare costs so much to go back and forth to see it." According to doctors, nurses, and charity agents, babies' health suffered needlessly as a result of their parents' refusal to permit them to go to the hospital. When infants died, physicians and nurses often blamed the parents for delaying treatment while the parents frequently attributed the deaths to the inability of medical professionals to provide adequate care. They might have both been right. Doctors lacked effective interventions for many deadly conditions, and babies died despite their efforts to provide supportive care. At the same time, parents sometimes kept babies from receiving effective treatments.[3]

The COS case records include numerous accounts of women who, understandably, resisted advice to wean their infants so that they could work, who rejected efforts to send disabled older children to distant

Figure 2.1 Four children in a tenement room, 1916
Photographer: Jessie Tarbox Beals
Credit: Community Service Society Collection, Rare Book
and Manuscript Library, Columbia University

facilities, and who refused to hospitalize ailing adult family members even when it meant exposing others to infectious diseases like tuberculosis. Families made choices, accepting and rejecting advice as it related to their beliefs and their needs. Not all of them refused institutional care. Some mothers placed desperately ill infants in hospitals, sought work outside of the city because they thought their infants might improve their health with fresh air, and broke up the family and sent younger children away, leaving them free to work and earn a living.

Beyond the entries in case records written by charity workers, the voices of poor mothers regarding infant care are hard to find. The observations of social welfare workers contain both valuable observations and biases. Medical records are similarly limited, revealing the ailments babies suffered, but less about the economic hardships shaping their lives and the lives of their parents and siblings. Poor infants' day-to-day existences are hard to excavate. What the case reports do reveal are the persistent efforts of philanthropic organizations to provide aid. Their child-saving work testified to the growing collective value of babies. Saving infant lives mattered not just to their families but also to Progressive reformers who viewed them as worthy future citizens. Reformers attacked problems ranging from an impure and contaminated milk supply, to the care of abandoned infants, to the situations of babies needing care while their mothers worked. Parents and social reformers did not form a partnership of equals, but they shared a common interest in preventing infant deaths.

Progressives, a loose coalition of political, religious, medical, and philanthropic leaders, embraced civic efforts to apply expert knowledge as a means of improving the lives of ordinary Americans. They believed the ascendant private interests characterizing the preceding Gilded Age needed to cede ground to a civic idealism that yielded social order and human betterment. As activists, Progressives stimulated a new public conversation about infant lives began in the opening decades of the twentieth century, endowing modern babies with new roles as symbols of the nation's well-being and future promise. Reformers built the scaffolding on which the federal government erected an agency devoted to the welfare of the young: the US Children's Bureau.

Many Progressives concentrated their efforts on improving the lives and life chances of the young, fighting for mandatory school attendance laws and legal limits on both children's work hours and the kinds of labor they performed. They advocated as well for supervised playgrounds as an alternative to city streets, and they created programs to prevent delinquency and to rehabilitate rather than punish children who got into trouble. Responding to the health threats facing the young and their families, reformers established neighborhood clinics and supported the work of visiting nurses. They erected seashore hospitals to provide treatment to the sick and preventive care to pre-tubercular children, and they urged municipal authorities to pass laws mandating the cleanliness of milk and to require its pasteurization.[4]

The deaths of infants functioned as measures of public health needs and failures, as statistical indicators of the nation's future, and as spurs to public action. As infant and child saving became modern established civic projects, discussions moved from whether to intervene in the lives of babies to what kinds of interventions would be most likely to succeed. Infants gained greater access to medical care, particularly if their families lived in cities and could make use of neighborhood dispensaries or obtain help from visiting nurses. But, as the example of the Tilton baby demonstrates, advice and access did not solve economic problems or cure diseases. Nurses, dispensary doctors, settlement house workers, and staffers from charitable organizations urged families to adopt scientific infant care practices and offered direct instruction. In some cases these well-meaning professionals appeared unable to recognize that they held poor families to middle-class standards that were impossible for them to meet. In other instances reformers provided infants without families – abandoned, institutionalized when they could not be cared for, or left with caretakers when mothers worked – a better chance at surviving.[5]

Progressive reformers, many of them women with a maternalist view of social welfare, looked outward and worked to inaugurate government programs to combat maternal and infant mortality. Both biased and well intentioned, the reformers, sometimes termed *child savers*, did not change the material circumstances shaping the lives of infants. Nevertheless, in promoting babies as social assets they implanted new ideas and created new institutions that would transform American culture. Their endeavors led them to investigate the lives of babies, to the education of mothers, to the provision of some clinical services and to the passage of new laws.[6]

When poverty, the shame of an out-of-wedlock birth, or other circumstances precluded women from raising their babies, they turned to institutions or, in some cases, to abandonment. In New York City alone, thousands of deserted babies ended up in foundling shelters each year. Most of them died; very few found homes. Families interested in adoption preferred older children whose health, likely survival, and character could be assessed. Perhaps in an effort to increase adoptions of the many available infants, an article appeared in *Harper's Bazaar* in 1912 with the provocative title "Bargains in Babies." It was not about economics, but fashion. The piece briefly highlighted a supposed new trend: single, middle-aged women "with more means and more leisure than they need" were adopting or arranging to support some of the 2,000 babies abandoned annually in New York City. There must have been a yawning gap between the supply of babies needing homes and the number of fashionable women demanding to adopt or look after them.[7]

According to a modern sociologist, children moved from being priced to priceless over the course of the twentieth century. As their potential economic contribution to the family declined, youngsters' emotional value soared. For infants, the historical arc differed. Babies made no monetary contribution to the household and were, in fact, always a drain on resources. Families invested in them as best they could. Collective social investments in infant welfare grew larger, spurred by evidence of a declining infant mortality rate. With growing recognition of the nation's future population needs, government agencies took steps to prevent infants' deaths and to enhance their futures. Babies became investments; they had public as well as private value.[8]

Calling babies a "bargain" raises several questions. What was the value of a baby and for whom? Visitors to expositions and amusement parks paid twenty-five cents to see infants in incubators; sometimes people paid $25 to $125 to give infants away to baby farmers – women who took babies into their homes to care for them. Abandonment imposed only possible emotional costs. Another question: was investing in babies worthwhile? The declining infant mortality rate made personal and civic investments in infants seem prudent as well as morally justified. But who would pay the costs of these endeavors and what kinds of investments needed to be made? Extraordinarily high poverty rates in the early twentieth century along with increasing income inequality meant that families living on the margins or falling into crushing poverty had little to invest. Larger collective outlays to save babies required both leveraging public funds and raising concern among those with social capital. This happened; but as one historian astutely documented, money went initially to infrastructure programs. Smaller sums went to charities, to erecting municipal facilities such as dispensaries, and to support for educational and health services. Ultimately, direct aid involved educational efforts that placed the final responsibility for saving lives on individual families.[9]

The subjects of babies and economics do not often overlap. There are estimates of the costs of rearing infants – of buying food, clothes, and medicine – but no detailed reports on what it costs to buy babies and which ones bring the highest price. The transactions, historically and today, are illegal and hidden and to the vast majority are abhorrent and heartbreaking. Yet, when accounts of baby selling appear they reveal not only the contours of the infant marketplace and the reasons people engaged in various transactions but also how babies acquired or lost value.

Hardship likely topped the list of reasons people sold babies. A poignant example appeared in a 1911 *New York Times* article titled "Will Sell One Baby to Save the Others: Husband Going Blind and Mrs. Monteque Fears Starvation for the Whole Family." To feed her children, pay the rent, and cover the costs of her husband's hospitalization while he underwent an operation to save his sight, Mrs. Monteque planned to sell the youngest of her four children, two-month-old Evelyn Grace. The economics made sense, but they upset the public. Distressed by the newspaper article, readers tried to help. A struggling "Colored" preacher in Trenton, New Jersey, sent one dollar; others sent different sums or offered to adopt Evelyn Grace. The story and its resolution, with the family receiving money, confirmed the power of the vividness response. Of course, it did not take much, probably only a few dollars, to keep Evelyn Grace with her family.[10]

How much did it cost to preserve thousands of infants' lives? Calculations of the benefits of investing in urban sanitation might be measured in such things as falling death rates from waterborne diseases, but aggregate mortality data typically concealed the variations among neighborhoods. Additionally, urban capital improvements, social benefit programs, and public health delivery efforts began within a short period of a few decades, making it difficult to discern the impact of each one. It proved equally difficult to assess the net gain from other investments. Did spending on maternal education programs save infant lives? A Buffalo, New York, visiting nurse paid to instruct immigrant families in infant care reported that it took months to teach women proper hygiene and feeding practices, and that only small improvements resulted. Was it an efficient use of funds? Or was money better spent on milk depots or on making sure that milk producers obeyed the hygiene laws? Vital statistics did not always supply the answers. At the household level, the economic calculus of investing in babies remained even more opaque.[11]

To attack the problem of infant mortality and to gain public support, social reformers offered both moral and economic justifications for their work. The moral arguments had deep roots. In the nineteenth century and earlier, religious organizations erected asylums and foundling homes in the hopes of saving infants' souls and possibly their lives. Their endeavors laid the foundation for future philanthropic and government programs by making a moral claim for the worthiness of infants. What twentieth-century reformers brought forward, in theory and in practice, was proof that saving babies paid social and economic dividends. The vulnerable infants of today, they argued, grew up to be the citizens of tomorrow. To make this claim, reformers offered both numeric data and anecdotal accounts that revealed the problems and possibilities of intervention.

The public knew well the threats to infant survival. "Summer complaint," the gastrointestinal ailment that nearly took the life of the Tilton baby, accounted for the majority of infectious disease deaths in infants. Numerous other deaths resulted from respiratory infections that often occurred in winter, and from communicable diseases such as measles, scarlet fever, and diphtheria that came in waves. Bowel disorders occurred most often in the hottest months of the year when milk spoiled quickly and bacterial infections spread easily. Public health authorities warned mothers against weaning in summer and told them to keep babies outdoors on hot summer nights. Reformer and muckraking journalist Jacob Riis observed the summer deaths in the slums of New York City in his 1890 book, *How the Other Half Lives*, writing "Despite all efforts, the grave-diggers in Calvary work overtime and the little coffins are stacked mountain-high on the deck of the Charity Commissioners boat when it makes its semi-weekly trips to the city cemetery." Other accounts tallying the hot weather deaths of babies seemed more prosaic but equally disturbing. In 1906, the *Washington Post* reported the deaths of fifty-six infants in seven days during a heat wave when an ice shortage led milk to spoil. Two years later, the death toll in the nation's capital reached sixty-one infants in a single week during another heat spell. Chicago's health department referred to the summer spike in infant mortality as "the annual harvest of death" and a pediatrician recalled a weekend when all the infants in a Chicago hospital died during a heat wave. Summertime deaths of babies, so visible and so numerous, led public health officials and reformers to call for new laws.[12]

A long and treacherous path led from the cow to the baby bottle. Bacteria sometimes entered milk from diseased animals suffering from bovine tuberculosis or from infectious organisms harbored in filthy, bacteria-laden barns. The organisms contaminating the milk multiplied inside the dirty metal cans transporting it from the barn to the train depot and continued to proliferate in unrefrigerated train cars as the milk made its way to the cities. In other instances, bacteria entered the milk and reproduced while it sat unrefrigerated in shops waiting to be sold. To enhance its profitability shopkeepers sometimes diluted the milk with contaminated water. To disguise its contamination and spoilage, they sometimes added adulterants. Once purchased and brought home, the milk could become even deadlier as germs grew inside unsterile and difficult-to-clean baby bottles. A 1907 study of workingmen's families in New York City revealed why poorer families faced greater risks: they bought loose milk at the grocery for five or six cents a quart. Households with a little more money purchased bottled milk for eight cents a quart, and those with even greater incomes obtained condensed milk in cans costing ten cents. An additional milk hazard facing indigent and low-income families was the fact that they had no iceboxes; their stored milk spoiled easily.[13]

Cities and states eventually passed laws that led to a safer milk supply, first by establishing nutritional standards and outlawing the adulteration and watering of milk, later through sanitary regulations placed on dairies and laws requiring pasteurization to halt bacterial contamination or growth and, finally, through laws mandating safe handling and storage. Municipal and state health departments also developed programs – often limited to the distribution of pamphlets – to educate mothers about the care and feeding of babies that included advice about how to store milk and how to clean baby bottles and nipples. In a few cities, milk depots supported by philanthropists gave away sanitary milk to poor families who had no iceboxes and this too helped to lower the risk of death from bacteria-laden milk.[14]

Efforts to ameliorate the conditions in which infants lived and died led reformers to focus on individual household problems rather than on broad economic challenges. Often they chose to educate mothers about proper infant care. But education could not make up for the loss of income if mothers stayed home to breastfeed and tend to their babies instead of leaving them in the care of siblings. Education could not provide families with the income needed to rent hygienic, uncrowded living quarters. Education could not produce the heat needed to keep babies warm in winter or provide the ice to keep milk from spoiling in the summer. So while deaths of infants declined over the course of the twentieth century, the gap in infant mortality rates between the rich and the poor, the white and nonwhite, and the immigrant and native born, remained wide.

The American population grew to nearly 123 million by 1930 from both an excess of births over deaths and from immigration. Between 1890 and 1929, 27.7 million immigrants settled in the United States, with their numbers peaking between 1900 and 1919. The demand for workers grew during World War I, when immigrants could no longer arrive by ship across the Atlantic. This helped spur the great black migration out of the rural South to Northern industrial cities as part of a larger internal migration from country to city that characterized the nation as a whole over the twentieth century. Immigration resumed after the war, but with limits, following passage of the Emergency Immigration Act of 1921 and the Immigration Act of 1924, both of which placed strict quotas on the number of people admitted based on their country of origin.[15]

Amid the great demographic changes, evidence began to appear showing that growing numbers of babies survived their first months of life. In 1910, the infant mortality rate per 1,000 live births stood at 104.2; it fell to 85.8 by 1920. The biggest decrease came in the rate of post-natal deaths (defined as occurring between one month of age and the first birthday) rather than neonatal deaths (occurring in the first twenty-eight days of life). Strikingly wide variations in mortality rates among infants of different races, classes, and regions persisted. In urban locales the health problems of African American infants and of the offspring of immigrants became increasingly visible, thanks in part to birth registration and to contact with public health programs. As they had in the past, the disparities provoked both civic responses and finger pointing; success in the aggregate left individuals to be accused of failure.[16]

Poor urban neighborhoods teeming with immigrants drew the greatest attention from Progressives, but reformers knew that rural living provided no immunity from the threats to infant life. As in cities, the failure or inability of women to breastfeed, the lack of clean water and clean milk, and unhygienic conditions threatened babies' health. Reformers who studied rural infant mortality put some of the blame on the mothers' need to engage in heavy farm work right before and immediately after giving birth. Investigations in factory towns, mill villages, and big cities similarly linked maternal employment to infant mortality. In the early twentieth century, socialist and political activist John Spargo went to a small town in New York State to study child poverty. There he viewed the situation of many families struggling to get by, including one with an immigrant father from Sweden and an Irish-American mother. They had two living children and five who had died before the age of twelve months. Spargo listed the causes of their deaths – two from convulsions, two from measles, and one from acute gastritis. And he observed that while the mother worked, the father, a laborer, was often unemployed. Reporting on other village households, he found families with both parents employed but with combined wages barely able to sustain their families.[17]

When both parents worked, older children cared for younger ones, a situation often described and decried by reformers. The problem led physician S. Josephine Baker, the director of the New York City Bureau of Child Hygiene, to create Little Mothers' Leagues to train girls age twelve and up to care for younger siblings, and the program spread throughout the country. It did not reach far enough. In many families, very young siblings with no training cared for babies, or neighbors tended to them sometimes while caring for large numbers of other infants and children.[18]

Infants without families – abandoned and institutionalized – faced the longest odds of all. For every incubator infant drawing a crowd, thousands of other babies lay unwanted in almshouses or discarded elsewhere: thrust down sewers, deposited in alleys, or handed off to strangers. Foundlings turned up in saloons, brothels, and churchyards, and on the steps of police stations. Newspapers throughout the nation recounted the arrests and sentencing of women and men who abandoned babies and told of the discovery of foundlings by passersby. In 1916, the

Evening Times-Republican of Marshalltown, Iowa, carried a story about a one-month-old baby boy left in the courthouse wearing dirty clothes. Whoever placed him there also left a doctor's typed feeding instructions. A Mitchell, South Dakota, newspaper recounted the abandonment of a two-month-old baby boy on the doorstep home of a Catholic priest in 1921. It was, the paper reported, the second infant found abandoned that week. Sometimes the articles noted where the authorities placed the babies or who took them in until they located the mother, and often the mothers were not found. In a 1914 column titled "In the News and out of the Ordinary," the *Alma Record* of Alma, Michigan, told of the six Philadelphia policemen who "matched coins" in order to decide "which would adopt an abandoned baby who was found on a doorstep." The departure or absence of the babies' fathers or households overwhelmed by need and lacking the resources to support an additional child explained many of the cases reported in the newspapers.[19]

Municipal poorhouses, private philanthropic institutions, and religious charities all took in foundlings. Before the Civil War, female reformers established homes for unmarried, abandoned, or widowed mothers, hoping to prevent them from deserting their offspring, and they too took in abandoned infants. The facilities remained part of the urban landscape through the early twentieth century and gave women a chance to care for their own babies while also nurturing a foundling. Though well intentioned, such efforts often proved futile, sometimes because the women who were asked to breastfeed and tend to the motherless babies had little additional milk or attention to give to them. As a result, many foundlings growing up in congregate institutions were bottle fed and died after contracting gastrointestinal infections. Turn-of-the-century economist Amos G. Warner put it succinctly: "It is not possible to raise babies by wholesale." He was correct. Of the 366 infants under six months of age admitted to the Randall's Island Infants Hospital in New York City in 1896, for example, 354 were dead by April 15 the following year. Other institutions posted equally horrifying numbers.[20]

Private facilities that took in babies for a fee did little better. In 1914, George Walker, chairman of the Maryland State-Wide Vice Commission, issued "The Traffic in Babies," a report that carefully scrutinized operations at two institutions. The facilities charged parents $100 to

$125 to relinquish babies. For one of them Walker calculated an infant mortality rate for babies less than six months of age at 100 percent. The other institution did little better with its charges: 97.5 percent of its resident infants succumbed by six months of age. Disposing of all the bodies posed no problem; one facility buried the infants in a large hole holding 75 to 100 bodies; Walker estimated 5,000 were buried this way. The other institution placed the bodies in a cemetery or handed them over for dissection.[21]

Facing criticism from medical experts and reformers, the leaders of some private charities shifted from institutional care to outplacement, a costlier but far superior arrangement. New York City's private Speedwell Society lowered its infant mortality rate from 100 percent to 10 percent by adopting a boarding-out scheme for the babies in its care. The keys to success, its leaders suggested, lay in the careful selection of foster mothers, their close and regular supervision, and, if possible, hiring women capable of breastfeeding the babies. Additionally, the separation of infants likely helped to stem the spread of deadly infections. For the babies, outplacement offered a chance at life, but not a family. After reaching an appropriate age, they left their foster mothers and returned to the institutions for education and training. They stayed until they found a job in domestic service, were apprenticed to learn a trade, or, in the case of some New York City youngsters, went west on "orphan trains" to be placed in farm families.[22]

Baby farmers presented another option for families unable to care for their infants. They housed babies for a weekly fee – so long as the payments arrived. Some of the caretakers provided a service as part of a web of mutual aid – earning a living while assisting neighborhood women who worked outside their homes or lived out as domestic servants. Other baby farmers operated solely out of greed, keeping large numbers of fragile infants in unsanitary homes, and failing to provide them with adequate nourishment or attention. Newspapers often followed the arrests, trials, convictions, and sentencing of what they often called mercenary baby farmers. A short item, "Johnson Jury Out; Fate of Alleged Baby Farmer Is Still Undecided," appeared in the *Minneapolis Journal* in 1905. The following year, the *Pensacola Journal,* a Florida newspaper, had a short front-page item about a New York baby farmer sentenced to two-and-a-half years in the penitentiary. She reportedly received the light sentence, as the headline deemed it, because of her age.[23]

A Chicago study identified many of the city's baby farmers as poorly educated older women who had no other means of earning a living. Many reportedly took in babies with the understanding that parents would not be troubled by their deaths. Mothers may have kept up the payments as best they could, but they understood that when they failed to make their weekly deposits their babies would likely die of neglect or be shipped off to the almshouse to meet the same fate. Neighbors knew which baby farmers did their best to tend to their charges and which ones did not – either by reputation or by counting the coffins leaving the house or the graves in the rear yard.[24]

Reformers sought to remedy the problem of an unscrupulous and unregulated traffic in infants and children by researching and reporting on the misdeeds of baby farmers and maternity home operators. Their probes into this somewhat hidden occupation uncovered the economics of the baby trade as well as the conditions that made it profitable. An investigator from the Massachusetts Society for the Prevention of Cruelty to Children found that Boston mothers paid $25 to leave their infants at a nursery and not return for them. In Chicago, the price was $15 or more to have a maternity home dispose of a baby. Unregulated maternity homes and baby farms in Minnesota charged even higher fees for a combination of maternity care and placement of the baby.[25]

In Baltimore, George Walker arranged for an investigator to visit the homes of women answering an advertisement for a home for a nine-week-old baby. A few replies arrived from childless families looking for babies to adopt as their own. The majority of offers came from women looking to earn money boarding a baby. They charged fees ranging from $3.50 to $10 a week. Investigators learned that families seeking to adopt apparently paid a premium for the pretty babies – sometimes as much as $100. As a pragmatic baby farmer astutely noted, "It's cheaper and easier to buy a baby for $100.00 than to have one of your own." Other babies, such as those adopted to be used as "heirs" in various legal schemes, presumably cost less. Recognizing the mostly deadly results of baby farming, progressive reformers pushed states and municipalities to enact laws and regulations requiring the regular inspection of the homes. Their efforts likely drove some providers underground.[26]

Poor families, especially those headed by single, deserted, or widowed women, had recourse to several other unsatisfactory infant care options. They sought help from relatives or neighbors when they went to work or, if they had older children, they sometimes removed them from school so they could take care of the infant and handle the household chores. In some places parents arranged for babies to be cared for at a day nursery run by a local charity or settlement house. Another option was a baby farm or an institution. Economists would describe the situation in terms of two competing systems of care. One consisted of private, for-profit, unregulated arrangements that were small in scale and neighborhood based as part of a network of reciprocity that enabled working-class and poor families to survive. The other consisted of a hybrid of public and philanthropic services that cost families little or nothing, but imposed social controls in the case of day nurseries or the likelihood of death in the case of foundling homes, unless they relied on outplacement arrangements.[27]

The charitable groups opening day nurseries expected their programs would prevent the severing of family ties that resulted from placing babies in institutions and would curb reliance on baby farmers. The nurseries charged a minimal sum and enabled women to go to work rather than rely on charity or tiny public relief payments and they kept the infants and children under the watch of responsible caretakers. The National Federation of Day Nurseries counted 618 such places on its rolls in 1914. Day nursery administrators sometimes demanded families undergo an investigation of their worthiness before being permitted to enroll their babies, and they had various other rules that deterred some families from enrolling their offspring. Nurseries imposed restrictions that neighborhood caretakers or older siblings did not, including rules about cleanliness and about assessing the families' worthiness for aid. They also, understandably, did not permit entry of sick babies who posed the risk of infecting the other infants and children and required extra care. Some families may have hesitated to use the nurseries because of the stigma of charity. During World War II, when the demand for workers grew, the US Women's Bureau reported that the long-standing association of day nurseries with charity dissuaded some working mothers from taking advantage of the care they provided.[28]

Social settlements as well as private charities and religious organizations ran day nurseries. Leading progressive-era reformer Jane Addams, founder of the Hull House settlement in a poor neighborhood in Chicago, added a day nursery to the array of services. Elsewhere in Chicago, the Catholic Women's League ran a number of settlements that included day nurseries. The DePaul Settlement and Day Nursery in Chicago reported it accepted babies as young as twelve days, and kept about twenty-five of them, observing that most were Italian, but that they had "many nationalities" in their facility. In Florida, the Methodist Episcopal Church South sponsored three settlements that included day nurseries. The lack of precise information regarding number of available spots and the number of infants enrolled makes it impossible to gauge the impact of day nurseries on infant care. Some day nurseries did not accept infants. Studies of wage-earning women found they preferred to keep young infants at home to be cared for by relatives, older siblings, or neighbors. A 1918–1919 investigation of 728 wage-earning mothers in Philadelphia revealed thirty of them had infants less than one year of age, but only four of their babies attended a day nursery.[29]

Records from the Chicago Nursery and Half Orphan Society reveal how infants sometimes bounced among family members, neighbors, unlicensed boarding homes, and day nurseries, depending on the household circumstances. One premature baby entered care because the mother had epilepsy and could not care for her infant. The mother subsequently had several admissions to the state mental hospital and her infant remained at the Nursery for several months before being discharged to the care of the paternal grandparents. A month later the infant returned to the Nursery because the grandmother needed to care for a sick family member. After a month she reclaimed the baby. In other instances, if the babies had no relatives to care for them they moved quickly from the Nursery to a boarding home. Typically, infants comprised only a small portion of the caseload at day nurseries. In 1934, the Chicago Nursery housed only sixteen infants out of a total of forty-eight children in its care.[30]

Many interpretations of infant value present themselves in institutional records. A careful reading of the notations in the case reports of the COS demonstrates that many parents valued their babies so much that they would not hand them off to strangers, whether it meant hospital stays or day nurseries. An analysis of the data about infant abandonment suggests that other parents valued their infants so little or so much that they abandoned them to the streets or the almshouse, wishing them dead or hoping they would be saved by caring strangers. Economics and emotion played a role in both decisions.

Reformers too valued infants; they attempted at various times to save babies' lives by erecting institutions, organizing day nurseries, or arranging for supervised outplacement. They advocated for changes in the law and they pressed for municipal and state services as well as charitable care. Reformers sometimes privileged congregate charitable care over family care, arguing that removing infants from households, even if only for a workday, or for a few weeks for medical treatment, would be in the babies' best interests. In some instances, charity workers saw babies left to be cared for by neighbors and siblings as proof that the poor did not value their infants enough. The judgment reflected the social and economic distance between poor families and those who wished to aid and educate them.

With infant mortality rates falling and with reformers increasingly committed to promoting babies' welfare, the early decades of the twentieth century saw new efforts to drive death rates even lower. Reformers asserted that the nation owed something to its most vulnerable future citizens; if saved and brought up right, they would become the next generation of soldiers, workers, and mothers, as one contemporary scholar explained. Progressive activists urged the nation's political leaders to invest in babies and they lobbied for the creation of the US Children's Bureau in 1912, the first national government agency in the world dedicated to the welfare of children. Under its auspices new programs began, but, hemmed in by political opponents, fiscal restraints, and a belief that families were ultimately responsible for their infants' survival, neither the Children's Bureau nor any other public agency possessed the means to address in a substantial way the many social and economic problems contributing to the deaths and illnesses of babies. Reformers valued babies, but they did not ultimately inspire the nation to pay the full cost of improving their life chances. Yet, thanks to the efforts of many reformers, in the twentieth century babies would become the connecting link between the federal government and the modern family, and their life chances would grow.

3

HELPING CITIZEN BABY

The US Children's Bureau, Good Advice, Better Babies

I N MAY 1932, THE US CHILDREN'S Bureau received a letter from Mrs. Lyle Davis of Port Orchard, Washington, seeking information about infant feeding. "Doctors I have consulted seem to be of different opinions on the subject," she wrote, "some say the vitamins are killed in evaporated [milk] – others say not." Despite having access to several medical opinions, Mrs. Davis turned to a federal government agency to settle the matter. She received a detailed letter in reply from a Children's Bureau physician, explaining the value of evaporated milk and how to compensate for the destroyed vitamins by giving her baby orange juice, tomato juice, and cod liver oil. Mrs. Davis's infant was one of an uncountable number of American babies whose mothers followed the advice of federal government employees. And the Children's Bureau was just one of many government agencies giving parents advice about infant care.[1]

Don't kiss babies. Let them cry. Make sure they get a healthy tan. Never give them pacifiers. Don't get them in the habit of being held. Over and over again mothers got this advice. And they learned the logic behind it. Kissing and pacifiers spread germs. Crying developed the lungs. Sunshine prevented rickets – a softening and/or weakening of the bones caused by a lack of vitamin D. Holding babies and playing with them got them overexcited. Instruction about tanning, crying, and kissing signaled a change in the lives of American infants and their parents. Bringing up babies required a new kind of work – defending infants against deadly pathogens, promoting their health with the assistance of professionals, monitoring their emotional and intellectual progress, and teaching them regular habits and self-control. But mothers couldn't do it all on their own. As infant mortality rates fell, the drive to push them even lower became a crusade. Public and private agencies stepped into the nursery to offer guidance and to criticize. Their reasons for doing so were moral and political: babies, they explained, were vulnerable future citizens. For this reason, in the opening years of the twentieth century, babies began to connect their families to local, state, and, most significantly, federal government agencies in new ways.

Certainly, many ordinary Americans encountered federal government agencies and services; for example, they served in the armed forces, they received mail from the US Post Office, and, after passage of the Sixteenth Amendment in 1913, they paid federal income taxes if their incomes were high enough. The creation of the US Department of Agriculture in 1862 and its elevation to a cabinet-level agency in 1889, along with the development of agricultural experiment stations and later cooperative extension services in the states, linked farmers to the federal government. By helping farmers, the federal government ensured the health of the nation's supply of food and strengthened the economy. In some ways, the history of the Children's Bureau mirrored that of the Department of Agriculture. The agency connected parents to the federal government and did so to assure that infants and children would grow up and contribute to an expanding national economy. The leaders of the Children's Bureau would draw the parallels between the two agencies when they attempted to gain support from Congress for new programs or to acquire sufficient funds for ongoing efforts. But the women leading the Children's Bureau and their supporters were never as successful as they hoped to be; unlike farmers, they faced powerful opponents. Nevertheless, the Children's Bureau's administrators did succeed in creating programs to educate mothers, helping to make infant care routines orderly and scientific, much as extension agents taught new agricultural practices and helped place farming on a scientific footing. Behavior in the nursery mattered, and while nursery hygiene practices were no substitute for adequate family incomes and healthy places to live, they did make a significant difference.[2]

Just as agricultural extension agents served to translate big federal efforts – supporting the nation's farm output – into small packages of individual assistance, Children's Bureau agents carved the child- and baby-saving project of the nation into a set of manageable programs, as other public health agencies had done. They gathered data, reached out via radio broadcasts, distributed pamphlets, and answered individual letters from worried mothers. Historians view the work of the Children's Bureau as both an example of social control as the Bureau's leaders endeavored to impose white middle-class cultural values on those rearing the nation's children and as a feminist effort that succeeded in improving the lives and status of women and children. Perhaps the Bureau's greatest legacy lay in connecting women citizens to federal officials. Babies played a critical role in cementing that partnership. In the same way that the federal government worked to prevent crop failures and animal diseases, it would take on the challenge of helping to preserve infants' and children's lives and futures.

The US Children's Bureau began its work in 1912. In entering a domain of action traditionally left to state and local governments, the Bureau's staffers tread lightly. Over the next decades cooperation between the Children's Bureau and state and local public agencies waxed and waned and a patchwork of programs began and ended in various cities and states according to political interests and financial resources. Racially segregated services remained the rule in many places.

In the first half of the twentieth century many social theorists argued that biological inferiority explained the high death rates of nonwhite infants and those born in immigrant families. The Children's Bureau's produced studies pointing to the economic and social conditions accounting for the excess of deaths. However, the Bureau's staffers never used their findings to make a full-frontal assault on inequality, even as they documented its impact. Instead, skirmishes in the war on infant mortality took place on other fronts and with limited weapons. Most often this meant some form of education, although, for a brief period in mid-century, the Children's Bureau supported direct services by delivering federal dollars to state agencies. The effort to combat infant mortality and improve the health and welfare of the young saw many battles won, but there was no final victory.

The ongoing work of the US Children's Bureau helped establish broad cultural and political support for the idea that children constituted a vital national resource. Patriotic rhetoric infused both baby-saving campaigns and organizations serving children. In an official letter sent to new mothers in Kansas, along with the pamphlet "The Care of the Baby," physician Samuel J. Crumbine, secretary of the Kansas State Board of Health and Collaborating Epidemiologist for the US Public Health Service, reminded:

> The State and the Nation rejoice with you upon the advent of this new citizen of the Republic and they, too, are anxious with you that his progress in physical and mental development be normal and natural, to the end that your baby may grow into a strong, healthy, and useful citizen.

Citizenship came to babies not as a political or civic right – the endowments of democracy given to adults – but through an implicit claim for social rights in the form of support for their health, education, and protection. In some nations of the developed world, civic rights would be bestowed on the young in the form of entitlement programs; in the United States, civic citizenship for the young gained rhetorical substance but limited fiscal underwriting. The Children's Bureau along with other federal agencies took small and necessary steps – not bold leaps – to ensure that babies survived and that children grew up healthy and educated.[3]

Wars are won with armed forces, ammunition, money, and the help of allies. The twentieth-century battle against infant mortality engaged these forces as well. Nurses, doctors, public health educators, charity agents, and social science investigators constituted the troops. Modern educational techniques became the bullets. Critical allies included manufacturers producing and selling products designed to fight germs, improve health, and make mothers' lives easier. The money came intermittently. The federal government funded new programs and then, after a time and in the face of changing political priorities, retreated.

The shaky marriage of public health and consumer culture gave birth to new household routines based on the application of the germ theory. Infant deaths, once seen largely as God's will, became evidence of insufficient adherence to the laws of hygiene and bacteriology. As a result, the nursery became the epicenter of middle-class household hygiene practices. Thanks to vigorous marketing of antiseptic products, articles in the popular press, and public health brochures and radio programs, American homes transformed into home fronts, where mothers battled germs – an invisible and threatening army. Ideally, near military-style order pervaded the nursery, with babies sleeping, eating, and bathing in regimented fashion.

In crowded urban neighborhoods, messages about proper infant care came directly from public health nurses who made the rounds teaching poor and immigrant mothers how to raise babies the "American way." Outreach to middle-class and wealthy mothers included exhibitions, department store displays, and a barrage of advertising in magazines. The resulting baby care practices imposed new burdens as "scientific motherhood" became dogma and rules replaced instinct.[4]

Raising infants, in some instances, evolved into a competitive effort. The magazine *Women's Home Companion* as well as state and local organizations sponsored Better Baby contests at state fairs or in gatherings organized by local groups. In some locales, Women's Buildings erected at state fairs housed the contests. There, experts judged the entrants on their physical and mental development according to detailed scorecards. In 1913, *Women's Home Companion* reported that experts assessed almost 150,000 babies. The contests appealed to parents because they combined elements of traditional baby beauty contests, which judged physical attraction and declared the cutest babies the winners, with an opportunity for a formal medical assessment.[5]

Better babies. What kind of parents would not want their infants to claim the title? *Women's Home Companion* promised, "If your baby is only a good baby this year, it can be a *better baby* next year," urging readers, "You study scientific farming and domestic science ... why not study better babies hygiene?" Parenting, and especially mothering, required training and hard work. Understandably, the mothers of winning babies, like the rearers of winning livestock, took pride in their accomplishments, even as they surrendered their own judgments of their offspring to outsiders who imposed rigid norms of health and development.[6]

As an infant, Nancy Ward attended the 1915 Better Baby event in Marietta, Georgia, sponsored by the Equal Suffrage Association. Her mother kept both her scorecard and her certificate of examination in her baby book. Sponsoring the Marietta event must have seemed like the perfect opportunity to convey the message that extending the vote to women would not lead them to neglect their maternal duties. As the contests spread, the phrase "better babies" became a commercial

Figure 3.1 Better Baby Contest, Indiana State Fair, 1930
Credit: Courtesy of the Indiana State Library

catchphrase. The Commercial Milling Company, the maker of Henkel's extra fancy flours, produced a 1920s baby book titled *Biography of a Better Baby*. Its fact-filled pages explained "how to feed the better baby," "how to care for the better baby," and "how a better baby should walk."[7]

Better Baby contests laid the groundwork for Fitter Families for Future Firesides contests of the 1920s, also held at state fairs but designed to judge the "eugenic health" of entire families in order to promote better breeding, or what some frankly labeled as race betterment. Turn-of-the-century progressive reformers believed that maternal education, investments in public health and welfare, and other environmental measures would succeed in reducing the infant mortality rate and make for a stronger nation. Eugenics advocates moved to prevent the breeding of the unfit and to promote the reproduction of white,

American, Protestant families in the face of an expanding and increasingly religiously and ethnically diverse society. Each side achieved victories. Environmentalists secured stepped-up efforts to educate, or more frankly, to "Americanize" immigrants and to instruct the poor in infants and childcare and saw the creation of the Children's Bureau. Eugenicists countered with legal measures aimed at controlling reproduction.[8]

Public debate about infants and eugenics flared with the release of the 1917 motion picture *The Black Stork*, which, as a historian noted, argued for physicians to withhold treatment from so-called defective infants likely to suffer before dying. The questions asked by the promoters of selective infanticide engaged professionals and elected officials as well as the public. They considered whether doctors should help disabled babies die in order to spare them from suffering and their parents from the burden of their care. To some, the elimination of damaged infants appeared to be a classic progressive solution – the application of science to a social problem. Supporters of eugenic infanticide viewed it as a reasoned response, contrasting it with futile efforts to keep severely disabled babies alive. Additionally, eugenicists saw the survival of the babies as imposing a cost on the taxpayers who supported their long-term institutional care, and as placing a financial and emotional burden on the families who took care of them and watched them suffer. Profound religious, public, and professional objections to the eugenic solution brought an end to the furor instigated by the film. For the most part, eugenicists' attention to the plight of disabled babies waned; they focused their efforts on enacting federal laws restricting immigration and state laws mandating institutionalization and sterilization of the unfit.[9]

The political interests of groups promoting infant health and those advocating eugenic breeding overlapped and diverged over the course of the twentieth century. Calling infants "future citizens" raised, for some, the question of whether they would grow up to be contributors to society, or a drain on the nation's strength and wealth. Eugenic language made its way into the 136-page life book first published in 1933, *Log-o'-Life: A Monument to the Faithful Co-operative Spirit and Parental Interest of Our Fathers and Mothers*, which served for many as a baby book. The volume's authors presented parents with the opportunity to record every possible event beginning at birth and on through college years, adulthood, and

old age. In their introduction, they offered parents a eugenic rationalization for keeping a careful account of their children's development:

> Every child has the moral right to demand a record of his ancestry as well as
> that of his own life, so much of which is utterly dependent upon his parents.
> Records are the building stones of the future whereby the superstructure
> of praiseworthy society, as well as a more splendid race displaying bodies
> patterned after a Greek Adonis with minds reflecting the noblest ideals,
> highest ambitions and truest Christian principles may be realized.

The grandiose language overlaid the simple idea that only the right kind
of parents created the right kind of babies.[10]

While they may not have identified a future Adonis, baby beauty
contests, as well as Better Baby contests, remained popular with the
public. Some of the competitions operated as fund-raising ventures,
collecting entry fees and distributing prizes and bragging rights. In
1925, the Washington DC National Association for the Advancement of
Colored People raised money with a contest that awarded prizes to the
babies whose supporters purchased the greatest number of coupons.
A World War II–era contest served to boost military and national morale
according to a newsreel from the Office of Emergency Management.
In addition to highlighting battles on Anzio Beach, Italy, in 1944 and
women in uniform, it offered footage of a baby show for the offspring of
military fathers.[11]

Far from fairground baby shows, social welfare advocates remained
busy investigating the link between family income and mortality and
morbidity rates. Eschewing simple eugenic explanations for poor health,
they sought to understand the living conditions that helped to determine if babies lived or died. The Russell Sage Foundation, founded in
1907 to improve social and living conditions in the United States, underwrote a study of four neighborhoods in Boston from 1910 to 1912. The
investigator, social worker Henry H. Hibb Jr., concluded, "the fundamental cause of the excessive rates of infant mortality in industrial communities is poverty, inadequate incomes, and low standards of living,
with the attendant evils including the gainful employment of mothers."
Regulating the employment of women before and after confinement
and instructing mothers and girls in domestic economy might help, he

conceded, but "the chief thing remains the provision of an adequate family income." Many experts diagnosed poverty as the ailment, but their prescriptions focused only on the symptoms. They argued for restricting women's employment and funding widows' and mothers' pensions for households without male breadwinners, but rarely addressed the subject of paying women sufficient wages or ameliorating poverty in female-headed households.[12]

Eugenics supporters countered with their own proposals, preaching the prevention of births to families of poor stock and advocating harsh measures to halt the "hereditary degeneracy" they viewed as responsible for poverty. Eugenicists did not wish to inoculate families against poverty, but to inoculate society from the poor. They viewed programs of income support as threatening established tenets that justified the market's control of workplaces and workers. Like generations of conservative social observers before them, social conservatives of the twentieth century perceived welfare as undermining a social compact with the laboring classes. They believed that material assistance to the poor would reinforce their habits of laziness and other vices, thus demoralizing the individuals who continued to work. The long-standing stigma of public relief so permeated American culture that families sometimes delayed asking for aid for their infants even in desperate situations. A 1928 study of the unemployed included a description of a baby, born healthy at nine-and-a-half pounds, whose weight plummeted to four-and-a-half pounds before the mother finally reached out for help. She hesitated because she did not want charity. It was a common story.[13]

Resistance to providing direct aid to needy families meant that chronicles of blighted infant lives sometimes became parables about bad parenting. A booklet from the Illinois State Board of Health, "Our Babies: How to Keep Them Well and Happy, a Booklet for Mothers," proclaimed: "Poverty does not justify the parents of children living in crowded tenement districts, in occupying dark and ill-ventilated rooms or in remaining where bad plumbing and bad sanitary conditions endanger life and health." Families, the author stated, should have known better and found "a clean and simple cottage [that] can be rented in the outskirts of a town or city for little more or quite as little as one must pay for the dark flat or tenement." The same finger wagging infused descriptions of families that failed to purchase clean milk or proper food for their babies, that neglected to screen their windows, letting in disease-carrying flies and mosquitoes, or that imported customs from the old country into their new American homes. Hard evidence linked infant mortality to poverty; deep-seated cultural beliefs and equally powerful political considerations deflected blame back onto the parents.[14]

Programs undertaken by the administrators of the Children's Bureau exemplified the tension between understanding problems and finding solutions for them. Launched with a limited mandate and little funding, the Children's Bureau staff made careful investigations of infant mortality and transmitted valuable information about infant and childcare to millions of Americans. In the 1920s, the Bureau became the granting agency for federal funds going to the states for maternal and infant services. During the Great Depression, the Bureau's leaders helped write important parts of the Social Security Act of 1935 and subsequently oversaw the distribution of funds to the states under Title V, which provided block grants to the states for maternal and child health and welfare services. Later, during World War II, the Bureau developed a model health insurance program covering maternity and infant care for the wives of servicemen. The Bureau's leaders hoped it would become a model for a peacetime initiative to provide health coverage to all infants and children. Instead, the program ended and the agency's mission shrank in the postwar years.[15]

Several years of political wrangling preceded passage of the legislation creating the Children's Bureau, which President William Howard Taft signed into law in 1912. Supporters included settlement house leaders, physicians, and public health activists, as well as former President Theodore Roosevelt. Opposition came from political leaders who objected to agents of government meddling in family matters; they believed it was up to the household breadwinner to provide for and protect his offspring. Absent a breadwinner, opponents of the Children's Bureau believed, families would find support from charities, relatives, neighbors, and churches. As a result, the Children's Bureau began its work with a limited mission – "to investigate and report on all matters pertaining to children and child life." Scholars describe the creation of the Children's Bureau as a temporary triumph of maternalist progressivism, in which domestic and feminist values and the belief that women had a special political role finally found public expression in programs and law. They note that the Children's Bureau became the first federal agency run by women. Through political acumen and effective coalition building, the Bureau's leaders, despite being under constant siege from political opponents, continued to reveal the needs of children and to fight on their behalf. The agency's survival was something of a triumph.

The Bureau's first director, Julia Lathrop, a longtime social reformer and child welfare promoter, maneuvered adeptly, well aware of the agency's delicate political situation. She directed staffers to gather data on infant mortality through community studies, to produce educational materials, to promote birth registration, and to engage in cooperative endeavors with states, municipalities, and voluntary organizations. Politically dodgy initiatives, such as attempting to outlaw child labor, had to be set aside. Similarly, the agency avoided actions that posed a direct threat to medical professionals. Careful to acknowledge the primary role of parents, to avoid political turf battles, and to not be judged as solely a welfare agency, the Children's Bureau asserted that its work focused not on the "poor child" or the "bad boy," but had a supportive, democratic mission:

> leading the parent to that interest in community action through which alone his own child may be safeguarded, and the citizen to a knowledge of the individual problems of heredity, ignorance, and poverty on the adequate solution of which depends the community's future.

The words sounded patriotic and nodded to both environmental and eugenic ideals, while providing few specifics.[16]

Birth registration, critical to understanding the nation's health, posed no threat, had no organized opposition, supported the work of the US Census Bureau, and garnered both popular and professional support. It had the additional advantage of aiding the enforcement of child labor laws, a keen interest of the Children's Bureau's leaders and of other reformers. When employers followed the law and demanded proof of age, increased numbers of children remained in school rather than entering the workforce. Additionally, as a baby book reminded parents, a birth certificate "may be used at any time to prove the child's citizenship, age, parentage, and genealogy, the right to inherit and own property, the right to attend school, to secure employment, to vote, to marry, to secure a passport, to hold public office." As the list implied, birth registration marked the initial step on the road to citizenship.[17]

Registration of births and deaths enabled public health experts to understand challenges to population health, to obtain a precise measure of the infant mortality rate, to attempt to discern its causes, and to observe variations by race, ethnicity, and region. Despite the value of the records, limited federal efforts meant that the United States lagged well behind other "leading counties" in registering births, according to the director of the census. Working to catch up, the Census Bureau expanded its data collection prior to conducting the 1910 census and in 1915 established a national Birth-Registration Area. Initially it included only ten states and the District of Columbia; by 1917, another ten states met the qualifications for inclusion. To obtain data the Census Bureau sent postcards to families asking about births, had employees scan newspaper birth announcements, and perused death records. As hospital births became more common, registration became easier.[18]

Another effort by the Children's Bureau designated 1918 as the Children's Year. As a home front program during World War I, Children's Year enabled the Bureau to join forces with the Child Conservation Section of the Field Division of the Council of National Defense. The finding that a large portion of draft registrants were physically unfit for service provided a rationale for the initiative beyond child saving, although that would be the Bureau's primary effort for the year. The Bureau's programming focused on promoting access to maternity and infancy care, improving recreation for children, and enforcing child labor laws in tandem with efforts to encourage adolescent workers to return to school. A major goal, to "Save 100,000 babies," won support from groups representing 11 million women. In 1918, the Chicago Health commissioner observed that "The number of men killed in war is not so serious an index of loss as is the high infant death rate or the falling birth rate," a sign that not even war could shift the gaze of reformers away from the cradle.[19]

Together with the Children's Bureau, reform-minded women attempted to plant the seeds that would yield a healthy crop of new public measures: the creation of state and municipal child hygiene agencies, the placement of sufficient numbers of public health nurses in all urban communities and rural counties, pensions for widows and even the "payment of wages which met the cost of a healthy, well-cared-for childhood." Some called for maternity benefits programs like those that existed in some nations in Europe. The Children's Bureau's leaders hoped that the agency's wartime efforts, including its strategic alliance with the Council of National Defense, would boost its political status and that wartime patriotism would stimulate funding for new programs for infants and children. However, when hostilities ended, the Children's Bureau administrators had to retreat from their aggressive efforts to reshape the public health and welfare landscape.

In arguing for local services as part of its Children's Year efforts, the Bureau's leaders tacitly acknowledged that babies and children would, at best, have state or municipal aid rather than federally provided or guaranteed care. This meant, in practice, that infants received help from a hodgepodge of programs that reflected the varying commitment of and resources available to government agencies and private organizations. In New York City, physician S. Josephine Baker, a city official, established a program of nurse visits to tenement house mothers and opened infant welfare stations where mothers received education and clean milk. In Chicago, a private voluntary organization, the Infant Welfare Society, ran baby stations that served more than 10,000 infants in 1921. Mothers brought their babies to be examined by a doctor and the welfare station supported home visits by nurses, which numbered more than 81,000 that year and more than 102,000 by 1926. Following Baker's example, Kansas public health leader and physician Samuel Crumbine arranged for county health visitors to make home visits, assist in registering births, distribute copies of "The Kansas Mother's Book," and provide information about the "care of crippled and defective children." Other state outreach programs included a health train that rolled through Kansas with an exhibition car and a compartment for well-baby examinations. In the South, a health train came to the parishes of Louisiana, offering health demonstrations. In Los Angeles, California, the College Settlement

Association, a private group, led the way in establishing public health nursing services in the city. Urban babies benefited the most from the new programs. By 1930, 100 cities had municipal maternal and child health agencies. Whether their work, along with the efforts of numerous individual charities, religious organizations, and state agencies, helped mute calls for broader federal public programs remains unclear.[20]

In 1920, the Children's Bureau released a report detailing the success of the Children's Year and discussing measures that lowered infant mortality rates in other nations. Recognizing political barriers to developing similar programs in the United States, the Bureau proposed providing federal funds to the states to administer child health programs. A federal-state partnership, the report pointed out, succeeded in the past, and it offered two examples: the Smith-Lever Act of 1914, which supported cooperative-extension agricultural services through land-grant universities, and the Smith-Hughes Act of 1917, which supported vocational education in public schools. The comparisons made strategic sense, given past congressional support for the state-based programs. However, farmers and schools lacked powerful, organized, and skillful political opponents. The proposal from the Children's Bureau aroused the anger and political might of organized medicine as represented by the American Medical Association, as well as opposition from political conservatives. Opponents argued that federal funds for maternal and infant services would overstep the divide between federal and state responsibility for public health and between elected officials and private citizens. Medical opponents complained that the Children's Bureau plan appeared to challenge the fee-for-service model of private medical care delivery, threatening the livelihood of physicians. Only pediatricians' and women physicians' groups spoke up in favor of the legislation being proposed.[21]

After a fierce battle, the Children's Bureau leaders and their allies in women's organizations won passage of the Maternity and Infancy Protection Act of 1921, commonly referred to as the Sheppard-Towner Act. It would be a short-lived but critical victory for maternalist advocates of expanded support for women and children. Secured in the wake of passage of the Nineteenth Amendment, it may have won support from elected officials who feared antagonizing newly enfranchised women voters. The legislation enabled the Children's Bureau to distribute funds to states to reduce maternal and infant mortality through public health programs including education and health demonstration projects, nurse visits, midwife training, and health examinations. Only three states – Connecticut, Illinois, and Massachusetts – rejected the federal funds offered to them. Other states put the federal dollars to good use. Ohio, for example, used the funds to support demonstration projects, including one designed to meet the needs of African American mothers and babies in Cincinnati, as well as health clinics, educational programs, and pre- and postnatal home visits by nurses. Sheppard-Towner dollars did not pay for medical services; clinic nurses referred infants and children found to need care to community doctors for treatment. The Sheppard-Towner Act underwrote outreach to millions of American babies and mothers. Funding ceased in 1929, due in large part to the efforts of the American Medical Association and as elected officials learned that women did not vote as a bloc.[22]

In 1930, a year after the demise of Sheppard-Towner, the White House Conference on Child Health and Protection focused on the needs of dependent and neglected children and the services available to them. The legacy of Sheppard-Towner as well as fears of big government overreach appeared in the opening address of Secretary of the Interior Ray Lyman Wilbur, MD. He acknowledged both the federal government's interest in the young – "Every child is now *our* child" – and the necessary limits on federal action – "No one should get the idea that Uncle Sam is going to rock the baby to sleep."[23]

Studies of infant, child, and maternal mortality remained a core part of the Children's Bureau mission before and after Sheppard-Towner. From its earliest days the Bureau's leaders partnered with old allies and recruited new ones to provide advice and to give credibility to findings certain to be challenged as reflecting the sympathies or the political agenda of the women running the agency. Among those advising the Bureau leaders were birth control advocate Ira Wile, physician and social work supporter Richard Cabot, nursing leader Edna Foley, public health leader and physician Charles V. Chapin, and public administration expert Luther Gulick, as well as professionals from the Census Bureau, the Russell Sage Foundation, the Prudential Life Insurance Company, and leaders of settlement houses and charities. The distinguished list of consultants likely inoculated the Bureau against charges of bias in its findings because the team helped to design impressive and detailed community studies of infant deaths.[24]

The first study took place in Johnstown, Pennsylvania, a site selected because it had no large factories employing women. Investigators interviewed more than 1,500 women who gave birth in 1911. The researchers asked numerous questions, except those deemed too personal – inquiries about alcoholism and venereal disease. Critical judgments of the subjects did, however, make their way into the findings with notations in the Appendix such as a "Slovenly home" and "Attending midwife in Johnstown says father has syphilis." The report contained demographic details, an analysis of community sanitary and housing conditions, assessments of mothers' literacy rates, and information about women's working lives, birth attendants, and household economies. Not surprisingly, the study found that families living in the poorest, most crowded, and unsanitary ward, with its largely low-income immigrant population (Serbo-Croatian, Polish, Slovakian, and Italian, among others), experienced the greatest percentage of infant deaths.[25]

Reports on infant mortality continued to appear as investigators traveled to communities around the nation. Researchers in Montclair, New Jersey, a comfortable suburban community with a lower-than-average infant mortality rate, reported the same findings as the Johnstown study – a significantly higher rate of infant deaths among the poorest residents, mostly African Americans and immigrants, living in the community's crowded fourth ward. The opening of a well-baby clinic and home visits by public health nurses, the report concluded, helped to lower the death rate. Other studies followed in Manchester, New Hampshire, in 1917, Waterbury, Connecticut, in 1918, and both Brockton, Massachusetts, and Saginaw, Michigan, in 1919. Over the years the findings grew more pointed; the Saginaw study linked poverty, as measured by the father's income, with infant mortality. A 1919 letter from Robert Morse Woodbury, director of statistical research at the Children's Bureau, to its director, Julia Lathrop, asserted that the methods used in the studies were the first to connect mortality in the first year of life with "the economic status of the family" by focusing on fathers' earnings and maternal employment.[26]

The Children's Bureau sent investigators to rural communities in Kansas, Wisconsin, North Carolina, Mississippi, Montana, and Georgia beginning in 1916. Their findings replicated the infant mortality studies in cities in terms of the measurable effects of income and ethnic, racial, and regional differences on life chances. Unlike the studies by social welfare agencies and the reports of philanthropic groups aiming to inspire or shame civic authorities and donors into action, the Children's Bureau issued lengthy publications filled with mountains of data but little information about the lives and deaths of individual babies.

Community isolation proved important in shaping the ways babies grew up. It determined not only access to care but, at times, the degree to which families relied on local healing traditions, their use of community birth attendants such as midwives, and their access to reliable information. A study of a mountain county in Georgia from 1916 to 1918 revealed that due to illiteracy or limited education, only 17 percent of the mothers reported having printed matter on infant care and those who had read about babies consulted "books of questionable value or worthless advertising materials." In this community, families lived far from medical services, in crowded homes with primitive privies and no running water.[27]

Children's Bureau agents used every possible medium to reach American families. In "hundreds of rural towns across the United States," they showed a silent film, *Our Children*, displaying the efforts of Children's Bureau nurses in Gadsden, Alabama, in 1919. There, nurses ran segregated well-baby clinics and the film's text noted, "The colored folk are equally enthusiastic over their conference." The film also highlighted the training of girls to take care of babies in the "Little Mother's League," showed school toothbrush drills, and captured scenes of the area women's club organizing to make the community safe for babies. Another silent film from 1925, *The Best-Fed Baby*, showed a neighbor and a doctor helping a woman increase her milk supply rather than having to wean her baby. It also emphasized sunbathing, consulting Children's Bureau pamphlets, and good health habits.[28]

Reports issued by the Children's Bureau never used the words *health disparities*, a term of relatively recent vintage referring to health differences among social groups, but they did explore the problem and produced

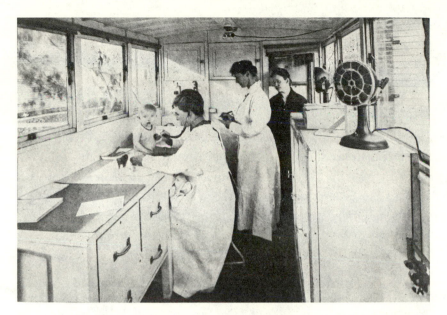

Figure 3.2 The Child-Welfare Special: A Suggested Method of Reaching Rural Communities, 1920
Credit: The Frances Sage Bradley, *The Child-Welfare Special: A Suggested Method of Reaching Rural Communities*, US Department of Labor, Children's Bureau (Washington, DC, 1920)

data identifying the variables that seemed to account for the varying rates of illness and death. A Baltimore field study of infant mortality published in 1923 documented the links among poverty, poor housing conditions, maternal employment, and infant mortality. It reported above-average infant death rates in African American families, in foreign-born Polish families, and in very poor native white families. Writing about the "isolation of a group from the life of a community as a whole," the report noted that if "it deprives men of economic opportunity, because they can not pass barriers of language or of color, the babies born into their homes will pay with a high mortality the price of the fathers' poverty." Elsewhere the report noted the legally separate and unequal health care facilities in the city and described the particular challenges faced by immigrant families. Subsequent studies such as *Causal Factors in Infant Mortality*, released in 1924, and "What Is Happening to Mothers and Babies in the District of Columbia?" published in 1928, reached similar conclusions about the social determinants of health. Racial differences appeared in many of the Bureau's reports and in the medical literature as well, especially as the African American population in Northern cities swelled in the years after World War I. An analysis by two physicians published in the *American Journal of Public Health* in 1926 concluded after a review of the literature and population data that the excessive infant mortality and morbidity rates of African American babies resulted from social factors. Their findings, like those of Children's Bureau researchers, pushed against the headwinds generated by social theorists asserting that humans existed along an absolute racial hierarchy.[29]

Although Julia Lathrop, director of the Children's Bureau, won praise as a friend of the "colored race" and spoke before groups such as the National Urban League, her personal activities did not translate into a programmatic effort by the Children's Bureau to address the particular problem of African American infant mortality. Given the limited mandate for the agency, the need to secure federal funding, and the racial politics of the 1910s and 1920s, the agency simply collected data about the effects of poverty and racial injustice and offered educational programs – many of them segregated. When social reformer Grace Abbott took over the leadership of the Children's Bureau in 1921, she confronted the same limits on her authority and at one point rebuffed an effort by Mary Church Terrell, a leading African American education and rights advocate who attempted to establish a "Colored Section" in the Children's Bureau. The Women's Bureau likewise rejected her overtures for creating a special section. Terrell reached out to officials in the Calvin Coolidge administration. Correspondence among the agencies and the White House resulted in the suggestion that Terrell seek work via a civil service examination – a brush-off wrapped in the cloak of rationality and fairness.[30]

Only after twenty-five years of work did the Children's Bureau publish in 1937 its first formal investigation focused on race and infant mortality: *Infant and Maternal Mortality among Negroes*. Rich in statistics and restrained in language, it noted that one of eight live births in the United States were of African American babies whose infant mortality rate was 86.1 per 1,000 live births as compared to 53 per 1,000 for white infants. Modern scholars understand and explain race as a social category, not a biological classification, but most Americans perceived race as a biological "fact." They viewed differences between groups as reflecting not only their presumed distinctive physical characteristics but also their collective destiny. The racism permeating American life inhibited the agents of the Children's Bureau, who documented its effects but had to leave it to those outside of government to propose solutions and develop programs designed to improve the health of the African American community.[31]

Relying largely on their own resources, African American organizations persisted in confronting problems of health in the community. From 1915 to 1930, under the auspices of National Negro Health Week, many communities held neighborhood clean-up campaigns, supported educational outreach efforts via newspapers, radio, film, and exhibits, and sponsored health demonstrations projects. Programmatic work included baby clinics, health clubs for mothers, and training programs for midwives. National Negro Health Week focused on combating all causes of excess mortality and morbidity with improving infant health a critical goal within a wider effort. In 1932, the US Public Health Service came on board and opened the Office of Negro Health Work as part of President Franklin Delano Roosevelt's New Deal programs. The health week evolved into a year-round program known as the National Negro Health Movement. The program eventually became part of the US National Public Health Service's Office of Negro Health, which disbanded in 1951 with the integration of Public Health Service programs.[32]

Minority group citizens faced substantial barriers to accessing care, especially in the Jim Crow South. Some white physicians refused to see African American patients. Restrictions on educational and training opportunities kept the number of African American practitioners in check. From the 1920s to the 1940s, the number of African American physicians remained stagnant. Hospitals serving African Americans were small and few in number and often lacked the resources needed to provide the best care. Poverty, racism, segregation, and social and geographic isolation also placed limits on African American families' ability to find and access medical care for their babies, and racism and segregation similarly restricted options for housing, schools, and employment that influenced overall community health.[33]

Children's Bureau staffers working in the rural South observed the severe, entrenched poverty in many African American communities. At times, offensive language littered the reports they sent back to Washington, DC, but their accounts often included trenchant observations about local conditions. In Cumberland County, South Carolina, Children's Bureau agents made home visits and opened segregated health conferences. The final report on this work, written by Dr. Frances Sage Bradley, lauded the African American community's interest in learning about modern baby care and in obtaining educational leaflets. Bradley also pointed out the lower incidence of rachitis (rickets) among African American children than among "the ignorant whites." Despite some disdain for community practices, Bradley responded in the affirmative when asked "whether or not the Bureau is making the right kind of noise." She wrote, "We are called 'the baby people,'" and reported that "fond mothers bring all their progeny wherever they expect to find us." The "baby people" found a receptive audience for the leaflets they gave away, including *Prenatal Care*, published in 1913, and *Infant Care*, published the following year. A Children's Bureau investigator in Cumberland County once discovered a bedridden old woman "entertaining herself with a copy" (of *Infant Care*) who said "she wished she had known some of these things when she was rearing her children."[34]

Children's Bureau publications entertained and educated several generations of Americans. Mrs. Max West, consulting with leading pediatricians, wrote the first edition of *Infant Care*, which appeared in 1914. It would be revised and published until 1989. A Children's Bureau correspondent called it "Uncle Sam's best seller." The initial compact volume had little new to say. The information it provided echoed *The Care of the Baby*, a booklet prepared by a committee of the American Association for the Study and Prevention of Infant Mortality and published in 1905 and later as a supplement to *Public Health Reports* in 1913. Nevertheless, it was *Infant Care* that became the nation's favorite baby care guide thanks to its widespread distribution. The Children's Bureau gave away copies, and senators and members of Congress used their free mailing privileges to send the booklet to new mothers in their districts. State and local health departments drew from *Infant Care* when publishing their own advice manuals, while women's magazines and infant care guides quoted or paraphrased its advice. Numerous baby books reprinted large portions of the slim volume. Despite the claims of opponents that in creating the Children's Bureau the federal government overstepped its proper role, ordinary Americans embraced the agency's advice about raising babies and children. *Infant Care* would be the federal government's most popular publication, with nearly 52 million copies distributed by 1965.[35]

The second and subsequent editions of *Infant Care* removed Mrs. West's name from the title page, replacing it with the names of the highly regarded physicians who helped to compile new material and suggest revisions. Unsurprisingly, the booklet emphasized the need to seek professional medical advice for all health matters. The idea that "doctors knew best" developed within a broader movement toward scientific motherhood in the early twentieth century. Ostensibly about giving mothers the tools to rear healthy babies, scientific motherhood pushed women to follow expert advice and to eschew the wisdom dispensed by friends and relatives. The modern infant care practices it promoted reflected the enshrinement of biomedical knowledge and the growing cultural power of physicians.

As a leading proselytizer for scientific motherhood, the Children's Bureau produced numerous pamphlets, among them guides to breastfeeding, booklets about keeping babies and children healthy, and instructions on sunbathing. The topics varied, but three core ideas appeared in almost all of the little volumes. First, prevention, such as sunbathing to prevent rickets, proved far superior to cure. Second, germs had to be vanquished, lest a deadly infection take hold. Third, infants' prescribed daily schedules required absolute allegiance. In addition to the implicit warning that disease or death might follow should these commandments be broken, Children's Bureau publications and the public health materials that reproduced their messages detailed the costs of haphazard parenting. The warnings evolved over time. Initially, the materials emphasized household control. Feeding babies on a strict schedule made mothers' lives easier as they cared for their homes and for other children than if they responded to the cries of hungry babies whenever they arose. As an advice book explained, a mother should "endeavor to so regulate her baby's habits as to leave ample time for her own rest and recreation." Later, physiological arguments, specifically preventing gastrointestinal upsets, validated the practice of strict feeding and toileting schedules. Finally, psychological needs became the principal justification for obeying the nursery time clock, as experts argued that babies needed to be taught to master their impulses in order to become successful adults. Failure to inculcate proper routines came to be seen as posing particular risks, including disobedient children who rebelled against parental authority.[36]

Like scientific management prescribed by business efficiency experts to maximize productivity through the strict regulation of the workday, nursery management aimed to impose discipline to reap profits – healthier infants and children – through order and regularity. The 1929 edition of *Infant Care* commanded that infants be given orange or tomato juice by the end of their first month to prevent scurvy, and that bowel training begin as early as the end of the first month and conclude no later than the eighth month. Replicating the time management guidelines insisted upon by efficiency experts, hangtags distributed by the Children's Bureau titled "Baby's Daily Time Card" gave detailed instructions by age for the ideal infant schedule. For babies up to four months of age, the day began with a 6:00 AM breastfeeding and ended at 6:20 PM with "bed, lights out, windows open, doors shut." There would be a 10:00 PM feeding and, for the first two months, a 2:00 AM feeding as well. By the tenth, eleventh, and twelfth months, the infant's day concluded in half-hour intervals, undressing for the night at 5:00 PM with the administration of cod liver oil and either tomato or orange juice. Next came supper at 5:30 PM: cereal, zwieback (a dry cracker) or dry toast applesauce, or prune pulp and boiled whole milk. Then, at 6:00 PM, the day ended with the familiar routine "bed, lights out, windows open, doors shut." Time and work discipline, so well charted in the history of the Industrial Revolution, came into the nursery.[37]

Ideally, nurseries operated like modern factories with mothers as managers who imposed discipline and assessed outcomes. Ideally, mothers fed their babies on age-appropriate three- or four-hour intervals and ignored cries of hunger that arose between feedings. Ideally, older babies received no additional sustenance between 10:00 PM and 6:00 AM and had their nighttime cries ignored. But just as assembly lines sometimes broke down or workers rebelled and forced managers to surrender to the culture of the shop floor, so too did mothers face rebellion and resistance and they sometimes surrendered to infants' demands. Women's letters to the Children's Bureau staffers would recount their violations of correct infant care protocols and the reasons for them.

Of course, some mothers held firm. A woman interviewed by a modern sociologist about her recollections of infant care in the 1930s and 1940s recalled that if her baby began to cry five minutes before the 2:00 AM feeding, she would let the wailing continue, even as her own mother who lived in the same house begged her to feed the infant. But the word of the doctor came before the demands of the infant. As she explained, "This was the way it had to be. If [the doctor] said every four hours, every four hours. It was the right thing to do." An African American woman interviewed about the same era also recollected her obedience to medical decrees with the exception of skipping the 2:00 AM feeding – but only after gaining the approval of her physician.[38]

If not all babies lived according to the prescribed ideals, it was not for lack of effort by the Children's Bureau. In addition to distributing printed advice, the Bureau reached out via radio. Starting in 1926, it supplied scripts about infant and childcare to the US Department of Agriculture's Radio Service program, *Housekeepers' Chat.* Infant care advice featured in episodes such as "Why Fruit Juice for the Baby," "Taking Baby to the Country," "How Much Sleep for the Baby," and "The Well-Behaved Baby." One hundred radio stations broadcast the shows to an audience of about 5 million. Women read the scripts on air, taking on the role of "Aunt Sammy," the implied wife of Uncle Sam. Aunt Sammy urged her audience to write for a copy of *Infant Care,* and in some episodes she read answers to questions sent from listeners and offered tips on infant care. "Aunt Sammy," a "friend" remarked in the script titled "A Sunshine Package for the New Baby," "I do wish you'd emphasize in your talks the fact that if babies are accustomed to the taste of cod-liver from the very first, they usually *like* it." That was pure government propaganda; numerous accounts in baby books and diaries make clear that babies loathed it.[39]

The airwaves carried lots of infant care advice into individual homes. In 1929, the second director of the Children's Bureau, Grace Abbott, began hosting radio broadcasts on NBC in a show titled *Your Child.* State and local health departments also produced programs for area broadcasters, taking advantage of this popular form of communication to send information directly into the home and deliver a message that seemed more personal when spoken aloud rather than conveyed in print. And the audience was growing. By 1935, 75 percent of American households owned radios. As a historian argued, by harnessing the same techniques as commercial marketers, health promoters competed with corporate interests to deliver messages to the public. However, food, beverage, and pharmaceutical manufacturers, which were among the leading radio advertisers, also offered information about infants' diet and health. Their goals were sales, not health.[40]

A survey of 2,758 white families and 202 African American families conducted for the White House Conference on Child Health and Protection in 1930 attempted to discover if the health messages sent in print and over the airwaves were received and followed. The study found that radio reached fewer African American families than Euro American families, and that African American households relied instead on child-care books and pamphlets. The research also yielded the unsurprising finding that social class determined much about infants' daily lives, from the likelihood they would enjoy a sunbath, to the length of time they were breastfed, to whether they attended day nurseries. The questions asked in the survey, not unexpectedly, dovetailed with the advice dispensed by infant care advisors.[41]

Boiled down to its essence, medical advice about infant care consisted of a few simple commands: breastfeed your baby, prepare bottles properly if you cannot breastfeed, carefully introduce other foods but only the right ones, and give babies cod liver oil and sunbaths. Sometimes printed materials and radio shows included additional instructions, typically about sleeping, bathing, and coping with teething and bowel complaints. Full-length infant care books often incorporated advice about household hygiene and the treatment of minor medical conditions as well as descriptions of conditions and symptoms necessitating a doctor or clinic visit. Care of babies in the summer merited particular attention because deadly infant diarrhea often resulted from improperly stored or prepared milk. Don't wean in summer, keep bottled milk cold and sweet, and open the window in the baby's room, the experts advised. The essential advice varied little from New York, Kentucky, Pennsylvania, or Texas.

Delivering these messages to new immigrants became a priority for public health officials. By 1920, native-born children of foreign-born parents comprised 22.9 percent of the US population. To reach their mothers and fathers, health departments printed infant care advice in many languages, among them Bohemian, French, German, Greek, Hungarian, Italian, Lithuanian, Polish, Portuguese, Slovak, Spanish, and Yiddish. Although public health experts presumed the foreign-born needed educating in the American way, they praised immigrant mothers for one custom: breastfeeding. Sometimes the compliment seemed intended as a backhanded slap at well-off American-born women who refused to suckle their infants. A brochure from the Chicago Department of Health with the lengthy and deliberate title "What Must We Do to Be Saved: The Slaughter of Little Babies in the City of Chicago Amounts to 6000 Yearly, at least 3500 of Those Deaths Are Avoidable, Education for Prevention" included a drawing of two women. One appeared to be an immigrant mother with a healthy breastfed baby; the other mother, who looked to be well off and wore a fancy hat, had a scrawny bottle-fed baby.[42]

The near-incessant complaints of medical authorities regarding women who refused to breastfeed their babies overlooked physicians' complicity in the act; many doctors subtly or not so subtly encouraged bottle-feeding by dispensing detailed prescriptions for scientific infant formulas. Regular management of bottle-fed infants kept patients in the waiting rooms. Well-child conferences, an established service in clinics and private doctors' offices by the 1920s, further fueled mothers' reliance on expert medical advice. Nurses weighed and measured babies and physicians examined them; mothers went home with instructions on infant care and feeding.[43]

Modern public health officials dispensed information about infant care in many forms, hoping to make mothers follow scientific practices. Did they succeed? Did families view advice from the federal government or other public agencies as unwanted or even invasive? Did parents attempt to shield their babies from the influence of the Children's Bureau and its allies? No. A significant number of citizens placed their faith in the "baby people" and tried to follow their advice. Citizens perceived the Children's Bureau as a partner in infant protection and as the possessor of useful knowledge. Families kept and cherished Children's Bureau pamphlets and wrote for help, barraging the agency with as many as 125,000 letters a year. Many correspondents referenced *Infant Care* and sought further information or help with matters the booklet did not address. In some cases, the letter writers turned to the Children's Bureau staff as the final arbiters after having consulted with several physicians; in other instances, they wrote because they could not afford to see a doctor. While the volume of letters declined over time, the lasting impact of the Children's Bureau's work appeared in letters from women complaining that their daughters-in-law did not adhere to the advice in *Infant Care*.

The missives arrived in Washington, DC, from the rich and the poor, mailed from rural hamlets and big cities, typed on fancy stationary or written in pencil on two-cent postcards. An historian's analysis of the correspondence from 1915 to 1932 determined that most of the letters came from native-born white women living on farms or in small towns, although residents of all regions and from all racial groups wrote to ask for help. Not all the questions concerned ailments. Mothers asked about patterns for baby clothes, whether to use baby powder or baby oil, and whether to circumcise their newborn sons, something the Children's Bureau refrained from answering. When the letters described disabled and seriously ill infants with complicated conditions, the physicians who replied referred the family to community doctors or clinics. In a few cases, agency correspondents wrote to state public health authorities asking them to help out the family.[44]

Letters from the Children's Bureau staff to local agencies increased as the Great Depression led families to write to President Roosevelt and First Lady Eleanor Roosevelt for help. The White House staff forwarded letters about child health to the Children's Bureau, and the staff there steered the writers to charitable agencies or gave them the address of their state or city public health department. Impoverished families also wrote directly to the Children's Bureau. A woman from Yarmouth, Maine, wrote in 1937 asking for a layette and received a reply with the address of the director of the Maternity and Child section in the state's Department of Public Health. An African American woman from

Magnolia, Mississippi, with a similar request had her letter referred to the Red Cross office in nearby McComb. The Red Cross investigator wrote to the Children's Bureau to report that after meeting with the family, assessing their farm and livestock, and determining they would produce six bales of cotton that year, that the agency would supply the family with a layette. The desperate letters often revealed the sacrifices parents made for their babies and the personal circumstances that led them to seek help. A woman from Brooklyn, New York, with a newborn suffering from a chronic illness, two other children, and a husband out of work wrote to Mrs. Roosevelt for help after borrowing money and pawning her jewelry. A mother from Coalwood, Montana, asked the Children's Bureau for help in a six-page handwritten letter detailing the medical bills she could not pay, including nearly $100 for the birth of a premature baby who spent a month in an incubator. With families struggling to pay medical bills and sometimes failing to do so, physicians struggled to earn a living. Understandably, some of the doctors resented the well-baby services provided by public clinics and charitable agencies. Acutely aware that physicians' organizations opposed its work, the Children's Bureau staffers appeared to go out of their way to abstain from diagnosis by mail, instead referring babies with medical complaints to doctors.[45]

Avoiding other entanglements, the Children's Bureau leaders eschewed corporate endorsements and politely rejected the companies that wrote hoping to secure their support. When mothers wrote to inquire about what brand of formula to purchase, or whether they had chosen the right brand of laxative, the Children's Bureau correspondents for the most part avoided direct answers. The letters from mothers, filled with the brand name products they bought for their babies, suggests just how effectively baby product advertisers reached consumers through their infants. The manufacturers' letters demonstrated how assiduously they worked to expand their sales by winning the endorsement of the trusted Children Bureau and because the manufacturers understood that mothers and fathers would invest in their babies, even in hard times.

Perhaps the dedicated efforts of the Children's Bureau staffers and their quick replies to anxious parents (usually within a day) as well as the vigorous efforts of the federal government to assist down-and-out Americans through federal New Deal programs helps to explain the answer to a question asked in a 1937 Gallup Poll: "Should the federal government aid state and local governments in providing medical care for babies at birth?" The pollsters heard a resounding yes. Seventy-four percent answered affirmatively, 16 percent no, and 10 percent had no opinion. The concept of the citizen baby, it appears, took root in American popular consciousness and culture thanks to the work of government employees, private organizations, and health and welfare professionals. Uncle Sam became a friend of the family. He didn't rock the baby to sleep, but he felt free to suggest when bedtime should begin.[46]

4

BRINGING UP BABIES I
Giving, Spending, Saving, Praying

I N 1900, RACHEL BIGGER'S MOTHER PASTED a lock of her hair into her baby book and wrote about Rachel's first shoes and her first haircut. At birth, Rachel received gifts of silver and silk; her baby book contained page after page listing items given to her, such as pearl bib pins – she got six – and elaborate items of clothing. Rachel's granddaughter Susan Scholotte, born in 1947, also had a lock of hair pasted into her baby book. However, by the mid-twentieth century, practical baby presents replaced expensive belongings made of gold and silver. Family friends and relatives gave Susan an impressive number of presents, but they tended to be useful items like a bassinette, bibs, and a bottle warmer, along with lots of clothes. Generational shifts appear in other baby books. Brian Smith, born in 1891, shared his baby book with his sons, born in 1921 and 1923, and his granddaughter Betty, born in 1954. Betty collected far fewer gifts than her grandfather, although she did receive some very elegant items and a lot of clothes. Grandpa Brian Smith collected $60 in gold pieces at birth; granddaughter Betty received $40–$65 in cash and a $25 savings bond – far less than her grandfather given the rate of inflation. As these examples suggest, baby books provide a window into the material and financial world of infants.[1]

Baby books, the large and small volumes in which mothers noted the details of their infants' lives, are close cousins to birders' notebooks. They record specific kinds of information – birth date, height, weight, gifts, physical milestones, illnesses, and religious celebrations, among other things – and they provide space for personal observations. Some baby books document an entire life from infancy through adulthood. Daniel Roebuck's baby book began with his birth in 1904 in Vermont, detailed his childhood battles with "summer complaint," mumps, chicken pox, and whooping cough, and then followed him through college, marriage, and the beginning of a career as a civil engineer in 1927. The baby book of Leroy James, born in 1901 in Gladstone, Michigan, became a full biographical record, including notes about his accidents, illnesses, schooling, marriage, and a bout of influenza during the tail end of the epidemic in 1919. A drawing pasted into his baby book in 1902 shows a boy holding a cigarette with the caption "On this day baby smoked his first cigarette – given to him by the artist, Mr. J. R. Walsh." On January 18, 1920, Leroy added a note: "I am still smoking."[2]

Most baby books record only a few days, weeks, or months of an infant's life, but they provide information that cannot be gleaned from other sources. In presenting daily events that would otherwise be unrecorded, the volumes illuminate the ways cultural beliefs and social forces flowed in and out of the nursery. They show how infants prompted their parents to learn or at least encounter prevailing medical theories and they reveal the deep well of community knowledge and ethnic group wisdom that also nourished nursery practices.

Infants introduced their parents to new products and habits of consumption, drawing them into modern consumer culture. Historians of capitalism investigate how standards of living changed, how culture shaped what people bought, how manufacturing shifted from home to factory, and how a growing number of products made their way into homes first as luxuries and later as necessities. Histories of babies reveal how consumer products – formula, toys, clothes, and other goods – appeared initially in the nurseries of the upper and middle classes and then made their way into working-class and impoverished households.[3]

In the opening decades of the twentieth century, growing numbers of Americans began participating in the consumer economy. The purchase of both durable goods (items that can be used for several years) and nondurable goods grew in the years after World War I, reflecting both an expanding economy and the growth of advertising. "Buy now, pay later" credit and installment plans enabled many of the purchases, including durable baby products like carriages, cribs, and high chairs, as well as quickly used goods such as baby bottles and baby clothes. Seizing the opportunity to buy more in flush times, Americans saved less than in earlier decades and borrowed more. Nevertheless, they put some money aside in savings accounts and bought insurance policies, another form of savings. Aggregate economic data tell this story; baby book entries provide a closer look at buying habits, economic conditions, the kinds of products manufacturers made and sold for infants, and how fashions went in and out of style.[4]

Mining the information in baby books yields some interesting nuggets. Gift lists show how, over time, particular products shifted from the category of luxury to necessity. Advertisement-laden baby books reveal the pitches made to parents based on the growing fear of germs and the desire to raise a healthy, "better" baby. Baby books promoted good fiscal as well as good hygiene habits with advertisements for life insurance policies and bank accounts. In some instances, the baby books functioned as account books, recording deposits and payments. Collectively, baby books make visible the small decisions that forged a consumer culture and they document the variations in spending and saving among families according to their income, ethnicity, and traditions.

Baby books varied in form and content; some mimicked scrapbooks, housing small keepsakes such as locks of hair, baby teeth, palm and foot tracings, birth announcements, certificates from schools, and items from houses of worship. Other baby books resembled diaries and contained the details of mothers' work and infants' daily lives. The vast majority of mothers used baby books with printed entries, although a few made their own. Often baby books served as photograph albums. They contained formal studio portraits and, increasingly, homemade snapshots as beloved babies helped make cameras household items.[5]

Kodak produced the original "Brownie" camera in 1900, expanding the ranks of amateur photographers. Affordable and aggressively marketed, the camera found its way into thousands of homes. The company produced an instruction manual for Brownie owners interested in taking baby pictures and made baby photographs a centerpiece of its marketing campaign. A full-page advertisement showed a mother photographing her baby and reminded readers:

> It makes no difference how often the baby goes to the photographer – and for the sake of admiring relatives his visits should be frequent – the record of his infant days is incomplete unless there are home pictures to supplement the more formal studio photographs.

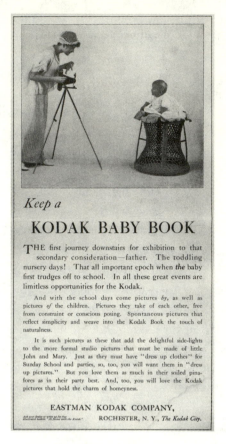

Figure 4.1 "Keep a Kodak Baby Book," advertisement, 1915
Credit: Wayne P. Ellis Collection of Kodakiana, John W. Hartman Center
for Sales, Advertising and Marketing History, David M. Rubenstein
Library, Duke University

Robert Newell Harris's family took a photograph the day after his birth at
the Chicago home of his grandparents in 1913, while Helen Pike's 1915
baby book contained a dedicated page for "Kodak pictures." The ease
and growing popularity of home photography did not end the tradition
of obtaining a professional photograph. The baby book of Christopher
Henley, born in 1917, recounted his visit to a professional portrait studio
in Bradford, Pennsylvania, on his way to church to be christened. Henley,
his elegant baby book reported, was "driven by Murphy, held by Maloney,
and had a McCarthy for a godfather."[6]

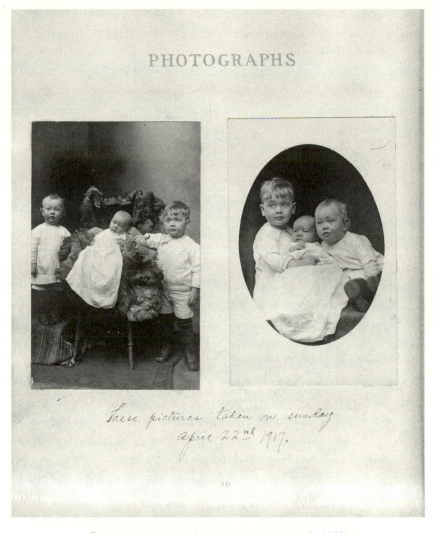

Figure 4.2 Photograph page from baby book, 1917
Credit: History and Special Collections, UCLA Library Special Collections

Decorated with paintings of cherubic babies and cute animals, fancy baby books typically included saccharine verses by romantic poets. Leading female artists illustrated many of them, including Maud Humphrey, the mother of actor Humphrey Bogart. With their silk covers, high price, and pages for recording things like "first appearance at table" and "first short clothes," elaborate and expensive baby books addressed the interests and household practices of a small set of wealthy Americans. They contained long lists of needed items of clothing and suggestions as to the ideal fabrics for them. The volumes' authors presumed that hired nursery maids would care for the newborns and so the text in one, published in 1899, advised, "under no circumstances allow the nurse to punish the child or scold it. All cases requiring discipline should be referred to the mother." Some of the fancy baby books had, along with drawings of an infant with a uniformed nursery maid, a place for recording her name.[7]

Upper-class families displayed their social position in myriad ways in baby books, from affixing their formal printed birth announcements on preprinted pages designed for that purpose to filling blank pages with photographs of homes and servants and accounts of travel. Irma Drescher's mother recorded in her baby book her first outing in an automobile in 1911, a time when only 5 in 1,000 Americans owned cars. Lily Brown's baby book from 1917 included fifty-two photographs of her family's large Victorian house in Montclair, New Jersey, and their summer place in Portland, Maine. It also contained a letter from a soldier in the American Expeditionary Force of World War I, thanking Lily for the Christmas package he had received in her name. Lily's wealthy family and their friends gave her many gifts, including a $10 gold piece used to purchase a silver bowl, a $25 bank account opened by her grandfather, and another $25 gift from a great aunt to purchase something for her room, such as "a desk or writing table," and two other gifts of $5. Lily's privileged start in life thus began with $70; the average industrial worker in that era made about $96 a month.[8]

The practice of keeping a baby record slowly moved down the social ladder. Publishers began printing less expensive volumes on cheap paper and retail stores, banks, insurance companies, and national brand manufacturers began giving away baby books to promote their products. Unlike printed advertising in quickly discarded magazines and newspapers, advertisement-laden baby books remained in the home for a long time; every time mothers opened them up to make notes they would be reminded that modern babies needed modern products.

Baby book advertisements reflected the boom in health consumerism spawned by growing "germ consciousness." In many instances, product information and health advice from government agencies appeared side by side, reinforcing their respective messages. A few of the advertisers resorted to fearmongering, suggesting dire results for babies not reared with the right products, but most took a positive approach. Buy the right products and your baby will be healthy; open a bank account and invest in education and your baby will be wealthy and wise. Manufacturers and retailers also sought adult consumers through baby book advertising. Coke Dandruff Cure and Hair Tonic produced a baby book in 1903. A 1913 baby book from Chicago included an advertisement for a billiards table. Other baby books hawked products ranging from carriages to corsets. Of course, infant images appeared in all kinds of marketing materials. "Salesbabies," as one author dubbed them, long predated the consumer revolution of the twentieth century and their adorable faces have kept them in business into the twenty-first century. Infant images appeared on product labels, trade cards, calendars, posters, and in print advertisements in newspapers and magazines. Iver Johnson marketed its revolvers as safe for babies, "accidental discharge impossible," and the Castle Hall Twins shown being carried by a stork promoted cigars of the same name. Cuteness sold.[9]

Most, but not all, baby books available to historians record the lives of economically secure, Euro American, nonimmigrant families, making it impossible to use them for statistical sampling or to inventory products in the homes of babies of various ethnic and racial groups. Baby books recounting the lives of disabled babies and of those who died in infancy are hard to find. Exceptions include the 1906 baby book of Ellen Forest, born in Norway, Maine, who became blind at the age of nine weeks, and the baby book of a boy born in Portland, Maine, in 1921. He died the following year shortly before his first birthday. The pithy and eloquent last words in his baby book reported he was "Born on Saturday, died on Sunday, buried on Monday." And "Thundered when born for one week and when dead." Though exceptional, baby books such as these document experiences that were far from extraordinary; the specter of disease, disability, and death hovered over all nurseries.[10]

Birth order proved to be a profound bias in baby books. Nearly all of them recount the lives of firstborn children. Many mothers seemed not to have had the time or energy to make entries in the baby books of later-born infants or twins – who also appear infrequently in baby books. This reluctance to keep a baby book for each new infant hurt sales, so a 1931 article in *Publishers Weekly* offered a few strategies for selling baby record books for siblings, including underscoring the importance of record keeping and encouraging firstborn children to help "keep little brother's or sister's book."[11]

Despite the efforts of publishers, the thrill of first-time events – baths, haircuts, utterances, meetings with relatives – seemed to be gone by the time the second, third, or fourth or additional infants joined the family. Later-arriving babies sometimes received only a brief line or two in the baby book of the firstborn child. Aviator Amelia Earhart, born in 1897 and known to her family as Millie, shared a baby book with her younger sister Muriel, born in 1899. With the arrival of a second daughter comparisons began to be made. Millie never sucked her thumb, her mother wrote, though a page in her baby book included a poem praising the habit as a way to relieve pain. Muriel took up the thumb-sucking habit at the age of seven months. Without referencing prevailing theories of character development, Mrs. Earhart made clear she recognized the differences between her daughters, writing elsewhere about their distinct temperaments and habits. Millie slept a lot and entertained herself; Muriel proved more demanding. Brothers Tom and Harry Warner, born in Bangor, Maine, in 1917 and 1920, respectively, also shared a baby book that recounted, among other things, the first automobile ride and moving picture show experienced by the elder boy and much less about his younger sibling. Playwright Arthur Laurents (birth name Arthur Milton Levine), born in 1917, shared a baby book with his younger sister Edith. Their mother noted that both wore short clothes immediately after arriving home following hospital births, but Arthur had the majority of entries.[12]

Fathers did not appear to keep records in baby books, but their infant care activities appeared in some of them. In 1906, Melanie Craig's mother described her time playing on the floor with her papa, who wouldn't stop and come to dinner. Other fathers became visible only in photographs; in some of the images they clutch their infants stiffly and appear uncomfortable as they hold their pose for the camera, but most of them look happy and proud. Fathers did write letters about their infants, sending inquiries to experts when they needed advice and keeping family members updated about their babies' growth and accomplishments. One man, worried about his baby's feeding problems, wrote to the leading pediatrician of the day, Luther Emmett Holt, for advice in 1908. Holt's small volume, *The Care and Feeding of Children*, published in 1894, reached best-seller status, and the father turned to him after consulting several physicians who failed to help with his child's difficulties. Three years later, the man wrote to Holt once again, about another child. Another father, Joy Morton, founder of the Morton Salt Company, wrote regularly to his own father about his daughters born in 1911, 1915, and 1925. From 1913 to 1936, a University of Wisconsin professor of Hellenistic Greek and Semitic languages kept notes in the book *Cute Things the Baby Says* on the verbal development of his six children, much of which began as they neared the end of babyhood. Perhaps his academic pursuits sparked his interest in his children's burgeoning linguistic skills.[13]

The majority of baby books contained only a few entries, usually made at the beginning of an infant's life: date of birth, height, and weight, as well as names of parents, grandparents, doctor, nurse, and the date of christening. Many mothers recorded the vital statistics – height and weight – for a few months or longer. Sometimes they made notes about their babies' outings or holiday celebrations with family. In a special case, a baby book began when the infant reached a few months of age. His mother, living in the oil fields of Texas in the early 1920s and using a baby book given away by the Borden Condensed Milk Company, explained, "No cards were sent as Baby came sooner than expected and no one thought he would live."[14]

Baby book entries suggest that the tentative first steps of poor and working-class families making their way into the modern consumer world often began with purchases designed to preserve or promote the health of their infants or to lighten the burden of newborn care as mothers coped with household chores and sometimes the demands of earning a living as well. Families bought bottles and nipples from stores or from catalogs and, when they could afford to do so, substituted manufactured baby foods and baby clothes for homemade items. In one instance, a father kept careful records of the expenses his newborn entailed. On the day of his son's birth, February 16, 1900, he spent $1.44 on telegrams and fifty cents on stamps, he bought a shield (presumably a nipple shield) for his wife for thirty cents, and he paid ten cents for cold cream and thirty cents for a bottle.[15]

Babies' costs figured into both personal household accounts and into larger political debates. A well-off father documented the expense of adding a baby to the household in a 1916 article in *Good Housekeeping* magazine. Expanding the family forced him and his wife to consider the expense and the need for economizing, even as relatives urged them to spend more on a layette. The new arrival cost them $131.16 for the first year, not including the cost of the doctor, amounting to $60, plus a hospital delivery and nursing services that came in at $144.45 for a three-week stay. Subsequently, a home nurse stayed for a few weeks at a cost of $33. The entire family budget totaled $2,540 for the year; the couple pinched pennies by making do without a maid and only the occasional services of a charwoman and laundress. Another calculation of the costs of a baby appeared a few years later in a booklet produced by the Voluntary Parenthood League, an organization that advocated for the availability of contraception. The booklet quoted the War Labor Board finding that it required a wage of $34.80 a week, or more than $1,700 a year, for a family of five with three children of school age to support itself, and reported that the costs for the birth, outfitting the baby, and prenatal care amounted to about $200 without luxuries. The League reminded readers that the government had "only two logical alternatives. Either it must guarantee a good rearing to every child born, or it must let the parents have a chance to understand how to have only those children for whom they can provide." The government elected not to follow either logical option.[16]

In 1901, the average American family spent 42.5 percent of household income on food, 14 percent on clothing, and 23.3 percent on housing, leaving just 20.2 percent for other items. Many families struggled to acquire even the basic necessities, coping with unemployment, sickness, and insufficient earnings. In the three decades from 1900 to 1930, the economy grew, enabling families to spend more on consumer goods. The infant clothing industry boomed, as did the toy business. Overall living conditions improved to the point that, by 1930, two-thirds of American households had electricity (and more acquired it later with New Deal rural electrification programs), and half of all American homes had flush toilets. Until the collapsing economy of the Great Depression left Americans with fewer discretionary dollars, Americans bought all kinds of consumer goods, from food and clothing to radios.[17]

Families who could afford to do so went shopping for their babies at department stores and neighborhood retail shops and by way of mail order catalogs. A 1925 manual written to train workers in retail sales reported "some mothers take such delight in baby things that they want as complete an outfit as possible and frequently those are customers of moderate means." Scholars point out that over the course of the twentieth century child consumers came to be seen as partially or fully independent subjects, able to indicate their likes, dislikes, and desires to parents and to sales clerks. In this way, children helped shape the way retailers operated and to influence the behavior of industries and advertisers. Babies too participated in the world of goods, but did so by directing parents to the marketplace rather than vocalizing their desires for particular items.[18]

Manufacturers marketed to the parents of babies the new, the cute, and the stylish, not just the practical and the healthful. New, must-have products came on the market and families with money bought them for their babies. Celluloid, a flammable plastic developed in the nineteenth century as a substitute for ivory, appeared in pedestrian products, like toys, in the twentieth century and seemingly had a bit of cachet. Writing in a 1910 baby book, a mother described a "celluloid" ball and "celluloid" ring presumably for teething, as if the designation conveyed something special. A small baby book made with a celluloid cover appeared in 1916, showing yet another use for this chemical compound. Celluloid apparently remained popular for some time; in 1925, Jennie Blue's baby book noted her birth in Cadillac, Michigan, and her receipt of "celluloid" rattles and "celluloid" dolls, carefully distinguished from the cloth and rubber dolls also given to her.[19]

Formula manufacturers quickly capitalized on baby books as advertising media. Well aware that infant feeding problems often stemmed from contaminated milk or water, they began advertising their products in women's magazines in the 1870s and 1880s as a safe alternative and later used baby books to reach potential consumers. In 1901, Just's Food Company of Syracuse, New York, published *Baby's Red Letter Day*, a baby book featuring the art of painter and illustrator Jessie Wilcox Smith. Eskay's Food for Infants, produced by Philadelphia pharmaceutical maker Smith, Kline and French, also reached out to consumers with a baby book. The Imperial Granum Company placed an image of "La Nourrice" by well-known American artist Mary Cassatt on the cover of *Our Baby's Own Book* published in 1914, which it distributed to physicians rather than directly to mothers. Along with copies of the book the doctors received a postcard with the suggestion "We hope the accompanying Rules for Nursing Mothers will meet with your approval and that you will clinically test Imperial Granum for such cases." Despite its beautiful cover and effort to reach consumers through professionals, the company achieved an artistic low with its doggerel:

> Don't have one bit of hesitation
> Insist on fresh air and ventilation
> Don't fail to show that you're perturbed
> If your sleep and rest time is disturbed …
> Demand Imperial Granum, baby's best food
> It won't tax Daddy's economical mood.[20]

Formula advertising promised healthy babies but in some instances implied that competing products might be reservoirs of germs. Advertising expert Helen Woodward learned, when she wrote copy for a baby food company in 1909, that cheerful advertisements sold more than "sob stories." Her client instructed her to "Tell 'em always to go to a doctor if they can and get a special prescription for their own baby. If they can't do that, tell 'em how bad the milk supply is in lots of places and that they'd better use this food." Her advertisements stressed the "scientific basis" of the foods, she explained, but also played to mothers' joys and fears.[21]

Challenged by the aggressive marketing of formula companies, dairies responded by distributing baby books filled with paeans to fresh milk. The Peavely Dairy in St. Louis, Missouri, first produced a baby book in 1908. Following the outbreak of World War I, it shifted its marketing strategy and came up with a patriotic pitch, adding a touch of Social Darwinian theory for good measure. Along with four pages promoting milk consumption and milk recipes, the text shamelessly aligned drinking fresh milk with victory overseas.

> The soldier or sailor, the marine or coast guardsman, who is in perfect health, is a more formidable enemy. He is capable of greater service to his country and the defense of those principles of justice and humanity, which today are under attack in all corners of the world. The colossal fight for freedom that is now being waged against the forces of tyranny must result in the survival of the fittest. To be fit for any emergency is our job. Good, fresh milk helps us in the attainment of this goal.

Most dairies facing competition from formula companies ignored both popular social theories and foreign wars, instead soliciting customers by presenting their milk as being of good quality. "Compliments of Triangle Dairy cream top milk, it whips. Tate Brothers, Gekeler Lane, Boise, Idaho," read the inscription in one baby book.[22]

The bacteriological revolution transformed public health efforts to combat disease, inspired entrepreneurs to market germ-killing and germ-free products, and challenged reformers to teach poor, immigrant, and rural families about infant and household hygiene. Families who could afford the expense invested in up-to-date bathroom plumbing and purchased window screens and other products designed to keep dirt and disease out of the home. Mothers who could afford to adopted the latest hygienic routines, dedicating themselves to following doctors' directives. Companies took advantage of the growing knowledge of and worries about germs to sell cleaning products as the chief line of defense against the invisible invaders. In seeding baby books with advertising, manufacturers, marketers, and retailers hoped to reap a rich harvest. When babies thrived, so did business.

Book of Baby Mine, illustrated by Melcena Burns Denny and published by the Simplicity Company in Grand Rapids, Michigan, beginning in 1915, epitomized the link between babies and consumer capitalism. Distributed throughout the country, it contained advertisements solicited from local merchants who gave away copies to mothers in their respective communities. After its initial success, the newly named Book of Baby Mine Company took over production and issued twelve updated editions in the years that followed, most recently in 1983. Of the ninety-six pages in the book, thirty-eight offered places for recording information, including notes on milestones, health, and events, such as birthdays and religious holidays. Like simple baby books given away by health departments and competitors, the volume included a significant amount of infant care advice. Like fancy baby books, *Book of Baby Mine* contained numerous pages for pasting in photographs and ones where mothers filled in responses to prompts such as "first time at Dancing School" and "first Christmas." Even as babies linked their families to the expanding consumer culture, they also kept them rooted in the world of religion. But houses of worship did not advertise; merchants did.

Community retailers placed advertisements throughout *Book of Baby Mine*, inviting mothers to come and buy. Oster Brothers Furniture supplied a copy for a girl born in 1915 in Youngstown, Ohio. One page interwove "Hints to Mothers" and "Proper Care of Baby" from the Infant Welfare Society with purchasing recommendations. Following the first bit of advice, "Be sure to get a comfortable baby carriage at Oster Bros," came suggestions on feeding and bathing. Another copy of *Book of Baby Mine* from 1930 included the reminder "Though the book would sell for $2.50, remember – it is given to you absolutely free by advertisers," quickly followed by a suggestion that recipients patronize the generous local businesses underwriting the publication.[23]

With its long history, wide distribution, and use by many middle- and working-class families, *Book of Baby Mine* offers a window into the lives of ordinary American infants. Dorothy, born in Council Bluffs, Iowa, in 1929, lost her father to "blood poison" at a young age and went to live with her mother on her grandparents' "acreage" west of Denton, Nebraska. Jane Jensen's 1935 *Book of Baby Mine* described her first outing to the Polish-American Citizen's Club in Albany, New York, and the first animals she petted – a cow and a chicken. It also held a sepia photograph of her parents. Seven Albany businesses advertised in Jane's baby book, including the Keller Baking Company – "Bread is your best food. Eat more of it" – the Central Dairy, and the Home Savings Bank of the City of Albany, which declared, "this bank is especially interested in teaching children to save … Have 'the Baby' get the savings habit. It may mean a College Education or business start." Focusing on the present rather than the future, the Little Folks Shop advertised its baby garments, blankets, and bonnets.[24]

Ideas about the new, the clean, and the scientific made hand-sewn diapers and hand-me-down infant wear seem unattractive, old-fashioned, and even dangerously unhygienic. Clothing makers frequently incorporated claims about hygiene into their advertising, along with promising the latest fashions. Merode Underwear for Infants marketed its products made from "Fine soft yarn and smooth flat seams with no rough edges," and informed potential purchasers the items were "cut by hand and sterilized by live steam." Vanta, another manufacturer of infants' and children's clothes, sold "hospital sterilized diapers" in "hospital sterilized packaging." Careful purchasing mattered if the nursery was to be a fortress against germs, rather than a receiving station.[25]

Families with sufficient resources purchased ready-made baby clothes rather than making them at home, which made baby books ideal media for apparel vendors. In 1936, the Tot Shop of Adrian, Michigan, gave away the sixteen-page baby book *My Diary*. Gregory McDonald, born in 1939, had a baby book from a nursery shop in Jamaica, New York. It contained a few pamphlets as well, including one from the New York City Department of Health, another titled "Hey mummy! Baby Deer Shoes sure are comfy," and a third with a "List of clothes and nursery needs for baby's health & comfort." The list of garments and goods needed by a baby could be lengthy. Even the federal government said so. The 1921 edition of *Infant Care* called for four to eight dozen diapers, as well as petticoats, nightgowns, and many other pieces of clothing for the baby.[26]

Clothing topped the list of popular gifts given at birth and Christmas. Families with money purchased or received a large supply of baby clothes or even a complete layette, including furniture, bath items (towels, soap, powder, oil, thermometer), "rolling stock" (a carriage), crib linens, and clothes. George Bryan Pitts II, born in 1923 to a wealthy couple, received at birth numerous silver items including cups, spoons, a plate, a dish, and a bib clasp, and hauled in a bounty of ten sweaters and fourteen dresses. The custom of dressing both male and female infants in white dresses began to shift in the 1920s, but George's family evidently followed tradition rather than fashion.[27]

Emerging ideas about the formation of gender identity at a young age meant that babies began to be dressed to express their gender with attention paid to the kind of clothing, its decoration, and its color. Robert Francis, born in 1934 at Our Lady of Perpetual Help Infant Asylum in Manchester, New Hampshire, and possibly an adopted child, received pink, blue, and white items as gifts. By the end of the decade, color-coding by gender became common, but with regional variations. In 1941, in reply to a query from Los Angeles, California, a correspondent for the Children's Bureau explained, "the local stores tell us that they sell blue for girls and pink for boys." Gender typing also appeared on baby book covers that used the words "his" and "hers" in the title and further distinguished the infant by blue or pink covers. The gender marking continued inside. *All Her Life*, a 1944 life book that included places for "My beau for life," "Showers," and entries about the wedding, honeymoon, and first baby. *All His Life*, issued in 1944, had an equal share of gender touchstones, with queries about "athletic interests," "bachelor dinner," and "first position." The pink-covered *All Her Life* baby book of Linda Jane Laubenstein, born in 1947 (who grew up to become a physician on the frontlines of the HIV epidemic), reported her trip home from the hospital wearing pink. She was ahead of her time. The identification of pink with girls and blue with boys did not become firmly fixed until the 1950s, when new ideas about infant development ratcheted up gender distinctions to an even higher level. Even furniture began to be gendered. The advertising booklet from Hochschild, Kohn & Co., the Baltimore Department Store for Babies, advertised nursery furniture in "pastel colors to harmonize with adorable 'boy and girl' nursery decorations." As a 1952 baby book reminded: "All babies are different; Boys are boys, Girls are girls."[28]

Many families lacked the means to purchase extensive infant wardrobes or even diapers. In those situations, babies wore homemade items previously used by older siblings or items pieced together from available material. Writers employed by the Works Progress Administration, a New Deal agency, collected the life histories of Americans and learned how parents fed, cared for, and clothed their babies. An interviewer reported on a mother-to-be who made diapers out of flour sacks. A nurse and teacher in rural North Carolina in 1938 described to an interviewer how she delivered baby clothes gathered from her friends to pregnant women she visited regularly. Another life history described a rural South Carolina mothers' club that sewed baby clothes for poor families.[29]

Rural and small town dwellers with money had the option of purchasing infant clothes, shoes, diapers, carriages, medicines, and toys by mail from Sears Roebuck or Montgomery Ward. The 1897 Sears catalog showcased goods for babies throughout its 700 pages; readers found infant items on offer in varying sections of the book, including baby foods, baby bottles, and baby cough syrup (reportedly compounded from "the prescription of a famous English physician who years ago attended the Royal Family of England"), as well as underwear, shawls, bonnets, and bibs. Baby carriages had their own section as well as a separate catalog. They ranged in price from $2.45 to $33, suggesting that Sears aimed to reach the broadest possible range of customers. The 1914 Sears Baby Book catalog offered clothing and supplies for maternity wear and infants, as well as three different baby record books. By the time Sears issued its Golden Jubilee catalog in 1936, the array of baby things grew even larger, from hats to shoes and from teething rings to toys.[30]

Urban dwellers with money could shop at downtown department stores to outfit their infants. Initially, department stores dispersed items throughout the store in the same way that Sears placed infant items by category with baby shoes in the shoe department, and baby medicines in the pharmacy department, rather than in a dedicated area. However, as sales of baby clothes grew, the stores moved all the infant merchandise to a single location. Linking shopping for babies to their health and welfare, department stores then went a step further, hiring experts to staff their infants' departments and provide professional advice. In a strategic effort to reach out to customers, Rich's Department Store in Atlanta went so far as to send a greeting card to every baby born in a Georgia hospital.

The creation of infants' departments reflected the overall growth in the number and size of department stores in the first part of the twentieth century, as well as the expanding array of services they offered customers, such as lunchrooms, beauty parlors, and post offices. By establishing infants' departments the stores took advantage of the fact that, thanks to advertising and to public health advice, families knew that nurseries needed to be stocked with the right goods. The bottom line for the stores thus involved securing customer loyalty by luring mothers to infants' departments staffed by trained salespeople.[31]

In 1914, the city of Chicago began hosting an annual "Baby Week" to raise funds to staff infant welfare stations. Two years later, the General Federation of Women's Clubs and the US Children's Bureau inaugurated a nationwide Baby Week – an enterprise devoted to educating mothers in infant care. Seizing an opportunity to connect with customers, department stores began sponsoring Baby Week events. They hosted lectures, gave away infant care pamphlets, and offered special promotions on baby items. In a letter to the Children's Bureau, one mother who wrote to ask for its publications reported she had learned about the publications from a store saleswoman.[32]

Baby Week exhibits and the newspaper, magazine, and radio advertisements promoting them made buying for baby seem virtuous, tying consumption to health. Merchants fully exploited the connection for many years. An executive from the Earnshaw Sales Company asserted in a 1933 letter to the Infant Welfare Society of Chicago that he had several hundred girls working in infants' departments and assisting new mothers. He explained, "Inasmuch as mothers oftentimes go to the stores before they see doctors or nurses, we consider this important work." In 1938, the Mother's Aid of the Chicago Lying-In Hospital established a "Baby Development Clinic" that traveled across the country offering department store demonstrations. The stores sponsoring the exhibits and lectures, the Mother's Aid group claimed, saw increased sales in the weeks and months that followed.[33]

The double lure of medical expertise and up-to-date products appeared in clever advertising copy from New York City's Macy's Department Store in the 1930s. One piece described a woman who turned to the Personal Shopping Service for help after adopting a six-week-old baby boy. The Personal Shopper at Macy's, the advertisement explained, received help from the Registered Nurse in the Infants Wear Department, who advised her about what to buy. A 1932 Macy's advertisement claimed that customers had purchased 300,432 diapers, "all hemmed, sterilized, and ready for action." Buying for baby wasn't merely about the accumulation of goods that marked the status of the family, as gold and silver pins and cups did for upper-class babies at the turn of the century. In the middle decades of the twentieth century, shopping meant selecting products that signaled the family intended to maintain a hygienic and modern nursery.[34]

Suffused with messages about saving for baby's future, baby books from banks and insurance companies aimed, like department stores, to build their customer base. The willingness of parents to invest in their babies in turn suggested their certainty that their infants would survive and have expensive needs in the future. In the nineteenth century, toy banks encouraged children to save their pennies. In the twentieth century, savings institutions touted the importance of placing babies' as well as children's and adult's savings in brick-and-mortar structures. Banks sprouted up in communities of all sizes. There were 13,000 banks in the United States in 1900 and double that number by 1913.[35]

After World War I, savings institutions assumed an increasingly active role in promoting the great American economic virtue: thrift. They reached out to customers via motion pictures and newspaper advertisements and developed programs to collect deposits from schoolchildren. Family members deposited funds into savings accounts for infants too young to drop coins into piggy banks. Baby books incorporated pages with headings like "Contributors to baby's bank account," "Into my bank account went ... " and "Finances." Later, a combination coin bank and baby book appeared, consisting of a metal container surrounded by twenty pages of advertising and places for recording information about the new baby. Bank formation slowed in the 1920s and subsequently savings rates declined as banks shut their doors and the economy spiraled downward during the Great Depression. Baby books nonetheless continued to promote the opening of savings accounts. A Baby's Savings Book from an unidentified Farmers and Mechanics' Savings Bank dated 1933 opened to two pages with slots for thirty dimes. Many parents took seriously the obligation to open savings accounts for their babies, perhaps viewing it as a marker of respectability. The baby book for Donald Goddall, born in 1912, lists the opening of his savings account at the US National Bank of Salem, Oregon, under his "Red Letter Days" along with his grandparents' first visit. Later, his baby book reveals his acquisition of two books, one poetic and one prosaic – Robert Lewis Stevenson's *A Child's Garden of Verses* and *Hints on Savings*.[36]

What did babies, or, more accurately, their parents, save up to buy? Bank advertisements answered: education. Schooling assumed a more prominent role in American life along with the shift from a rural agricultural economy to an urban manufacturing and service economy that required an educated workforce. Baby books given away by banks responded by encouraging parents to save for their infants' schooling. *Baby's Bank and Record Book* published in 1926 included a section on college savings estimating a need for about $1,000 – a figure it reported deriving from the University of Pennsylvania catalog. A helpful chart showed that saving $1 a week would, with compounding interest, yield $1,065.72 in fifteen years. The baby book of Wendy Little, born in Montrose, Colorado, in 1929, made it easy to start saving on her behalf – it included deposit slips on perforated forms.[37]

The year 1929 was hardly an auspicious time to open a savings account. Between the stock market crash of that year and the beginning of the New Deal banking reforms in 1933 more than 5,000 banks failed, wiping out the savings of millions of Americans. The coins in children's toy banks might have been the only liquidity of some unfortunate households. The baby gift of $12.50 deposited for Bernice Ranger in the Fifth Avenue Trust and Savings Bank in Moline, Illinois, in 1920 and the $15 placed in the Canton, Ohio First Trust and Savings Bank for William Dorn in 1921, who had $118.61 saved by 1926, probably disappeared, along with many other cash gifts so carefully recorded in numerous other baby books. At least William got his picture taken for free after the first deposit was made for him.[38]

Life insurance offered another method for securing the future. Policies held on children became popular with working-class families because it offered a way to pay for burial costs. However, the sales infuriated reformers who believed insurance purchases made youngsters' deaths profitable, thus incentivizing neglect, or worse. Critics also took offense at placing a monetary value on the life of a child, viewing it as threatening their efforts to make childhood sacred. The sacrilization of childhood succeeded nonetheless and as a scholar noted, the pitch by insurance companies shifted from burials to saving for the future as mortality rates declined and consumer culture expanded. Nevertheless, well into the twentieth century, fear of pauper burials in potter's fields led families to buy insurance for their children as well as for the household breadwinners. Initially, families were not able to insure infants in the first year of life because their mortality rates were too high, but later they could buy policies for them. The family of Jane Little, born in Jefferson City, Missouri, in 1937, enrolled her as a member of the National Life and Accident Insurance Company's "Shielded Baby Family," at the age of five weeks. Organized in Nashville, Tennessee, in the 1920s, the company sold policies to African Americans who could not purchase life insurance from other national companies.[39]

Other sources of insurance included mutual benefit societies operating within immigrant and ethnic communities. Many of them became insolvent during the Great Depression as the savings institutions holding their collected funds collapsed. The sermons about thrift included no warnings about placing too much faith in banks. Large national insurance companies such as Prudential Life Insurance, Western and Southern Life Insurance, and Equitable Life Insurance survived as many families kept up the premium payments. To entice policy buyers, the companies advertised in baby books or gave away their own inexpensive volumes that typically included both infant care advice and a ledger for recording payments.[40]

Like banks, insurance companies pitched education as a reason for buying a policy, explaining that it could later be exchanged for cash. A 1915 Equitable Life Assurance baby book advertisement in *Book of Baby Mine* began, "Say, Dad, what about my college education?" The come-on played to parental dreams, not realities. High school graduation rates for seventeen-year-olds hovered below 13 percent and college attendance and graduation was much lower. Nevertheless, families had aspirations for their babies and acted upon them. A 1919 investigation of infant mortality in the city of Brockton, Massachusetts, by the Children's Bureau found an Italian immigrant mother saving to send all four of her children to college. Furthering parental hopes, a shift in educational attainment saw high school completion rates grow to 40 percent by 1935, as large numbers of children withdrew from the workforce due to a lack of jobs and as laws began to limit their employment opportunities and mandated school attendance.[41]

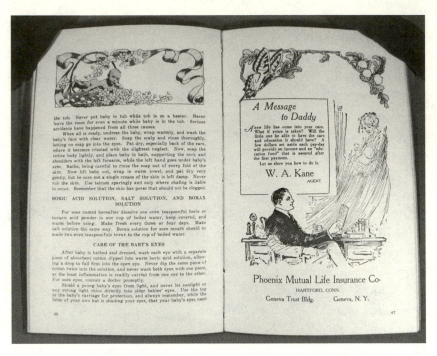

Figure 4.3 Insurance advertisement from *Book of Baby Mine*, 1915
Credit: The Phoenix Companies, Inc. and History and Special
Collections, UCLA Library Special Collections

Other motives, besides paying for an education, may have spurred
life insurance sales. The mother of a boy born in 1925 wrote on the
bank account page of his baby book, "We took out an insurance of about
$300 or over at 3 months old in the Prudential Co." Later the family
purchased more insurance from the same company, perhaps feeling the
need to do so because of their son's propensity for accidents. According
to his baby book, he fell out of his high chair at five months. Subsequent
tumbles down the cellar stairs and an episode at twenty months of age
that knocked off a piece of his tooth made him seem a good candidate
for insurance, lest a future accident end with his death.[42]

Burial costs haunted families, and they continued to make insurance payments even when coping with strained finances. Interviews
with unemployed families revealed that while some gave up their policies as money ran short, others did their best to hold on to them. An

Irish-American family reported being able to buy milk for their six-month-old twins and two other children because of the payment they received following the death of a child. A Polish-American family with seven children let policies for the older children lapse and cashed out their savings to support a new baby. In 1939, a South Carolina housewife told an interviewer from the Federal Writer's Project that she carried insurance on herself, her daughter, the daughter's baby, an orphaned grandchild, and another member of the household "to put us away in case of death." Proper burials mattered. An interviewer recorded the words of an African American pastor who presided over many funerals: "The thing that's been the greatest benefit to our race is insurance. I knows of more'n one instance where it provided a funeral where the corpse would-a had to lay out till somebody got out and raised the money to pay for the buryin.'" Reformers who loathed the selling of life insurance policies on infants and children seemed not to understand the fear and shame of being unable to provide a proper funeral for a loved one.[43]

Whether banks, bakeries, or baby clothes sellers, commercial and financial organizations of all types used discussions of babies' needs to teach families about fiscal discipline and consumption, two conflicting habits of modern life. Families listened, or put another way, modern infants helped turn parents into both savers and spenders. They opened accounts at savings institutions and purchased advertised factory goods that guaranteed protection from germs and promised to promote healthy development. Buying for babies and saving for their futures occurred amid an expanding economy with fresh habits of consumption propelled by advertising. The professionals writing advertising copy offered assurances of convenience, thrift, and aesthetic modernism and messages about maternal love and obligation.

The advertising message "buy for the sake of the baby" rested on a demographic certainty: each year brought more customers. As Christine Frederick, an expert in household management and advertising, wrote in her 1929 book *Selling Mrs. Consumer*:

> It is estimated that in 1929 there will be approximately 2,500,000 babies born. The first year expenditures for the little newcomers will amount, in all probability, to about $150.00 each, which makes a total of $375,000,000 a year which American women spend every year for just the little one-year-olds.

Frederick detailed the growth in expenditures for milk and insurance, and predicted a growing interest in health. She was wrong about the latter: interest in infant health wasn't growing; it was a sustained priority.[44]

Despite the growing cultural power of consumerism, baby books made clear that babies connected their families to God as well as mammon. A 1936 volume distributed by advertisers presented on succeeding pages prompts for "I open a bank account" and "I pray." The juxtaposition appeared in many baby books. Even as infants helped forge new connections between families and the marketplace, they also helped sustain generational ties and religious identities. *Book of Baby Mine*, like nearly all the fancy and commercial baby books, included pages for reporting on religious activities and holidays. Other baby books included religious poems, such as "God Thought about Me." Mothers wrote entries on pages titled "Prayers," "Questions Pertaining to Religion," and "Religious Education," and for declaring "Religious Affiliations." Several Protestant denominations produced their own baby books, including the twenty-four-page *Nursery Log* from the Lutheran Brotherhood, published around 1920, and the eight-page *A Book for the Cradle-Roll Baby*, which appeared in 1929. Baby books for Catholic and Jewish babies appeared in later decades.[45]

Descriptions of baptisms and christenings appeared in baby books along with memorabilia from these and other religious ceremonies. The baby book of a girl from Texas born in 1909 held her Baby Roll Certificate from the Women's Home Mission Society Methodist Episcopal Church, South Texas Conference and her confirmation certificate from 1923. The book *All about Me: Baby's Record* had entries for "I was christened at" and "Was I good?" sparing the need to write a lengthy description of the event. One boy's mother answered: "First M.E. Church, October 4th, 1925 by Rev. Walter Atchinson" and "Very good. Sleeping all the time." Mary Linda Peale's baby book from 1929 recorded her membership in the Cradle Roll society at Grace Methodist Church, while Ronald Trevert's baby book included his many Full Gospel church pins marking his family's participation in this Pentecostal movement. Baby book entries do not make clear whether the arrival of an infant induced families to become more involved in organized religious life or if religious families were more likely to record their babies' early religious activities. It seems likely that the religious themed entries reflected the overall growth in church and congregation membership that occurred in the first half of the twentieth century.[46]

Private as well as public celebrations of religious holidays appeared in baby books. Entries referenced the spiritual and the secular by recording gift giving and family gatherings as well as prayers. Many baby books contained pages for "first Christmas" and "first Easter" along with places for recording secular holidays like Valentine's Day. One mother personalized an entry page by crossing out "Christmas" and writing "Chanaka 1927 Dec. 18." Frequently mothers pasted Christmas cards and valentines into the baby books, continuing a tradition of card collecting that went back to the nineteenth century.[47]

Despite recent lamentations about the commercialization of Christmas, the long tradition of buying for babies meant that gifts as well as religious sentiments marked the holiday. Babies in wealthy families collected many expensive presents. For her first Christmas, Edna Nicholson, born in Troy, North Carolina in 1914, received a gold bib pin, gold dress pins, a gold ring, a nightingale (crocheted) towel and washcloth, a dress, shoes, two pairs of silk hose, a rubber kewpie doll, five rattles, and toilet water. Equally impressive gifts had arrived five months earlier to mark her birth. Five-month-old Ella Pierce, born in 1921, also took in quite a haul at her first Christmas, collecting fourteen dolls among the many other presents. Christmas gift lists, like baby gift lists, revealed the social class of the recipients and the material world they inhabited.[48]

Baby books served many purposes, as ledgers for listing gifts, as places to keep records of bank deposits, as repositories of vital records, and as diaries of family activities. They housed keepsakes, photographs, locks of hair, and ribbons. Entries made by mothers often gave clues or direct evidence about the lives of individual babies and about the broader culture in which they lived. And they recorded tragedies as well as joyful events. Baby Edna, who received so many gifts in gold, had only a short record of her life. She died young and her baby book resides in the papers of a sister born eight years later. Death continued to strike in the nurseries of the rich and the poor, even as their mortality rates varied and the death toll dropped over the century thanks to improvements in public health and private hygiene practices. Baby books as well as statistics tell that story. They reveal the extent to which infants were brought up according to the health advice delivered by experts. Were they? The answer to that question was, not surprisingly, yes and no.

5

BRINGING UP BABIES II
Health and Illness, Food and Drink

MARY GOODRICH'S GRANDMOTHER KEPT A DIARY detailing Mary's birth in 1896 and her early life as well as that of her sister's. A few days after her arrival, Mary's family sent for "old Mrs. Bakens' butter scale." Mary weighed seven-and-a-quarter pounds. Weighed two months later, she delighted her family with the results, having reached the "full weight proper for little ones of this age according to Dr. Starr's book which is our authority." (Physician Louis Starr published one of the earliest American books on nursery care, *Hygiene of the Nursery*, in 1888.) Families understood that every ounce and pound gained by a baby signaled her good health and proper nourishment. Understandably, weight loss caused alarm. Writing to her husband, Alexander Graham Bell, in 1906, Mabel Hubbard Bell reported that his grandson, named after him, had "gained an ounce yesterday but lost it again this morning," and they sent for the doctor. Other babies appeared to have no trouble putting on weight. Malcolm Kerr, born March 1917 weighing a hefty nine-and-a-half pounds, soon outgrew his family's scale. By October of that year, he weighed twenty-two pounds when weighed at the butcher shop.[1]

Scales became a well-used pediatric medical technology in the middle of the nineteenth century. Physicians used them to assess the status of individual infants and for collecting data that would become the foundation of widely used growth charts. The idea of weight as a critical medical assessment began with French physicians, who recorded babies' progress in the context of a broad national interest in increasing the size of the population. The French custom spread across the Atlantic. The family of a baby boy born in Roxbury, Massachusetts, in 1872 kept notes in a translated baby book distributed to French mothers: *The Mother's*

Figure 5.1 Mother's record photograph from *Babyhood Days*, 1915
Credit: History and Special Collections, UCLA Library Special Collections

Register: Current Notes of the Health of Children (Boys). The Mother Records for the Physician to Interpret. Written by J. B. Fonssagrives, a professor of hygiene in Montpelier, France, it included places for recording weight and growth as well as family history ("descent and consanguinity") and "physiologic conditions and hygienic habits." The medical practice of weighing babies on a regular basis spread throughout Europe and the United States. Advice books urged regular weighing and suggested what kind of scale to buy. "If regular baby scales are too expensive," one author wrote, "a good counter scale such as is used in grocery stores – will answer the purpose admirably." Numerical data, so important to the development of medical science and social epidemiology, also mattered to individual households.[2]

The biomedical revolution of the twentieth century and the technological advances it generated made their way into households in baby steps. The new technologies, defined as applied knowledge and processes, became part of babies' lives. They ranged from birth certificates used by the government to accumulate vital statistics to soap sticks inserted rectally to assist in toilet training. Unlike municipal water systems or vaccines, which offered collective and individual protection from disease, many of the new individually applied technologies made little impact on infant mortality rates. Yet they shaped the daily experiences of babies and parents.

Mothers who once used close observation to determine if babies failed to thrive learned to make judgments by reading scales. Baby Eleanor, born in 1917, received a daily weighing until she reached eight weeks of age, and had a twice-weekly weighing after that. The results appeared on a homemade weight chart. Her father, who was away much of the time, wrote home to his wife to express his concern: "Hope baby shows some satisfactory progress on the scales." According to his baby book, James Harper Jr., born in New York City in 1919, got a daily weighing until he reached the age of one month and then weighing became a several-times-a-week custom for the next two years. Unlike their late nineteenth-century predecessors, which typically contained a single entry place for birth weight, twentieth-century baby books contained pages for daily or weekly gains of ounces and pounds. A few medical advice manuals went so far as to instruct mothers to weigh their babies before and after each feeding. The growing emphasis on nursery surveillance and record keeping led mothers to offer observations as well as numerical accounts. The "Baby gained right along so I had no worry about him being underweight," one woman wrote in her son's baby book in 1937.[3]

Education in the mathematics of infant care came to low-income households via visiting nurses, clinic physicians, and public health booklets. Some mothers, recalcitrant or slow learners, ignored the lessons and practiced older customs alongside or instead of the new regimens. In other cases, families lacked the means to purchase the necessary tools and took their babies to clinics to be weighed. Writing to another rural farm woman in North Dakota, one mother asked whether she had taken her children to the schoolhouse, reporting there were more than 200 babies there to be weighed and measured when she took her own children.[4]

To help mothers track their babies' weight, the Children's Bureau distributed weighing and measuring cards organized by age and sex. The mother of Nina Robinson, born in Keokuk, Iowa, in 1917, tucked one into her baby book and kept a record of her growth. During the 1918 Children's Year, the Bureau made instructions about weighing a priority. Better Baby contests reinforced the message, giving entrants scorecards that included a "Table of Standards" for height and weight and stressed that underweight babies need professional help. Clinicians, including nurses staffing infant-welfare stations, kept an eye out for underweight babies and referred them to physicians.

Manufacturers and retailers leapt at the opportunities provided by the professional directives on weighing. A 1928 baby book published in Los Angeles advertised scale rentals, promising economy and playing up new expectation with the come-on: "You will only need the scales for a few months – but those few months count, ask your doctor." The following year, Macy's department store placed scales, along with bassinettes, cribs, and play yards, in its new department of nursery furniture.[5]

The consumer revolution abetted the transformation in infant care practices, as manufacturers convinced families to buy instruments, such as infant scales, that aided record keeping, and products, such as commercial baby foods, that promised to be nourishing and hygienic. Advertisers recast common nursery items such as soap, canned milk, scales, and patent medicines as important nursery technologies. Their marketing often melded interest in infant health protection to the promise of domestic science – a set of applied skills intended to make women's household work easier. However, the extent to which the educational efforts of public health experts and product manufacturers transformed household practices depended in large part on family income. Some babies grew up with infant scales and other nursery equipment; others depended on homemade items.

Changing infant care practices, such as regular weighing, did not signal the medicalization of the nursery. *Medicalization* refers to the process by which conditions become defined as problems to be studied, diagnosed, prevented, or treated by health care professionals. Infant deaths and illnesses did not need to be medicalized; they were understood as medical problems as well as challenges to faith, family, and community. What shifted over the course of the twentieth century were the ways families responded to conditions threatening their babies' lives. Biomedical science became the predominant way of explaining and responding to those threats. Seen from the perspective of the crib, it becomes evident that babies played a critical role in making medical authority paramount in the nursery and the home, driving Americans to accept new ideas and practices derived from an understanding of germ theory and from acceptance of the advice of health care experts. Thanks to their vulnerability and to the possibility of reducing the risks they faced, infants assisted medical professionals in gaining dominion over a broad swath of cultural practices.

Babies' and parents' first introduction to scientific infant care increasingly occurred in hospitals. The growing safety of medically managed deliveries, the attraction of anesthesia, safer surgery due to aseptic operating theaters, and the advantages of hospital nursing care meant that by 1938, approximately half of all deliveries took place in hospitals and the percentage grew larger in the ensuing years. Baby book entries acknowledged and promoted this transition. To mark the occasion of her birth, the mother of a girl born in Blessing Hospital in Quincy, Illinois, in 1932 pasted into her baby book a photograph of the hospital nurses along with a color postcard of the hospital. Perhaps she wanted her daughter to know, when she grew up, that she had been born in the most up-to-date setting. In another mark of the hospital as a place for giving birth, the Mothers Aid of the Chicago Lying-In Hospital supported its charitable work by selling a baby book, the advertising-free *Our Baby's First Seven Years*, beginning in 1928. The volume came filled with scientific advice from the hospital's team of medical experts and would be revised and reissued for decades.[6]

Publishers quickly recognized that hospitals made ideal locations for distributing baby books and would be important sources of advertising revenue. In 1937, hospitals began distributing under their institutional names *Congratulations: A Magazine for Mothers*. Filled with advertising from national brands, the magazine included a few places for recording information, making it something like a hybrid baby book and periodical. Although new issues appeared regularly, the articles, such as "Babies are like puppies," "Six bottles and all is well," and "The diapered dictator," rarely changed even as the advertisers regularly updated their copy. The articles, understandably, directed parents to rely on physicians when their babies became sick. The pieces also encouraged shopping, with titles such as "Complete Layette" and "Glamour for Baby," and saving, with "Of course he'll go to college." A perforated "for easy removal and use" birth certificate appeared on the magazine's first page. With birth registration becoming standard practice, other baby book publishers also included places for birth certificates. Libby's, an infant food manufacturer, gave away a baby book that included a page instructing mothers to "paste birth certificate here."[7]

In addition to functioning as repositories of personal keepsakes, baby books became designated places for storing official medical documents and the volume of ephemera tucked into baby books increased over time. Quarantine cards, formula prescriptions, dietary advice, and lists of illnesses joined the Christmas cards and photographs. Some baby books offered places for recording diseases and some mothers kept a record, although they rarely recounted what their babies experienced by way of symptoms and treatments. The baby book of George Roberts, born in 1913, noted the rickets he had from birth that he outgrew, as well as his subsequent bouts of measles, whooping cough (pertussis), chicken pox, and German measles (rubella). All but rickets were common infectious diseases of infancy and childhood with diphtheria, measles, and respiratory illnesses such as pneumonia and bronchitis being the most dangerous. Epidemics also took a toll, but like short bouts of illness, they resulted in few detailed entries. Georgia Ellen Baker, born at home in Grand Rapids, Michigan, in October 1918, died in March the following year; she was probably one of the 675,000 American victims of the influenza pandemic that took 30 million to 50 million lives across the world. Nona Baldwin Brown contracted "Spanish influenza" at the age of five months, suffering with convulsions, bronchitis, and abscessed ears.

She ultimately recovered. Another baby, Peter Stone, avoided that fate because his mother almost never left the house during the outbreak and, she reported, the family received no visits from the physician following her confinement because the doctor "was afraid of bringing germs."[8]

As medical knowledge grew, baby book publishers incorporated ever-larger amounts of information about disease prevention and treatment into their volumes, typically by reprinting material from public health agencies. *Baby's Health: A Practical Handbook for the Young Mother*, published in 1916, included advice from the Children's Bureau as well as the New York State Board of Health and the health agencies of New York City, Chicago, Illinois, and Providence, Rhode Island. The thirty-third edition appeared in 1927, announcing: "Over one million copies distributed to the mothers of the United States." The *American Baby Book: Health Record* from 1921, reportedly "compiled after years of study by leading surgeons and doctors," provided information on common conditions, among them measles, whooping cough, malnutrition, and tuberculosis, as well as advertisements from a pharmacy, a savings and loan, a photography studio, and a baby carriage shop. At a time when public health educators worked to take the lead in presenting information to the public and yet often failed to achieve the same audience and impact as commercial advertisers, the inclusion of their material in baby books, often alongside advertisements, must have seemed a welcome opportunity to reach mothers.[9]

The Metropolitan Life Insurance Company's baby book and health pamphlets, as well as its services to policyholders, exemplified the overlap between commerce and medicine. Families purchasing insurance received the Metropolitan Life baby book first published and distributed by the company in 1900, as well as numerous booklets such as *Baby's First Days, Home Nursing Care of the Babies*, and *How to Dress the Baby*. The baby book explained: "From time to time the METROPOLITAN AGENT leaves a book at our house which shows us how to keep well and how to prevent disease." New editions appeared in 1923, 1936, and 1942. Met Life, as it was known, distributed a staggering 3 billion pamphlets on health topics to its policyholders and for a time provided them with care from visiting nurses, presuming that prevention and treatment would be cheaper than paying out death benefits. Between 1909 and 1953,

Met Life nurses gave health information and direct services to more than 30 million policyholders. When their one-year-old baby contracted whooping cough and pneumonia in 1931, an immigrant Italian family living in New York City, for example, received daily visits from a Met Life nurse. Other insurance companies did not provide nursing services, but they did publish and distribute baby books that laid out the basic rules of infant care. The Prudential Life Insurance Company gave its policyholders copies of *Our Babies* written by Chicago Commissioner of Public Health and public health leader Herman Bundesen.[10]

The fusion of professional medical advice and consumerism appeared in the pages of women's magazines as well as in baby books, with strategically positioned articles about health care placed alongside advertisements for medical products. In 1925, *Baby's Album: Presented by Leading Merchants of Louisville, KY* positioned a discussion of "Baby's dinner" adjacent to an advertisement promising "Even father makes biscuits with Ballards' Self-Rising Flour," while the advertisement for the Vogt Refrigerator Company ("Perfect refrigeration for baby's food and mother's") came sandwiched between information about artificial feeding and baby's dinner. Dietary advice appeared in nearly all public health materials, as well as in magazine articles and in baby books distributed by formula makers and baby food manufacturers. Borden's astutely named Baby Welfare Division produced *The Care of the Mother and Baby's Welfare: Proper Care and Feeding*, which included health advice, a height and weight chart, and numerous testimonials about and pictures of babies raised on Borden's. Despite the winning come-ons, infant food and canned milk producers did not have a large market share in the first decades of the twentieth century; most families that bottle fed their babies used fresh milk formulas (typically made with milk and added sugar and then diluted with water).[11]

Rates of formula feeding increased over the twentieth century thanks to the vigorous and sustained marketing efforts of canned milk and formula manufacturers. Their heavy advertising led to brand recognition, but it did not guarantee brand loyalty. Henry John, born outside of Dallas, Texas, in 1916, still nursed at the breast, but also drank Mellin's food once or twice a day. He then switched to Holstein milk mixed with dextrimaltose (a carbohydrate-based milk modifier) and then to

Horlick's Malted Milk. Letters to the Children's Bureau commonly mentioned product switching like Henry John's as a response to digestive problems.[12]

Some of the commercial infant foods appeared to gain a regional or local following. In 1932, an Indian Health Service nurse working in Reno, Nevada, reported that the mothers she worked with favored Borden's Eagle Brand Condensed Milk. Speaking to a Works Progress Administration interviewer in 1938, an older woman in Burlington, North Carolina, recounted that Borden's milk restored the health of her sickly granddaughter, and some of the other people interviewed referred to Borden's as a food for the sick. Most babies growing up during the Great Depression on reservations and in poor Southern towns probably received breast milk; those who could not do so and relied on Borden's or some other commercial product may have been the only members of their household to receive store-bought sustenance.[13]

Infant feeding problems prompted many pleas for help in letters to the Children's Bureau. Mothers reported breastfeeding difficulties such as engorged breasts and they inquired about correct bottle feeding and how to keep milk from spoiling in the summer. "Contrary to the general opinion," a correspondent learned in a reply to her letter, "thunderstorms do not cause milk to sour." Happy to stamp out superstitions, but fearful of provoking the ire of fellow practitioners or manufacturers, the women physicians answering the letters never gave advice about what to buy or how to properly blend milk, water, and sugar. "It is impossible to prescribe formulas for individual babies without examining the baby," the Children's Bureau writers frequently explained in their replies. Mothers inquired less frequently about the next stage in babyhood – weaning – and the subject received minimal attention in published material on infant care. Having learned that milk sometimes harbored colonies of dangerous bacteria, aware that it could spoil quickly, and perhaps unable to afford ice or mechanical refrigeration, the few women who wrote about the subject reported that they avoided weaning their babies in the summer. In this instance, health professionals reinforced popular folk wisdom about not taking babies off the breast in the hottest months of the year. Other traditional beliefs about weaning, such as commencing it "on Good Friday, unless the trees are in bloom," as one correspondent reported, or by zodiac sign, as another noted, had no equivalent in the biomedical world.[14]

The question of when to introduce solid food appeared in numerous letters to the Children's Bureau. In the 1910s and 1920s, experts advised transitioning from an exclusively liquid diet to one with solid foods in the second six months of life. By the 1930s, the age for starting solid foods dropped to four months and later experts suggested starting at even younger ages. An additional push came from scientific findings about the importance of vitamins and minerals, the proper balance of fats, proteins, and starches, and the caloric values of foods. As a result of these discoveries, dietary advice for infants and children became increasingly detailed. *Diets for Children*, published in 1924 by physician Lulu Hunt Peters, the author of the syndicated newspaper column "Diet and Health," summarized the latest scientific findings for readers. Peters argued for introducing babies to new foods by their fifth or sixth month, but not feeding them table foods, a practice she called "pernicious." She suggested starting babies on strained vegetables in their seventh month, explaining to mothers how to steam or cook them until tender and then puree them through a strainer, until the babies' molars arrived sometime between twelve and sixteen months. The work of preparing meals for babies undoubtedly helped sell mothers on the value of commercial foods, and the sales figures indicate that increasing numbers of families purchased them.[15]

Baby books supply details about infants' shifting diets, seemingly prompted by the expanding pages for recording each new addition to the menu or by presenting timetables for introducing new foods. Martha West, born on a ranch in Jackson Hole, Wyoming, in 1921, began her life consuming Mellin's Food, then graduated to formula mixed with water and later expanded her diet in the precise order suggested by experts: prune juice and orange juice at six months, followed by vegetables, broth, and crackers at eight months. Born in 1917, Edith Roosevelt Derby, granddaughter of President Theodore Roosevelt and daughter of physician Richard Derby, began eating vegetables and cereal at four months and hard-boiled egg yolk, prune pulp, applesauce, spaghetti, rice, celery, squash, and turnips at nine months. Despite Edith's dietary deviations from what many physicians and infant health experts advised, her mother wrote that she gained weight slowly and steadily and slept six hours without interruption.[16]

Rather than listing the foods that babies needed to avoid and in keeping with its generally encouraging tone, the Children's Bureau's 1914 pamphlet *Infant Care* provided a timetable for adding new foods. At nine months, babies could enjoy meat broths and at ten months, part of a soft egg, a small piece of crisp toast, or zwieback. At twelve months, infants graduated to strained cereal and after celebrating their first birthdays, they could partake of meat and cooked vegetables. Noticeably absent from the list were fruits. As explained in a letter from a Children's Bureau correspondent to a mother in Kellogg, Idaho, who inquired about her baby's diet: "Raw fruit should never be given to a child under two years of age, it is extremely dangerous under one year." Subsequent editions of *Infant Care* offered slight modifications to the timetable.[17]

Dietary advice from medical experts, though well-intended and scientifically up to date, ignored the fact that poor and working-class Americans sometimes struggled to put food on the family table, lacked access to clean water for cooking, and may have had no stoves or iceboxes. Many parents had no other choice but to serve table foods to their infants, and some struggled to provide even a minimal diet. The medical literature took note of this fact, documenting the numbers of infants and children who suffered from malnutrition before and during the Great Depression. Even as some mothers wrote to the Children's Bureau for advice about canning their own vegetables for their babies, other families could not even provide this kind of nourishment. Rural families kept gardens and livestock, but others living in mill towns and villages could not grow their own food and instead relied on the overpriced company store. Low-income urban families purchased foods from neighborhood bakeries and small shops, or turned to produce sold by pushcart peddlers.

The first foods given to babies fed from the table, such as mashed potatoes and cornmeal gruel, closely resembled commercial infant foods in their consistency. In some cases, mothers made foods palatable by chewing small bites of food and then spoon-feeding the now-softened items to their babies. A researcher in the Ozarks observed this practice, one that vexed public health experts who worried about germs. Medical professionals responded by producing materials instructing mothers not to taste milk from the bottle (presumably to test the temperature) before giving it to babies and not to chew food for babies. But both practices made sense, especially for mothers who didn't own a thermometer, lacked the time or equipment to strain food, and had no funds to purchase commercially produced foodstuffs. Infants' diets reflected their families' economic resources and customary practices as well as the clout of food industry advertising and widely dispensed infant feeding advice from professionals.[18]

Infant feeding customs in immigrant communities frequently disturbed health experts, and they responded with explicit warnings and sustained efforts to Americanize the diets of new American babies. Wisconsin authorities, mindful of their large German-American population, gave stern warnings to mothers, instructing them not to feed babies sauerkraut as well as other "bad" foods such as candy, cake, pork chops, and dill pickles. The New York State Department of Health scolded immigrants with the warning that "Ham, bacon, or pork, cabbage, pickles, tea, coffee, or beer, bananas, berries, cake, candy or ice cream should not be given to babies or little children." Nevertheless, infants consumed all kinds of forbidden items. Experts would have blanched at the diet of a baby born in 1928 who, according to his baby book, enjoyed coffee at age seven weeks given to him by his grandpa, and consumed pumpkin pie, cranberry sauce, and turkey at his first Thanksgiving, when he was seven months old. Folk medical beliefs as well as family income, ethnic traditions, and medical advice determined what infants ate. Giving the baby a "taste of everything the mother eats will protect him from colic," a woman told investigators from the Children's Bureau visiting rural North Carolina.[19]

In her 1905 book about the mountain people of Appalachia, writer Emma Miles reported that babies began to eat a whole range of table foods – grease, sugar, strong coffee – from the age of one month. Conducting a study of immigrant health sponsored by the Carnegie Foundation, social reformer Michael M. Davis Jr. met a mother who brought her sick baby to a clinic where the staff discovered that she followed the custom of feeding her infant what she fed herself. Back home, this was buttermilk and soup; in America, she relied on the available beverages: coffee and beer. Another researcher observed that Portuguese-American families fed "sopa" (soup with softened crackers in it) to their infants. Again and again, studies found that immigrants raised their American-born babies as if they were still in the old country, producing much hand-wringing among professionals.[20]

The Children's Bureau investigation of infant mortality in Johnstown, Pennsylvania, in 1915 made an example of the mother of twelve children, eleven still living, whose baby consumed soup, milk, coffee, and crackers at six months and sauerkraut, cabbage, and pie beginning at nine months. Despite the rather remarkable survival rate of her offspring and the work it must have taken to maintain her household, the investigator condemned her feeding practices as well as her "dirty" house. Other investigations also found that most babies ate what their families had on the table, whether they grew up in the Polish community of "Packingtown," the name for the stockyards community in Chicago, or in rural Mississippi, where a Children's Bureau researcher found an African American infant who ate "everything" since her eleventh day, including all the meat she wanted beginning at two months. Another study in the rural South highlighted the racial differences in infant diets. By four months of age, 60 percent of African American babies she studied were consuming solid food compared to less than 35 percent of white infants.[21]

What went into infants came out of infants, making toilet training another shared concern of parents and experts. Baby book pages prompted mothers to make detailed notes, as they practiced what a writer called "hygienic surveillance." In the first half of the twentieth century, both laypeople and professionals endorsed early toilet training, but for different reasons. Success freed mothers from repeated changing of diapers, from treating diaper rash if they lacked sufficient time or supplies to make regular changes, and, most importantly, from the constant drudgery of laundering. Recounting her satisfaction in freeing herself from that chore, Jessie Silver's mother wrote in her baby book in 1917 under the heading "Baby's First Lesson" that she was "sitting on her little chamber at five months." Later, Mrs. Silver added, "At one year baby is wearing little drawers and keeps them clean." For health care professionals, success in training indicated self-mastery, an important step in proper psychological development; for mothers, success meant less laundry.[22]

Ideally, bowel training began in the third month. It often involved inserting thermometers or soap sticks – two seemingly essential toileting tools – into babies' rectums. Of course, toilet training also presented a marketing opportunity. What kind of soap for the baby's bottom? The baby book *How to Bring Up a Baby: A Hand Book for Mothers* published by Proctor and Gamble in 1906 and written by nurse and author Elizabeth Robinson Scovil answered unequivocally: Proctor and Gamble's own Ivory soap. Additional uses for Ivory ranged from washing the baby's bottle to treating various medical conditions such as colds, fevers, and convulsions, which were, Scovil explained, "often caused by undigested food." Proctor and Gamble not only employed a nurse to write its baby book, it reached out to health providers working with low-income families. In an advertisement with the heading "The baby the stork left 'four flights up'" in the *American Journal of Nursing* readers met Mrs. Lamperti, the wife of a day laborer. From a settlement house nurse, Mrs. Lamperti learned that only Ivory would do for her four-month-old Mario.[23]

Most babies learned to control their bowels the old-fashioned way, by being held over a bowl when they were too young to sit on their own and later on by sitting on a pot by themselves and being given assistance with a soap stick, or some other appliance, such as one invented by a physician as a substitute for soap. When they got a little older, babies graduated to the toilet or the outhouse. (As late as 1940, 35.5 percent of American homes lacked a flush toilet and in 1950, a quarter of American homes still did not have them.) Toilet training required the literal hands-on assistance of adults and the inconvenience and work involved created an opportunity for the makers of infant toilet seats that held babies in place. By the 1920s, the Little Toidey company was selling baby toileting equipment in infant departments and in plumbing shops. A 1939 baby book mailed by the Gertz Nursery Shop in Jamaica, New York, included its brochure "Training Is Fun with Little Toidey" providing instructions on the use of soap suppositories when toilet training began at the age of three weeks and a list of Little Toidey products to buy. Just as the baby food manufacturers emphasized starting babies on solid foods in the early months of life, toilet equipment manufacturers endorsed early bowel training.[24]

Little Toidey, manufactured by the Juvenile Wood Products Company, competed with a growing number of training products, including the Doo-Tee Infant Trainer and the Up-See-Daisy toilet seat. Thanks to their targeted advertising and perhaps to their clever or cringe-worthy names, the toileting products became well known. Little Toidey appeared in the advice book *Mother and Baby Care in Pictures*, along with other images supplied by commercial manufacturers. In an exchange of letters during World War II, one father observed of his five-month-old daughter, "These early years are so important in habit formation," going on to note, "Already she is using a little toidey seat." In that brief passage he gave a nod to a successful advertising campaign and to the emerging emphasis on infant development as habit control. Whether or not babies or parents found training "fun" remains unclear.[25]

Babies' reactions to a core commandment of infant care and an essential tool for health – a daily dose of cod liver oil – suggested that many were heretics. They expressed their dislike effectively enough for their objections to be noted, but could not halt its application. Along with daily sunbaths, doses of cod liver oil constituted a second front in the war on rickets, a common nutritional disease that could lead to fractures and skeletal deformities, among other problems. It was a serious concern. One study found rickets afflicted 75 percent of babies born in New York City in 1921. An investigation by physician Martha May Eliot, who would later become chief of the Children's Bureau, documented the importance of vitamin D as a means of preventing the condition. She conducted research in New Haven, Connecticut, in 1923 and in Puerto Rico a decade later, confirming the prevalence of rickets in infants and children.[26]

The first edition of *Infant Care* attributed rickets to "faulty food and improper living conditions." A subsequent finding that rickets indicated a vitamin D deficiency resulted in a five-page discussion of sunbathing in the revised edition issued in 1929 along with instructions for administering cod liver oil. Although relatively inexpensive, cod liver oil required a cash outlay and its strong, unpleasant taste made it unpalatable to the young (and the old). To help mask the fishy flavor and to simultaneously prevent scurvy, *Infant Care* recommended giving cod liver oil with orange or tomato juice. In a tacit admission that it had neither a pleasing odor nor a pleasant flavor, the booklet told mothers to pretend that it was not offensive: "The mother must not let him know by her facial expression that she does not like the smell of the oil because that will teach the baby not to like it. She must take it for granted that he will like it even if she does not." Cod liver oil, the Children's Bureau materials insisted, was "bottled sunshine."[27]

Attempts to teach babies to like cod liver oil did not always go according to plan. Hugh, born in 1930 in Colorado, got his first dose of cod liver oil at the age of one month, but it did not agree with him. His mother wrote in the diary she kept about him, "we will depend on sunshine alone for a source of vitamin D. Hugh's digestive apparatus rebels against this essence of dead fish so popular for babies at present." Other babies objected as well, but resistance proved futile and they received their bottled sunshine regardless of whether they liked it or even needed it. Public health authorities inculcated the cod liver oil regimen so effectively that long after vitamin D supplementation of formula began and vitamin D-irradiated milk came on the market, mothers continued to dose their babies and to take them outdoors to develop a tan.[28]

Public health authorities preached the gospel of cod liver oil; family diaries, baby books, oral histories, and sales records indicate their success in spreading the word. Manufacturers reaped a bountiful reward, with a threefold growth in sales from 1926 to 1937. Claims for the healing power of cod liver oil often went beyond the evidence, with lists of its virtues that made it seem more like a magical elixir than an extract from the organ of a fish. Early purveyors advertised it as a cure for consumption (tuberculosis) and listed other ailments it allegedly treated, including colds, rheumatism, skin diseases, and general disability. The federal government backed up its faith with dollars; on Native American reservations, the Bureau of Indian Affairs field nurses distributed cod liver oil both to prevent rickets in infants and to boost the health of older children.[29]

Oral histories from the Works Progress Administration include references to cod liver oil, suggesting how effectively health officials and manufacturers persuaded the public of its virtues. A poor Bridgeport, Connecticut, mother told an interviewer in 1939, "I have to get Vitamin D for the baby," and mentioned later, "I haven't been able to get the baby any Cod Liver Oil but I'm going to try very soon. She needs it." Evidently, domestic science teachers expounded on its merits. A North Carolina millworker reported that his wife knew that "My babies and ourselves too have to have the right kind of vitamins" because she "took home economics in school." Perhaps regretting what she did not know at the time, a forty-year-old blind woman whose children had been born decades earlier told an interviewer that in earlier years, "You did not give them so much cod liver oil and things like that." The perception that infants and children required a daily dose led some charities to give it away. Hospitals and well-baby clinics sometimes did so as well, providing it to impoverished families or selling it at cost, presumably because prevention was cheaper than cure and untreated cases left compromised bodies.[30]

The perceived value of sunbathing preceded knowledge of rickets as a vitamin D deficiency; people understood tanning as healthful in ways not fully explained by scientists. The Metropolitan Life Insurance Company gave its subscribers a small booklet, "Sunlight the Health Giver," published in 1928, that included an historical account of the healing power of sunshine, which made one feel "better and stronger." In an explanation that seemed more imaginative than clinically grounded, it told readers that the sun "works mysteriously through the skin and causes certain chemical changes in the blood," resulting in an "increased number of red cells of the blood," thus preventing anemia. "The Perfect Baby Has a Healthy Tan," a chapter in the 1929 instruction manual *The Perfect Baby*, made clear that infants needed daily sunbaths to achieve a healthy color. For the well baby under five months of age, the Children's Bureau recommended two lengthy periods out of doors daily beginning at age three to four weeks. For some households, cold weather, tenement housing with little access to sunlight, and northern latitudes made sunbathing difficult. One ingenious solution to these problems, the "baby cage," consisted of a cage-like box made of wire that could be placed outside a tenement house window. Another option, for families with money, was a commercial sunlamp.[31]

Seasonal changes in sunlight led Mrs. C. Lekowski of Cleveland, Ohio, to write to the Children's Bureau in 1938 to ask what time of day to set her baby in the sun as the days grew shorter. She reported that she read *Infant Care* and listened to Children's Bureau director Katherine Lenroot's talks on the radio. A reply came from Marion W. Clarke, MD, director of the Division of Research in Child Development, who enclosed a copy of the 1929 revised edition of *Infant Care* and suggested: "During the Spring and Fall in order to obtain the full benefit of the sun's rays, the sun bath should be given during the middle part of the day." The answer suggests that health experts successfully harnessed sunlight, turning it from a natural element into an applied technology to be used according to precise directions. With the Bureau's enthusiasm for sunshine it was no wonder that manufacturers wrote to the Children's Bureau for endorsements of their sunlamps and products such as Vita glass, which "admits the beneficial rays of the sun." Cod liver oil producers did the same. The corporations hoped for but failed to win official certification from the nation's baby experts.[32]

The modern medical products, applied technologies, clinical services, and prescribed regimens that shaped the everyday experiences of babies appear in baby books, in reports from government agencies and foundations, and in community studies. Broader in scope than baby book records but less statistically sound than expansive demographic portraits produced by large-scale organizations, community studies often provide more details about the experiences of babies from low-income families or contrast the experiences of infants living in different situations within the same community. The studies do not focus on babies per se, but they reveal important aspects of babies' lives and explain the medical and commercial services shaping their upbringing. A study of Muncie, Indiana, in the 1920s, published in 1929 as *Middletown: A Study in Modern American Culture* by sociologists Robert S. Lynd and Helen Merrell Lynd, showed that community members relied on many kinds of medical care. The Lynds found abundant patent medicine advertisements in the local newspaper, including one for a "non-opium" baby syrup, as well as advertisements from older physicians working outside the medical mainstream. When the Great Depression tightened its grip on the nation, the need for free or subsidized health services grew, and this became evident to the Lynds when they returned to Muncie in the 1930s. They produced *Middletown Revisited: A Study in Cultural Conflicts*, a follow-up volume to their earlier work. It appeared in 1937. The Lynds discovered that by the 1930s, sales of patent medicines declined, although the newspaper advertisements for them continued. Many Muncie families struggled to get by; the authors observed that many of them relied on half-day free baby clinics, one for Euro Americans and one for African Americans, run by the Visiting Nurse Association.[33]

The transition from home to hospital births and the role of medical advice appeared in community studies of "Plainville," the pseudonym of a southern Midwest farm community of about 1,000 people living in sixty-five households. The Social Science Research Council of Columbia University sponsored the first study conducted in 1939 and 1940. A different investigator made a second study in 1954 and 1955. The first study, simply titled *Plainville, U.S.A.*, reported residents' recollections of twenty-five years earlier, when midwives and granny women attended most of the births. In 1939 and 1940, 89 of 103 births occurred under a doctor's care at home. After World War II, the follow-up study, *Plainville Fifteen Years Later*, reported that all deliveries took place under medical supervision, with the vast majority of babies being delivered in the nearby "Largetown" hospital, and only a few delivered at home by a physician.[34]

In the 1939–1940 period, some Plainville mothers raised babies "by the book," while others followed a combination of "granny lore" and "modern methods." As a mother explained, she read books and magazines about childcare and "agreed with what the books said," but she raised her babies the old way, "because it was easier." The study noted that most babies slept in their parents' beds, were breastfed on demand, and were cuddled and carried when they cried. All of these practices ran counter to medical advice, which underscored the need for separate sleeping quarters, scheduled feedings, and taking care not overstimulate or overindulge babies. Other Plainville customs at odds with contemporary professional instructions included starting babies on solid foods late, at about six to eight months, and initiating toilet training later than experts advised. The medical advice dispensed by nurses and physicians, on radio, in pamphlets, and in baby books did not always shape nursery experiences. Infant care practices did become "modern" over time, but parents, not experts, set the pace of change.[35]

The follow-up study in Plainville revealed how residents began to be influenced by urban social values and modern ideas about infant care. Nursery practices increasingly conformed to medical guidelines. Families labeled "high status" moved their babies to cribs, and more frequently than in earlier decades bottle fed rather than breastfed their offspring. In the 1950s, Plainville babies enjoyed both commercially prepared baby foods and table foods, suggesting the effects of both vigorous marketing and a higher standard of living. Despite the change in diet, babies continued to be fed on demand rather than on the clock. The strict scheduling favored by professional infant care experts gained little traction in Plainville; knowing the latest advice did not always mean following it. One mother reported learning about toilet training from pediatrician Benjamin Spock's book on baby care and from the *Better Homes and Gardens Baby Book*, but, she reported, their techniques did not work for her baby. She gave up her efforts to train the baby and resolved to try again later.[36]

Babies' physical and emotional needs led parents to pray for them, to buy for them, and to learn from medical experts how to care for them. By introducing or connecting their families to biomedicine and to consumer products promising good health, babies served as agents of the modern. Entries in baby books and reports from community scholars and government researchers make clear that adoption of baby-rearing techniques took place in fits and starts, according to the needs and resources of individual families. The same sources also reveal that even as babies pushed their families into new practices, they also anchored their households in traditional customs, helping their families and communities sustain their reliance on long-standing healing practices. Babies could be engines of modernization and they could also act as brakes.

6

HELPING BABY CITIZENS
Traditional Healers, Patent Medicines, Local Cultures

I N THE 1930S, A MOTHER IN Adams County, Illinois, recalled how, when her baby was dying of brain fever years earlier, a physician arrived and "He said he could not help my baby." What happened next convinced her of both the fecklessness and ignorance of doctors.

> A neighbor came in. We peel [*sic*] onions, chopped them up fine, put salt over them, and made a poultice; put one on each wrist, one on the bottom of both feet and one across the chest. And we saved my baby. Of course, we worked all night, when a doctor would not do that.

A folklorist studying the Ozarks reported on a Tulsa, Oklahoma, baby with summer complaint that the doctors reportedly failed to help. The father returned to Missouri, harvested artichoke roots, and came back to make a tea that relieved the baby in hours. Many other individuals recounted stories of physician ineptitude, while praising homemade remedies and alternative healers. A North Carolina widowed grandmother who used turpentine and corn liquor to cure her granddaughter of stomach trouble described the futility of orthodox medicine, telling an interviewer from the Federal Writers' Project of the Works Progress Administration (WPA): "Doctors don't do so much good."[1]

Popular complaints about physicians contained both truths and exaggerations, often lacking in context. Some doctors avoided treating babies whose families were unlikely to pay and who lived far out in the country, decisions that kept practitioners solvent but earned them scorn. Some poor families called doctors too late to be of help, hesitating to spend their dollars or incur debts and leading physicians to blame the families for their infants' illnesses and deaths. Beyond the decisions made by each party was the fact that medical treatments worked in some cases and not in others.[2]

Traditional methods of preventing and treating infant illnesses survived the efforts of public health providers to make orthodox medicine the only choice. Babies both pushed their families into the world of biomedicine and restrained them from fully embracing all of its claims and practices – sometimes by dying under medical care and sometimes by recovering with the aid of community-based healers and home remedies. Unquestionably, scientific infant care became the dominant practice in the twentieth century, but it was by no means uncontested, nor did it drive competitors out of the marketplace or competing ideas out of the nursery. As folklorists revealed, infants received treatments that their parents, grandparents, and great-grandparents had received for the same afflictions.

Twentieth-century medical literature extols the value of physicians, nurses, and public health officials in supporting infant health. Accounts of traditional practitioners found in the folklore literature and oral histories do the same for wise women, midwives, medicine men, and other community healers. The makers of patent medicines praise themselves in their advertising. Even as the cultural power and scientific foundation of modern biomedicine expanded, two other sources of health provision – community-based providers and a robust and a lightly regulated pharmaceutical industry – continued to answer the needs of families with sick infants. Evidence for this appears primarily in individual stories rather than statistical tables.

Families sometimes pulled medical books and pamphlets from their shelves and doctored babies following the written instructions. On occasion, these contained up-to-date, if not necessarily useful, instructions, but often they did not. The author of a Children's Bureau study in rural Montana complained about families relying on information from "works purporting to be of medical value to laymen but whose whole reason for existence seems to be to give employment to book agents." Children's Bureau experts also aimed criticism at patent medicine makers and folk medicine practitioners, loosely defined as nonprofessionals supplying health care. Their doctoring often involved the application of natural remedies from plants.[3]

Studies of folk medicine typically explored the practices of minority group members and people living in poor, rural communities, making it easy to conclude that reliance on traditional remedies reflected an economically marginal status or geographic distance from doctors and hospitals. However, the selection of presumed outsiders as targets of study masked the continuing reliance of middle- and upper-class families on folk practices and treatments. Later, research among urban immigrants countered the rural bias of early folklore studies and, along with reports from social welfare workers, demonstrated that despite access to hospitals, clinics, nurses, and doctors, many city-dwellers preferred unlicensed caregivers from their own communities. Additional findings regarding the choices of well-off families documented that they too relied on non-accredited caregivers.[4]

Both community-based practitioners and scientifically trained professionals constituted folk communities of healers. Each group possessed bodies of knowledge and core beliefs. The members maintained their respective identities through rituals and by using a vocabulary that promoted cohesion and served to demonstrate their social status and expert knowledge to patients. Doctors and nurses used the language of science and argued that laboratory research, controlled studies of population health, clinical observations, and university-based training gave them special skills and useful data. They had a theory of disease drawn from their knowledge of germs and they regarded those who did not understand their explanations of illness causation as unsophisticated or, frankly, ignorant. However, many professional theories and treatments rested on little more than professional folklore, especially in the realm of baby care. The advice physicians and nurses dispensed about the right age to initiate toilet training and introduce solid foods as well as the warnings they gave about the dangers of rocking babies to sleep or picking them up when they cried had no scientific underpinnings. In these cases, health care professionals employed folk knowledge handed down from their teachers and their medical and nursing books, supplemented by their observations and experiments. Like their competitors, orthodox medical providers benefited enormously from the fact that many conditions they encountered resolved on their own. Rocked or not, babies eventually fell asleep.

Traditional healers operated much the same way as orthodox physicians, but they often gained an advantage from being fully integrated into their patients' communities. Their advice drew from the teachings of other experienced healers and from observations of their patients. They had theories of disease and they possessed knowledge that physicians did not have regarding ailments particular to their communities. Local healers used herbal remedies as well as other treatments, including ones used by doctors, to relieve aches and pains. In some cases, herbs used by folk practitioners later proved to be effective pharmaceutical agents; in other instances, the remedies they used would be shown to be useless or harmful. The same was true of many professional medical interventions.[5]

Commercially manufactured patent medicines generally fell into the useless or harmful category, and this was more often the case for products marketed before the era of government regulation over their labeling and contents. Cure-all elixirs that claimed to halt deadly diseases or promised to alleviate other symptoms usually did neither, succeeding only in enriching their manufacturers, advertisers, and retailers. When the remedies proved helpful, thanks to the placebo effect or to the alcohol and narcotics they contained, which succeeded in dulling pain, manufacturers benefited from word-of-mouth endorsements. Seeking the largest possible market, proprietary remedies claimed to be broad-spectrum treatments, assisting individuals suffering from both chronic and acute ailments and assuring users the contents were strong enough to cure any adult and safe enough for any infant or child. The grandiose declarations on their bottles and in their advertisements undoubtedly spurred sales and most likely resulted in babies (and others) finding relief in some cases and experiencing dangerous overdoses, an incipient addiction, or even death, in others.[6]

Patent remedies offered two distinct advantages over professional practitioners: lower cost and easier access. Families living far from pharmacies purchased and kept on hand patent remedies sold by mail order and by traveling salesmen. Among other remedies, the 1897 Sears Roebuck catalog offered Mrs. Winslow's Soothing Syrup – a popular teething preparation containing morphine – and it also sold Castorline – a supposedly narcotic-free mixture that promised to destroy worms, allay fever, prevent vomiting, cure diarrhea, and relieve teething, constipation, and flatulence in infants and children. Letters to the Children's Bureau reveal that parents tried many over-the-counter medicines to treat common problems in infants. Only when the nostrums failed to provide relief did mothers take the next step and visit a doctor, clinic, or community practitioner or seek help from the Children's Bureau.

The author of an infant care book published in 1938 observed that "If an aboriginal visitor could read our language, a glance at the advertising sections of our magazines or a trip downtown on the street cars would leave him astonished at our preoccupation with the subject of constipation." The same visitor would have been equally impressed, or astonished, by the volume of letters to the Children's Bureau addressing this topic and detailing the various treatments babies endured. Many of the letters listed the patent medicines given to infants and frequently noted that doctors had recommended them. A mother writing from Fort Benjamin Harrison, Indiana, in 1917 told how she followed the advice of a physician who suggested castor oil and soap sticks and glycerin suppositories for her baby's constipation. Evidently unable to solve the problem with those measures, the mother sought help from another doctor, who prescribed Milk of Magnesia and told her that if that failed, she should use Castoria. From Chipley, Florida, a mother wrote in 1929 about using Castoria, castor oil, and paregoric (a very dilute opium tincture that could actually cause constipation) for her baby's bowel troubles. While the Children's Bureau correspondents frequently dispensed boilerplate advice, when necessary they gave specific responses to questions raised in letters. Tacitly admitting the popularity of various remedies for constipation, the Bureau advisor wrote to the Indiana mother that Milk of Magnesia did the least harm of all the methods suggested to her. More importantly, although a physician had advised giving the baby paregoric, the Bureau agent instructed the mother not to use it.[7]

In the early twentieth century, muckraking journalists and medical professionals exposed and crusaded against the deadly or worthless ingredients in many popular medications and pushed for their regulation. Reports calling for control over drug marketers echoed the larger, ongoing crusade to outlaw sales of unsanitary and contaminated foods containing dangerous and disgusting adulterants. Magazines targeting well-off female subscribers, among them *Women's Home Companion, Good Housekeeping,* and *Ladies Home Journal,* helped to rally support from readers for government intervention in the patent medicine trade. After public outcry about hidden dangers in food reached a crescendo following publication of Upton Sinclair's exposé of the meatpacking industry, *The Jungle,* Congress passed the Pure Food and Drug Act in 1906. It required, among other things, that the makers of over-the-counter medicines reveal their contents.[8]

The new law, in theory, enabled parents to know what they were buying for their babies; however, many dangerous but properly labeled products remained on the market. *Nostrums and Quackery,* a 1911 collection of articles from the *Journal of the American Medical Association,* listed a number of opiate-laced teething products available for purchase, including Kopp's Baby's Friend and Morell's Teething Syrup. Because they contained opiates, which were constipating, soothing syrups met multiple needs, treating common infant diarrheal diseases as well as relieving the discomfort of teething and colic (a common poorly under-stood condition leading to abdominal pain and sometimes hours of sustained intensive crying in the early months of infancy). Despite the new law, a Children's Bureau study of maternal and infant care in rural Georgia begun in 1916 turned up a number of misbranded products, as assessed by the US Bureau of Chemistry (a precursor to the US Food and Drug Administration). The Georgia remedies contained large amounts of alcohol as well as other substances certain to quiet babies and children including chloroform, opium, and morphine.[9]

Over-the-counter remedies and doses from the whiskey bottle kept at home for medicinal and other purposes sometimes quieted babies too much. Public health pamphlets and medical advice books warned about deadly overdoses and dangerous habits resulting from their use. A baby-saving booklet from the Chicago Health Department explained: "Motherly love often becomes motherly murder through the use of soothing syrups." Aiming to reach a broader audience, the Better Babies Bureau of *Woman's Home Companion* magazine provided a guide to baby health exhibits, including information on setting up a display of "baby killers," among them patent medicines, soothing syrups, and par-egoric, as well as pacifiers, cheap colored candy, painted toys, and nursing bottles with long tubes (which were hard to clean and thus encouraged the growth of bacteria). Accounts of infant deaths linked to soothing syrups appeared in newspapers as well, but advertisements for the very products that were killing or intoxicating babies vastly outnumbered the news stories. In 1908, two years after passage of the Pure Food and Drug Act, the *New York Times* published a two-line story about twins in St. Paul, Minnesota, whose deaths from syrup poisoning were being investigated by the coroner. The same paper carried daily advertisements for Mrs. Winslow's Soothing Syrup.[10]

Babies benefited from passage of the Harrison Narcotics Act of 1914, which restricted the manufacture, importation, and distribution of opiates and coca and prevented the sale of laudanum (tincture of opium). The Act permitted continued sales of paregoric, classifying it as an exempt narcotic. Alcohol remained on the shelf even after enactment of the Eighteenth Amendment in 1920. While the legal manufacture and transport of alcoholic beverages stopped, physicians could write prescriptions for medicinal alcohol and, of course, alcohol continued to be available through illicit channels. Perhaps for that reason, a 1923 baby book that included medical advice from Oregon physician Estella Ford Warner offered information about poisons and their antidotes, including those for both opium and alcohol.[11]

Families turned to folk remedies to prevent or cure infant diseases that physicians could not treat. Whooping cough, the common name for pertussis (a highly contagious respiratory infection caused by bacteria), was the deadliest infectious disease for infants in their first year of life in the decades from 1900 to 1920. Its frequency, seriousness, and easily recognized cough followed by a "whooping" sound inspired many protective measures and treatments, most of them useless. Pennsylvanians of German background as well as African American and Euro American families in North Carolina reportedly placed infants in grain hoppers (devices used for transporting agricultural products) in order to prevent whooping cough. When faced with a case of the disease, families tried various cures. One, recounted in a 1939 study of Tennessee folklore, involved a complex set of procedures: "Take it (the baby) out to a graveyard, dig a hole three feet deep, hold the baby by the heels, put it in the grave and shake it well. This will cure the cough." A different Tennessee resident described making tea from a hornet's nest with honey added and administering it twice daily for two weeks in order to cure a case of whooping cough. Physicians had nothing better to offer. An effective pertussis vaccine did not appear until 1939 and routine immunization did not begin until the early 1940s. Effective antimicrobial treatments came later.[12]

In some instances, community healers appeared to offer more help to babies than their scientifically trained competitors because they could treat conditions that regular physicians did not recognize. Families in the South sought care for infants with "bold hives" (an eruptive skin disease) and for "livergrown" (a presumed dangerously enlarged liver). Both ailments appeared in homeopathic and other alternative medical texts from the middle of the nineteenth century, but not in regular medical books. Physician Willis P. King, writing in 1891, attributed the practice of treating livergrown to "grannies" and midwives in the West. An account from a study of Ozark folk medicine described the treatment:

> A stout old woman grasps the baby's left hand and right foot and twists them together behind the back, then does the same with the right hand and left foot. She has to pull pretty hard sometimes, and the child hollers somthin' terrible, but it's the only treatment for a liver-growed baby.

The description from the folklorist concluded, "physicians tell me that it does not seem to do any particular harm." A milder remedy for livergrown, recounted in a study of the Pennsylvania Germans, involved passing the baby through a horse collar. In rural Georgia, some mothers reportedly used bloodletting through scarification to treat what they simply referred to as hives. One baby received nine such treatments – with only a few drops of blood extracted each time – during his first month of life. Bloodletting may have entered community practice by way of regular medicine. It was once a common procedure in an earlier era of heroic medicine when doctors used powerful and immediately active treatments like emptying the stomach and bowels along with extensive bloodletting to treat an array of ailments.[13]

The boundary between healers could be porous. Astute doctors understood that securing the trust of patients required acquiescing to favored traditions and learning from other providers. Amy Lathrop, wife of a small-town physician in Kansas who began his practice in 1905, published an account of pioneer remedies and recounted the ways practitioners learned from each other. She reported that drinking cider vinegar, a preventive recommended by a doctor during a smallpox epidemic in 1899, came to be seen in the community as an effective means of halting the spread of the dreaded disease. In the case of an infant with cholera infantum and thrush, she observed that six physicians called to the bed-side failed to cure the youngster, who ultimately was successfully treated with prayers and a cooked chicken gizzard. Lathrop also described how a local physician incorporated traditional remedies into his practice. Learning from a midwife that mothers gave their babies two teaspoons of cold water shortly after birth to prevent colic, the doctor tried it on his next confinement case and reported, "Believe it or not, that baby never had colic." Vinegar did not halt smallpox epidemics and cold water did not prevent colic, but in each case observed coincidences led to new clinical practices. The medical treatment of infants drew from laboratory findings, from community customs, and from observed recoveries often attributed to the most recently applied remedy.[14]

Despite occasions when physicians learned from community practitioners, trained doctors most often viewed their rivals as dangerous and ignorant. Writing about female health advisors, Willis P. King found it "astounding what influence those women often acquire over families, and more especially over young mothers. They say 'she is an old lady an' knows more about babies than the doctors; what does a *man* know about a baby, or about a woman either?'" He pointed in particular to the custom of "these women" dosing newborn babies with saffron tea and catnip. Johns Hopkins physician Leonard Keene similarly warned readers of *The Farmer's Wife* magazine in 1913 to "be on guard against the procedures that 'Mrs. Smith has used for three generations' or that explains how Mrs. Jones 'raised thirteen.'" But why should families be distrustful of healers with years of experience and demonstrated skill who provided direct care over long days and weeks and who charged very little or nothing at all? All of these reasons helped explain why midwives in particular remained active and respected in many communities even when other childbirth options became available.[15]

Midwives not only delivered babies, they cared for mothers and infants after the births. Many physicians resented them as competition, but some supported their work. Like doctors, midwives varied in their skills and training, but unlike doctors, they typically came from the same communities as their patients. The category of midwives included African American "granny" midwives in the South, Japanese-American midwives known as *sanba* in the West, immigrant midwives in urban enclaves and Midwestern farming regions, and Mexican-American midwives called *parteras* in the West and Southwest. Despite the value of their services, midwives declined in number as childbirth shifted to home deliveries by physicians and, more significantly, from home to hospital. By 1930, midwives attended only 15 percent of all deliveries in the United States, most often in the South.[16]

Recognizing midwives' role as community health care providers, the Children's Bureau inaugurated midwife training programs run by nurses using Sheppard-Towner funds, and many states began licensing and registering trained midwives. Their education emphasized the application of modern, sterile delivery techniques and placing silver nitrate drops in the eyes of newborns to prevent venereal ophthalmia. Classes also focused on getting midwives to jettison their herbal remedies, including homemade teas and salves used to support labor, delivery, and postpartum healing. A racial divide existed between the state officials administering the training programs in the South and the midwives who enjoyed the trust of their respective communities. Margaret Charles Smith, a trained Alabama African American midwife licensed in the 1940s reported having to give up the use of common medicinal plants in order to avoid losing her license or her liberty, but she informed her biographer that other midwives continued to use botanical treatments.[17]

Field nurses' reports from Native American communities detail both acceptance and rejection of modern biomedical care. The disturbingly high infant mortality and morbidity rates on reservations concerned government agencies; they addressed as best they could the medical problems, but not the underlying poverty that was outside their mandate. In 1916, the Children's Bureau produced a little booklet, "Indian Babies: How to Keep Them Well," offering advice about feeding, daily care, treatment of lice and scabies, and when to seek hospital care for

Figure 6.1 Midwife wrapping her kit to go on a call in Greene
County, Georgia, 1941
Photographer: Jack Delano
Credit: US Farm Security Administration, Office of War Information

serious illnesses like tuberculosis, trachoma, and pneumonia. On the reservations, nurses and physicians ran hospitals, clinics, and educational programs. The Indian Field Service nurses sent monthly reports to the Department of the Interior headquarters in Washington, DC, in the 1930s and 1940s. Their accounts included both statistical data about the patients seen and conditions treated and detailed descriptions of their work.

On many reservations, the nurses offered classes in scientific baby care. The lessons at the Elko, Nevada, reservation included such things as "how to clean a wash basin" and "how to put drops in babies' eyes." Nurse Helen Kelso, working on the Warm Springs Reservation in Oregon, promoted infant feeding schedules to her clients and reported she taught two women to nurse babies on the clock, every three hours, rather than on demand, as was apparently the custom. However, Kelso failed to get the mothers to stop carrying their babies "on the [cradle] board." The march toward modern infant care took some steps forward, but the pace proved slow. Generally, reports from nurses noted good attendance at infant care classes and friendly receptions during home visits where they taught infant feeding and other skills. A nurse on the Red Lake Chippewa Reservation in Minnesota reported a successful intervention after finding an unwashed two-day-old baby and the parents fearful of bathing him. She explained the infant needed only a warm oil bath and clean clothes, not full immersion in a pan of water as the parents feared. In other situations, the nurses failed to persuade families to abandon traditional customs. Although they met with resistance, the nurses persevered. An assessment of nurses' efforts in Southern California, which included well-baby conferences and transporting infants to medical facilities as well as support for immunizations, concluded that the assistance provided to infants, children, and adults succeeded in lowering death rates from communicable diseases in the years from 1928 to 1948. Nevertheless, the numerous challenges of reservation life, including extreme poverty, high rates of contagious diseases, and distant and limited health services, kept overall infant mortality rates very high.[18]

Field service nurses, like urban caseworkers, sometimes encountered defiance when they attempted to remove babies from their families and place them in distant hospitals. The nurses' reports mention families hiding sick infants, refusing institutional care outright, or removing babies from hospitals after a short stay. Writing from the Morongo Indian Reservation in Banning, California, a field nurse with the Mission Indian Agency claimed the reluctance to hospitalize babies stemmed from families being "under the influence of the Medicine Man."

Official condemnation of medicine men was neither consistent nor universal. A 1937 survey of the health and social needs of Native American children conducted by the Children's Bureau acknowledged that medicine men possessed some knowledge and skills. Women healers on the reservations, on the other hand, earned no such respect; the Bureau report belittled their skills, explaining, "in many tribes the older women understood the application of herbs, which were employed in much the same way as our grandmothers and grandfathers used them as simple home remedies." The author paid limited attention to the enormous variations among tribal groups in terms of their physical environment, cultural traditions, and economic resources, and similarly neglected to explore the kinds of treatments provided by community healers and the effectiveness of their remedies. Trained in biomedicine, nurses and doctors stressed to their patients the value of the current rules of infant care and the need to obey them without question or deviation. They sometimes observed many practices outside the scientific mainstream and made an effort to distinguish which ones were worthwhile or might be overlooked in order to gain the trust of parents.[19]

Community-based healers used remedies they found effective and their knowledge came from what might be deemed long-term observational studies. They conducted experiments with various substances and practiced personalized medicine, with care regimens adapted to the circumstances of the patients and their environments. Community practitioners did not, of course, hold accredited professional degrees or publish their findings in professional journals. But, in many instances, physicians and nurses who claimed scientific expertise provided advice about the treatment of infant illnesses that rested on fewer clinical observations and broader assumptions than their nonprofessional peers. Did babies really require soap sticks to learn to defecate over a pot beginning at the age of two months? Did they need to be burped to prevent colic or spitting up? A recent medical study of burping suggests they did not. Burping was medical folklore promoted by doctors.[20]

Community studies as well as baby book entries indicated that not all babies lived by medically sanctioned rules, and it appears that many were no worse off for it. This was particularly true in the case of regimented daily care. Modern baby books along with physicians preached habit training as character building and eschewed the old-fashioned techniques that one writer labeled "the method of sympathy" in a chapter on sleep entitled "No Lights, No Toys, No Bottles." Many parents remained ignorant of or willfully disregarded the advice about scheduling. Baby books, social work case records, and community studies reveal frequent cases of babies indulged by parents who found modern baby care ideas not to their liking. It appears that, despite warnings from experts, the babies experienced little harm to their physical or mental health as a result.[21]

A study of the white working-class families in the "new South" from 1880 to 1915 found extensive violations of the modern rules for bringing up babies. Infants consumed table foods at three months, far earlier than was then recommended, and their mothers began to wean them once mixed feeding became an established pattern. The laxity appeared in other areas as well. Toilet training did not begin at a fixed early age, despite the belief of medical experts that it needed to commence in the first six months. Thirty years after the appearance of the study of white working-class Southern families, another researcher, Margaret Jarman Hagood, found the same infant care practices among Southern white tenant farm families. The women she investigated relied on a variety of healers and medicines, including home remedies and quacks. The mothers turned their backs on the heavily promoted schedules for feeding and sleeping and delayed toilet training their babies. Eschewing the rigid and unemotional upbringing that medical experts advised, the mothers did not let infants cry themselves to sleep and instead rocked them in their arms or in their cradles. Indulgence of this sort horrified medical professionals, who were certain it opened the door to future emotional and developmental difficulties. Hagood, a sociologist, not a physician, offered a different view, finding "an absence of the continual struggle and conflict which often accompanies the forcing of an infant to an arbitrary routine and this period of life appears to be relatively free from frustration."[22]

Two common problems vexed infants, parents, doctors, and traditional healers, while enriching patent medicine makers: colic and teething. Colic, marked by loud, constant crying, understandably unnerved parents. Mothers' efforts to relieve their babies' discomfort led them to document their reliance on multiple remedies and healers. They bought patent medicines, cooked up homemade concoctions, followed measures prescribed by doctors, and tested treatments recommended by friends and family members. Babies endured all sorts of efforts to ease their discomfort, sometimes experiencing one remedy after the other or many at once. With the exception of narcotic- and alcohol-laced treatments, none of the measures quieted the crying or provided relief. Among the relatively benign treatments reported in a study of Tennessee folklore were blowing tobacco smoke on a baby's stomach and pouring hot water into a shoe and then giving it to the baby to drink. North Carolina folk remedies included saffron tea, calamus (a wetland plant) root tea, and tea made from the scrapings of the inside of the father's hatband. Even physicians suggested herbal treatments along with other interventions. In 1912, Dr. Ralph Oakley Clock suggested treating colic by rectal irrigation followed by soda mint tablets, cinnamon water, and then a "spice plaster" of ginger, cloves, cinnamon, and allspice in a flannel cloth dampened with hot whiskey and applied to the abdomen. At the very least, the baby smelled good.[23]

Mothers of colicky babies wrote to the Children's Bureau for help, sometimes after physicians and over-the-counter medicines failed to resolve the problem. In 1915, a Kentucky woman described her baby's distress, reporting that the physician's prescribed treatment – colic tablets to digest her milk – did not work. After the doctor's suggestion proved fruitless, she gave the baby popular home remedies: "asifrettive & whiskey," "calimel tea," and "caster oil," and then purchased the popular patent medicine she called "Charles H. Flitcher's castoria." None of them worked. Her efforts illuminated her desperation and signaled the popu- larity of traditional herbal treatments. The asafetida she dosed her baby with was a foul-smelling plant with now-recognized medicinal properties that was commonly used to treat constipation. It had other applications as well. Dr. Samuel Crumbine wrote in his autobiography that many people believed "a bag of asafetida around a child's neck" prevented diphtheria. In Louisiana, people used asafetida to prevent smallpox. The whiskey given to the Kentucky baby functioned as a common household anesthetic used by parents and prescribed by physicians for colic and many other conditions. Proper dosing, for whatever purpose, posed a challenge. A baby given some whiskey water shortly before his circum- cision in a Colorado hospital in 1930 reportedly became "shockingly drunk."[24]

The company producing Fletcher's Castoria engaged in an early, sustained, and effective mass-marketing campaign to win over con- sumers. Initially, its advertisements played to parental fears. One fea- tured a dead infant and a maudlin poem followed by the statement "Oh, what a pity that Mrs. Vowels [the mother of the seven-month-old baby eulogized in the poem, and likely given a name to rhyme with bowels] did not know about CASTORIA." Subsequent promotions took a positive turn and the company began producing a baby book in the 1920s in which it marketed the product as a "harmless substitute for castor oil, paregoric drops, and soothing syrups." As mildness became a selling point, a competitor, Teethina, produced an advertisement-laden baby book mostly consisting of advice about infant care, including the many uses for the "kindly laxative for babies and little children."[25]

Not all remedies were kindly; many harmful substances remained on the market to treat fretful babies. A one-year-old Connecticut infant received soothing syrup for his bowels and the cutting of teeth and what his mother called "nervous," in addition to the paregoric she purchased to help him sleep. Despite being dosed with several products, he continued to have difficulty sleeping at night, as explained in a letter to the Children's Bureau asking for help. Other mothers also attacked small problems with a large arsenal, only to move on to even heavier weapons when the treatments brought on new difficulties. Writing to the Children's Bureau from Oneida, Wisconsin, in 1916, a mother reported having tried castor oil and then Calomel (a mercury compound) before moving on to Milk of Magnesia, Epsom salts dissolved in water and prune juice, Dike's Compound Laxative Fig Syrup, and Entona (a wheat gluten suppository) to cure her baby's constipation. In the same letter she inquired about using "worm seed tea (as recommended by old ladies)" for a child with round worms, a dangerous parasite. Wormseed, an herb commonly used to treat worm infections, was highly toxic and even deadly. Not surprisingly, the Children's Bureau respondent warned her against its use and also advised abandoning other homemade and commercial remedies.[26]

Infants' teething pains provided both sales opportunities for nostrum makers and a chance for doctors to earn consultation fees. Although a normal part of infant development, many practitioners and laypeople considered teething a highly dangerous period of life and believed it could provoke convulsions among other serious problems. Physician Luther Emmet Holt listed common symptoms of teething in his late nineteenth-century advice book as fretfulness, loss of appetite, possibly a slight fever, and loose bowels, but he concluded the difficulties lasted only a few days. With parents worried about babies' weight gain and fearful that fevers signaled dangerous infections, they understandably sought help when teething began. The baby book of Ruth Buchanan, born in 1905, listed doctor visits for both colic and teething. The shared baby book of Ronald Matthews, born in 1919, and his brother Charles, born in 1923, contained a detailed discussion of their teething difficulties.[27]

Concerns about teething ebbed in the twentieth century, but they did not entirely abate. Babies vocalized their discomfort and in response parents trekked to the pharmacy or opened the medicine cabinet. The first edition of *Infant Care* rebuked parents who gave patent medicines for teething, and warned that they contained narcotics. It suggested consulting a doctor about lancing the baby's red and swollen gums. The warning may have been sensible, but the remedy – taking up the lance – was unproven. The booklet advised parents not to attribute all ailments to teething, and it suggested that often the actual source of discomfort was overfeeding. Many parents clung to the popular belief that teething posed a danger and seemingly had the evidence to prove it. A man recalled his son's death in 1922, telling an interviewer from the Federal Writers' Project in 1938 that "He died at eight months, and Martha says it is because something went wrong with his teething and his gums were poisoned." The 1929 revised edition of *Infant Care* continued the effort to persuade parents not to engage in excessive worrying, explaining, "teething alone rarely counts for illness or fever." Nevertheless, babies continued to express their discomfort and their parents persisted in believing the eruption of teeth signaled the beginning of a dangerous stage of infancy.[28]

Remedies for teething difficulties collected by folklorists included supplying the infants with things to gnaw on, rubbing their gums with various substances, and giving them items to wear in order to ward off pain. In Louisiana, babies gnawed on alligator teeth and sheep bones (among other things) as they cut their teeth. In middle Tennessee, tying a mole's foot around the baby's neck reportedly brought relief from teething pain. Mormon pioneers in the Rocky Mountains ended their babies' teething problems by rubbing the brains of a rabbit or other animal on their gums. A study of Pennsylvania Germans found they used rabbit brains as well as rattlesnake rattles for this purpose. Belief in the medicinal power of animal brains was long-standing, widespread, and enduring. A 1908 memoir by a country doctor attributed the custom to "colored" nurses and washerwomen who advised their employers to try it. When all the teeth erupted and the babies' pain ebbed, the cures all made sense in retrospect.[29]

Scientific medicine advocates and patent medicine makers held no monopoly on nursery care, but the cultural respect earned by the former and the advertising might of the latter left many local healers to work in the shadows by the middle of the twentieth century. Descriptions of traditional cures appeared in family records, oral histories, and folklore accounts or in the dismissive writings of medical professionals. The application of herbal cures and homemade teas and the accepting of care from wise neighbors and relatives existed in a sphere of mutual support and exchange, and outside of the expanding market economy. A WPA interviewer working in the mountain town of Brevard, North Carolina, observed that catnip tea was a medicine for babies, apparently unaware that it grew wild in the mountains, making it a thrifty choice. A mother from Whitaker, North Carolina, wrote to the Children's Bureau (addressing her letter to the "Better Babies Bureau") and mentioned giving her son a cupful of catnip tea daily, along with breast feeding him, describing yet another use for an accessible plant believed to offer multiple health benefits. The Children's Bureau physician replying to her letter urged her to abandon this custom.[30]

Poor families did not shun needed medical care for their babies; they struggled to obtain it when their home treatments did not work and they pursued free services when they were too embarrassed to ask community healers for charity care. As a result, growing numbers turned to hospital clinics. A study conducted between 1928 and 1931 by the Committee on the Costs of Medical Care documented the economic strains on medical services and providers as well as the problems many people faced trying to access care. Composed of leading physicians and researchers and supported by several foundations, including the Carnegie Corporation, the Milbank Memorial Fund, and the Rockefeller Foundation, among others, the Committee's investigators studied nearly 9,000 white families of varying incomes living in eighteen states. The findings offered no surprises: poor families saw doctors less frequently and asked for free care more often than households with more money. The researchers documented that people living in rural areas struggled to gain access to services, that the quality of medical care varied, and that often physicians faced challenges trying to earn a living.[31]

Understandably, consumers looked for inexpensive treatments and had a difficult time navigating through the maze of available services. Investigators found an "excessive use of self-prescribed pharmaceuticals, resort to quacks and charlatans, and – among urban people – a helplessness and incapacity to search out the medical service needed from the welter of practitioners and agencies." The well-to-do received criticism in the report for seeking help from what the authors labeled "cult healers." The study condemned the patent medicine sales that accounted for 10 percent of all expenditures on medical services and commodities – a sum the authors considered wasted – but patent medicines may well have been the only affordable treatments available, and some families lacked the means to afford even cheap nostrums. In a study of childcare in rural Mississippi, Children's Bureau researcher Helen M. Dart observed that white mothers sometimes overdosed their infants with remedies from the medicine chest while African American mothers made frequent use of teas when treating their children. Economic resources as well as cultural traditions likely explained the difference.[32]

In the interwar years, modern "citizen babies" helped to connect households to scientific practices, the consumer marketplace, and government programs. At the same time, "baby citizens" kept their families rooted in traditional healing practices and household customs that reflected local cultures, community norms, and economic conditions. Even as trained nurses, physicians, and public health practitioners worked to promote prescribed nursery routines, household hygiene regimens, and regular consultations with orthodox medical practitioners, some families remained deaf to their counsel. Weaning mothers from infant care practices and popular nostrums suggested by friends, family members, and community healers proved challenging.

In the post–World War II years, investigators turned to studies of Hispanic groups as their percentage within the overall population grew. Immigrants from Mexico and their children led the growth in the Hispanic population in the second half of the twentieth century as it expanded from 1.63 percent of the population in 1940 to 3.24 percent in 1960, followed by more rapid growth in the years after 1970. Studies of health practices in Mexican American communities revealed long-familiar themes: reliance on community practitioners, use of both herbal remedies and patent medicines, culturally specific theories of diagnosis and illness, and difficulties accessing and placing faith in medical professionals. As an informant in Texas told an anthropologist "Doctors can't cure a person of mollera, or empacho, or susto, because they don't believe in them."[33]

When their babies became ill, families understandably sought help first from traditional healers who shared their cultural knowledge and who had the needed skills to select and use herbal remedies to treat common afflictions. A 1950s study of Spanish-speaking people in the Southwest found teething babies received onion leaves and stems to chew. When they had a cold, infants received a cough syrup made from the juice of fried or roasted onions, sweetened with honey or sugar. Community members shunned traditional medical services much of the time; *parteras* delivered twice as many babies as doctors and children had low immunization rates. Recognizing this, the New Mexico State Department provided training to *parteras*, partly in the hope that they would become liaisons between Anglo practitioners and rural Spanish-speaking patients. Families did seek help from doctors. Hospital-based practitioners observed that infants sometimes returned repeatedly for treatment of malnutrition, which the doctors blamed on both poverty and poor dietary choices. Researchers observed the effects on infant health of the lack of health insurance, poverty, and geographic isolation, as well as the linguistic barriers and cultural traditions that marked infant care practices in many Hispanic communities.[34]

Families shopped for infant care. They preferred to buy from those who knew their language and culture and whose fees they could afford. As active health consumers engaged in the modern marketplace, they purchased over-the-counter medicines such as laxatives and aspirin as well as turning to various practitioners. An example of this appears in a detailed account of an infant, Lupita, suffering from a gastrointestinal problem. It appeared in a study of the Mexican American community in San Jose, California, conducted in the mid-1950s. Lupita's care revealed the range of treatments available, the intersection of traditional and modern medicine, and the ways personal encounters with healers shaped the family's assessment of their value. Lupita's odyssey began after several days of growing distress. Her mother took her first to a woman who diagnosed a teething condition and offered a rag dipped in whiskey. The treatment failed and Lupita's symptoms continued and eventually grew more severe. Several days later her mother took her to a *curandera*, a traditional healer who diagnosed empacho, defined as food stuck in the digestive tract. The *curandera* treated Lupita with a warm olive oil massage and a dose of powdered chalk (a form of calcium carbonate still used as a remedy for stomach complaints). The problem did not resolve and Lupita received a second treatment, which also failed to cure her. After that, Lupita's mother, following the advice of her sister-in-law who was a practical nurse, took Lupita to a doctor. The physician prescribed antibiotics and Lupita recovered. In her mother's recollection, however, it was the *curandera*, not the doctor, who cured her. Perhaps it was the literal hands-on care and fact that the *curandera* provided two treatments that made them more memorable than the prescription from the physician.[35]

The tug from biomedicine proponents, baby product manufacturers, and government agencies slowly succeeded in pulling most babies and their families into the orbit of modern infant care and consumer culture. Parents learned to want what doctors promised in large part because medical science offered increasingly effective methods for preventing and treating infants' illnesses, especially with the development of antibiotics and new vaccines in the post–World War II years. Nevertheless, infants continued to swallow over-the-counter medicines and homemade remedies, and to undergo treatments from community healers. The choices reveal that the attractions of the biomedical world were never proved so powerful that families jettisoned other alternatives. New ways of raising babies did not sweep aside old customs; instead, they partially overlaid them.[36]

In the middle decades of the twentieth century, infant care began to reflect findings made by psychologists in infant development laboratories. The new studies of babies led experts to renounce old orthodoxies. Doctor-recommended strict scheduling and restrained affection gave way to more relaxed styles of parenting as psychologists discovered that it stymied infants' self-mastery and need for comfort. Practices once scorned by professionals came to be seen as beneficial. By the 1950s, when the researcher studying the Mexican American community in San Jose, California, observed families holding their babies, playing with them, and soothing them when they cried, she found it neither shocking nor remarkable. It was what the experts advised. Of course, the psychologists and physicians who promoted affectionate parenting never acknowledged endorsing practices commonly found among generations of urban immigrants, Native Americans, and rural farm families. Nor did they concede that the new methods of infant care they advocated reflected assumptions as well as verifiable findings. Many new ideas about how to raise babies were, like many of the old ones, professional folklore.

7

THE INNER LIVES OF BABIES
Infant Psychology

FORTY-FOUR MILLION PEOPLE ATTENDED THE 1939–1940 World's Fair in New York City. The Fair's official theme, "The World of Tomorrow," offered an optimistic vision to a nation still reeling from an economic depression and warily watching events in Europe and Asia that would soon lead to World War II. On the fairgrounds, the promise of the future enticed viewers to several shows and events featuring babies. The manufacturers of Karo Syrup and Gerber Baby Food cosponsored the "First Year of Life" exhibit along with the Maternity Center Association of New York City. More than 660,000 people viewed the display, picking up 400,000 free pamphlets, including "Baby's First Year of Life" and "Father Plays a Leading Role." Another corporate sponsor, Mead Johnson, presented an exhibit on "Child Health, Normal Growth and Development," while Junket's Food Products sponsored a "personality baby contest." There were special events as well, including a baby crawling contest that ended in controversy because the infants were left crawling and crying in the broiling sunshine for more than an hour. A more successful effort drew fairgoers attracted to a fundraiser for the "Free Milk Fund for Babies" featuring well-known stars Abbott and Costello, Cab Calloway, and Irving Berlin, among others.[1]

The New York World's Fair, like so many of its predecessors, included an incubator exhibit organized by Dr. Martin Couney. Visitors found it in the amusement area rather than in the health and medicine exhibit hall displaying scientific marvels. Shortly after the fair opened, *New Yorker* writer A. J. Liebling published a profile of Couney, portraying the elderly doctor as "a Patron of the Preemies" and describing the "bantam weight babies" in the incubators. Liebling observed that one of Couney's first

American preemies, from the Omaha Exposition in 1898, survived to win a Croix de Guerre in World War I.[2]

At the door of the incubator building, a sign announced, "All the World Loves a Baby." Maybe so, but the financial statement suggested that the public no longer loved incubator shows. One disappointed viewer, a young boy, stood outside the exhibit warning would-be paying customers, "They don't do no tricks. They just sleep." Despite overall good press, including articles in the *Brooklyn Daily Eagle* and the Washington, DC, *Times Herald,* Couney's exhibition struggled to make money, leading to some testy exchanges with the fair organizers. It was an ominous sign. Failure to draw a crowd at the World's Fair in 1939 presaged the closing of Couney's Atlantic City boardwalk summer incubator show in 1943 and the end of the Coney Island Incubator exhibit two years later. Incubators saved lives (98 of the 108 babies housed in the New York World's Fair exhibit survived), but in the 1940s, the public considered them hospital technologies, not commercial entertainment.[3]

Perhaps incubator babies no longer fascinated viewers because other weakling babies – multiples – eclipsed them as public showpieces. The first surviving set of quintuplets, the identical Dionne girls born in Canada in 1934, became tourist magnets at their government-built compound known as "Quintland," bringing in about half-a-billion dollars in the midst of the Great Depression. Manufacturers produced Dionne dolls, books, and other souvenir items and their faces appeared in advertisements for Gerber's baby food, Palmolive soap, and other products. The doctor caring for the quintuplets, Allan Roy Dafoe, became famous and published both an infant care advice book and a baby book. Other multiples, like New Jersey's Kasper quadruplets born in 1936, followed in the Dionne quintuplets' footsteps to become product promoters. But surviving multiples remained rare enough that the press continued to offer human interest stories about individual premature babies struggling for life. In 1947, for example, a Chicago newspaper profiled Carol, "a negro baby" who weighed one pound, seven ounces at birth. Decades earlier, Carol might have grown in an incubator exhibit, but Carol was a modern baby; she spent ninety days in a hospital incubator.[4]

With more premature babies surviving, questions began to be raised about the long-term consequences of their early arrival. Did their frailty at birth signal a lifetime of poor health? Did it foretell intellectual impairment? Arnold Gesell, pediatrician, psychologist, and founder and director of the Yale Clinic of Child Development, sought answers to these questions. Along with his team, he conducted research at the New York World's Fair incubator exhibit every other week and with the cooperation of Couney filmed the babies and observed and recorded their development. The team followed up with regular calls at the homes of the incubator graduates. Gesell's investigation exemplified the expanding scientific interest in the early awakening of the human mind. He and other psychologists asked whether infants' behavior stemmed from their genetic endowment, individual personalities, instincts characteristic of the human species, environmental influences, learned patterns of conduct, or some combination of these elements. Gesell scholars concluded that, in the end, "He believed in the individuality of the child but chose the dictates of the genes over the whims of the environment."[5]

With the declining rate of infant mortality, scrutiny of infants' emotional and intellectual development increased, or, more succinctly, babies became scientific objects. Studies of human mental development grew in number and sophistication over the twentieth century, gaining scientific rigor and public interest. Investigators looked to map language development and intellectual growth at each stage of an infant and child's life using observations, laboratory experiments, and longitudinal studies. Research institutes devoted to child study began. Scholars produced textbooks for peers and students, founded professional journals, and wrote articles for the public and guides to childrearing. The formal studies of infant development led to a flood of articles in professional and popular journals codifying what many mothers already knew. Most babies cooed and then they talked; they crawled and then they walked; they learned to sleep through the night, to control their bowels (with proper training), to wave bye-bye, and to smile in response to others. From the beginning, infants showed researchers that they had distinct personalities.

Babies introduced many households to the science of psychology, and many families applied what they learned. Middle-class parents hoped to transmit class advantages and cultural capital by preparing their off-spring for success in the modern industrial economy. Personality, understood as an outward manifestation of the self, in contrast to the notion of character, a part of one's inner life, mattered. By the second half of the twentieth century, it was a truism that successful people had good personalities, and it was understood by many that parents needed to nurture personality development in their infants from the beginning of their lives. Psychological perspectives on infancy increasingly infused childrearing manuals, popular culture, and baby books.[6]

Commercial, medical, governmental, and psychological interests in babies were like spokes on a wheel. They rotated together over the course of the twentieth century and revolved around a single axel – but remained distinct from each other. Developmental psychology was the last spoke added. The concepts it introduced shifted parents' gaze from the weight and height of their babies toward their developmental milestones, rebalancing their attention. As a result, experts in infant development gained social status and cultural authority. The theories they disseminated changed the daily work of parenting and led babies to undergo a new kind of scrutiny.

Home economists, public health nurses, educators, and public intellectuals translated the findings of developmental psychologists into instructions for parents. Using the same outlets as medical experts – parenting manuals, women's magazines, radio broadcasts, classroom instruction, and public health booklets – they taught fathers and, more importantly, mothers how to nurture the intellectual and emotional growth of their babies. The question of how to develop healthy personalities in the young even commanded attention from the federal government in the postwar years. But the inner lives of babies, though increasingly scrutinized and discussed, remained hard to fathom.

Studies of infant lives, refracted through simplistic discussions of nature versus nurture, had long fed into political and cultural debates – about eugenics, immigration, and social welfare. On one side stood intellectual and scientific leaders who viewed genetics as determinative. They raised questions about what kinds of couples should have babies (or be prevented from having them), and who ought to be admitted or barred from the United States based on the characteristics that would

be manifested in their children. Hardcore eugenicists believed fundamental biological differences existed, and they and others used this
supposedly scientific argument in support of racial segregation as well
as in promoting immigration restriction and sterilization of the unfit.
They believed investments designed to improve the well-being of individuals and groups would prove futile because an individual's life course
had already been plotted out in one's genes. Intellectual and scientific
leaders on the other side of the debate believed environment shaped
development and they pondered different questions. They inquired as
how to best ensure the mental hygiene of children, asked what kinds
of interventions prevented delinquency, and investigated how social
programs enhancing the economic stability of families enabled them to
raise emotionally and intellectually healthy children. The debates grew
more complex over time, but continued to reflect established and, in
the case of eugenicists, unproven presumptions about how race, gender,
and genes influenced intellect and personality. In drawing from scientific findings about infant development, advocates from each side made
babies into rhetorical touchstones in political debates about human
potential. The speculations and arguments shaped the culture in which
babies grew up and the resources available to support their needs.

The findings of infant psychologists challenged long-held cultural
beliefs, influenced educational practices, and infused public rhetoric,
but had little effect on the daily lives of most infants. Babies received
professional assessments of their development with increasing frequency
and parents answered an expanding list of questions about whether
their infants attained certain skills or reached particular milestones, but
the measurements did not for the most part shift babies' experiences.
As developmental experts realized and parents knew, babies could
not be made to crawl, vocalize, or perform other tasks according to a
schedule. What changed were the accounts mothers kept and the kinds
of inspections babies received.

Psychologists and mothers used different vocabularies but faced similar
challenges in trying to determine what various movements and cries actually signaled about babies' developing minds. Early investigators scrutinized individual infants and developed grand theories from their slim
base of evidence. They asked whether personality and intelligence came

fixed at birth or if the infant brain demonstrated what modern scientists call neuroplasticity – meaning it could be shaped by experiences, by the environment, and by illnesses. A subsequent generation of researchers undertook studies of large numbers of infants. The more observations they recorded and the more infants they followed over long periods of time, the more they recognized that while infant development followed a general sequence, individual infants developed at their own pace.[7]

Twentieth-century psychology grew from the studies of Freud and his contemporaries who worked with adult patients to explore the unconscious, the development of the mind, and the power of early life events to shape personality and behavior. It emerged as well from early psychological investigations of babies, often case studies investigators made of their own offspring. Following the birth of his son William Erasmus in December 1839, Charles Darwin kept a diary of his development published as *A Biographical Sketch of an Infant* in 1877. Another Englishman, William Preyer, who spent his career in Germany and was known as the father of scientific child psychology, studied his son's development, and in 1882 published *The Mind of the Child.* American scholars also observed infants and children. Among the most notable were James Mark Baldwin, philosopher and psychologist at Princeton and later Johns Hopkins University, who studied his nine-month-old daughter, and psychologist and Clark University president G. Stanley Hall.[8]

The findings of Hall, a pioneering American psychologist, met with early acceptance but later came to be criticized for their lack of scientific rigor. His studies relied on questionnaires and rested on disproven theories. Despite their shortcomings, his works led to the child study movement, a lay effort that found a receptive audience among well-to-do women. Hall's followers examined their own offspring using his methods and employing his questionnaires. Members of the American Association of University Women and the National Congress of Mothers organized study groups to discuss articles published in *Child Study Monthly.* The magazine, founded in 1895, addressed "every one interested in the health and education of the child." Conservative in its intent – that mothers would devote themselves to rearing children – the child study movement made observations of offspring into a kind of calling for elite women. They embraced its tenets and became early practitioners of scientific motherhood, keeping detailed records of their children's development. Other experts also held out their hands to mothers interested in keeping precise developmental records. Beginning in 1910, physician Evelyn Lincoln Coolidge ran the Young Mother's Registry for the magazine *Ladies Home Journal*. Women sent the magazine monthly letters with information about their infants (weight, health, sleep, etc.) as a requirement of membership in the registry, and as members, in turn, were free to write with questions about infant care.[9]

Child study proved to be a mission for some women and an obstacle for others. Commercial artist Anita Parkhust Willcox recalled in an unpublished autobiography asking her mother-in-law about books about childcare right after World War I.

> The big expansion of child study had barely begun. So I read what I could find. There were scientific books to be had. They did not address young mothers but conveyed some useful information. Watson's behaviorism, Freud – I read what there was. Nowhere was the problem presented in the terms I confronted. Yet millions of women faced raising children while holding down a job.

Willcox chafed under the demands of child study and scientific infant care; other mothers approached the work with zeal. Mrs. Winfield Scott Hall, the wife of a Northwestern University Medical School physiologist who wrote several books on sex and reproduction, made her own mark by recording in detail the first 500 days of her son's life. She claimed to have left him during his waking hours only half-a-dozen times during his first sixteen months – showing more dedication to the task of infant study than any trained psychologist. In 1896, she reported her observations in a series of articles in *Child Study Monthly* and in painful detail described her son's physical and intellectual development. A typical entry described his fifty-third day: "When a rattling box of matches was held before him, he stopped fretting and looked uninterruptedly at it for six minutes."[10]

Two other notable studies of infant life appeared in the late nineteenth century. Millicent Washburn Shinn made a careful observation of her infant niece and presented her findings at the World's Columbian Exposition in Chicago in 1893 in a lecture entitled "The First Two Years of the Child." Although she subsequently earned a PhD in psychology and published *The Biography of a Baby* in 1900, she went no further with her investigations. That same year, Henry Olerich, a utopian author, published *Viola Olerich: The Famous Baby Scholar*. In it he recounted the educational training he called the "Natural Method," which he provided to his eight-month-old adopted daughter. Olerich weighed her, measured her, photographed her, recorded her intellectual and emotional growth, and trained her so that she would eventually be exhibited on the stage performing various intellectual feats at the age of two. Olerich used his adopted daughter to test his theories of education and although not part of the child study movement, his careful diary keeping emulated its favored practice.[11]

Women frequently used baby books for recording their infants' intellectual awakening, and the entries made by well-to-do mothers suggest the influence and reach of the child study movement. The mother of writer Ernest Hemingway kept her observations of his accomplishments in a scrapbook she began after his birth in 1899, making entries on his sequential physical achievements as he progressed from standing to walking. Likewise, the mother of Frederick Lewis Allen, who grew up to become editor of *Harper's* magazine, recorded his awakening senses following his birth in 1900. She observed as he responded to noise and light, reacted to different tones of voice, and learned to kick and to smile.[12]

Baby book manufacturers responded to the emerging science of infant development by including more detailed entries for recording babies' "firsts." Printed pages inquired about such things as language acquisition and the transition from crawling to walking. An 1899 publication, *The Babyhood Journal: A Record of Baby's Doings from the Day of Its Birth,* suggested the influence of the child study movement in its title, letting mothers know it would allow them to document more than gifts, weight, and height. Later the term *milestones* replaced *firsts,* and baby books incorporated more space for mothers to enter observations of their babies' intellectual development. Even without written cues from publishers, mothers increasingly charted the acquisition of new skills such as holding a toy and recognizing the "baby in the mirror." Some mothers seemed aware of what they were expected to observe, whether from reading about infant psychology in books and magazines or from discussions with peers and family members. A few wrote in a defensive tone when their infants omitted certain stages such as standing without having first tackled crawling. Women's baby book entries showed both an awareness of the expected sequences of development and relief when any unusual patterns did nothing to impede their babies' overall progress.[13]

In the same way that families employed traditional cures along with relying on scientific medicine, so too did they continue to employ assessments of development derived from folk customs as well as from modern psychology. Baby books reveal that for parents, an age-old question mattered most of all: what does the future hold for my baby? Publishers responded to parents' interests and to their own need to appeal to the largest possible market by incorporating new entry pages while retaining old favorites. Traditional folk verse linking personality to the day of one's birth – "Monday's Child Is Full of Grace" – remained alongside pages that reflected ideas drawn from the child study movement. A 1912 baby book had entries for "first definitive signs of emotion at visible things," "first attempt to reach for something," and "first signs of reason," as well as an astrological chart. Curiosity about their infants' characters and futures presumably led parents to look to the skies for guidance, as well as to earth-bound science.[14]

In his baby book, the parents of James Walker, born in Buffalo, New York, in 1914, noted his first journey – up the stairs – and the things brought along with him: a Bible and some silver. A first trip upward, according to popular belief, would lead a baby to rise in the world. From Adams County, Illinois, came a woman's recollection of two such journeys made by families of different economic stations. "When Mrs. R's son was born, the grandmother carried him up a ladder into the garret of the one-storied house to make sure he would rise in the world." For a wealthier family the trip was different: "I remember that the nurse who attended the mother of our prominent citizen Mr. K., insisted on performing the same ceremony, which was in that case made easier by the existence of stairs."[15]

Like in a game of telephone, as the custom spread over time and place interpretations shifted. A Maryland resident reported, "It is bad luck to carry a baby upstairs before it is carried down"; but another declared that failure to take a baby upstairs first would make it "low minded, and it would never rise in the world." A 1907 baby book included a line for recording the person who first carried an infant upstairs, the date, and the baby's age at the time with the explanation, "It is an old superstition that a baby should be carried upstairs that it may rise in the world, before it is taken downstairs." The mothers of Louise Groff, born in Hillsboro, Texas, in 1907, and Ida Brick, born in New Brighton, Pennsylvania, in 1912, dutifully filled in the page.[16]

James Walker's family not only took him upstairs, they attempted to get a precise sense of what lay in store for him by offering him a choice – the silver or the Bible. Which item would he crawl to and grasp? The former foretold wealth; the latter predicted a career as a preacher. A folklore account from North Carolina explained, "Place a baby on the floor with a bottle, a Bible, and some money before it. If he picks up the bottle first, he will be a drunkard when he grows up; if he takes up the Bible he will be a minister; if he plays with the money, he will be rich." Other objects also signaled the future – crawling toward a deck of cards prophesied life as a gambler, while reaching for a hammer predicted a future as a carpenter. Perhaps because many paths were perceived as closed to women, the baby book of Eloise Hunt, born the same year as James Walker, reported, "Her grandmother Elliot put a dollar on the floor and she immediately went for it." Wealth seemed to be her only choice and she chose it. But was she to be rich or greedy? North Carolina folklore suggested that clinching a coin foretold a love of money and avarice. The custom of predicting an infant's future through the use of objects continued late into the twentieth century. A Kansas folklore study in the 1950s and 1960s uncovered many such examples of babies choosing their futures, and in 1992, the *Los Angeles Times* published an article about a Korean-American baby's first birthday during which a little girl chose her future by selecting items presented to her: string, books, money, and pencils.[17]

Natural curiosity and hopes for their offspring led parents to employ various techniques to discern their infants' futures and it led baby book publishers to offer all possible options for discovering what lay ahead. Disproved and now discarded, the so-called mental science of phrenology once claimed to be capable of revealing character and personality through the assessment of the topography of the cranium. From the

Victorian era to the 1920s, phrenology held sway among some thinkers and members of the public who believed practitioners successfully used the so-called science to determine an individual's mental faculties. But phrenology could also be a do-it-yourself science, and so an expensive baby book published in 1891 contained a phrenology chart enabling parents to read their infants' character traits by assessing their heads. This was a rare example of phrenological science in a baby book; most publishers stuck to traditional pseudosciences.[18]

Astrology was a more popular and equally unempirical practice presumed to divine the future through a study of the placement of the sun, moon, and planets at the time of birth. Several baby books included horoscopes predicting infants' personalities and offering advice according to their zodiac signs. One explained that Cancers should not marry young and should guard against selfishness, vanity, and despondency, while Virgos made good writers and musicians but were apt to be conceited and critical. Daily newspapers as well as weekly and monthly magazines also published horoscopes with forecasts about life, love, and opportunities awaiting individuals born under each sign. Pasted into the baby book of Bernice Inman, born in Lakewood Hospital in Cleveland, Ohio, on July 13, 1921 (and therefore a Cancer), was her astrological chart for the day taken from the local newspaper. Baby book horoscopes remained fashionable through the twentieth century, spurred in later decades by a resurgent interest in astrology during what some people called the Age of Aquarius – the "new age" cultural movement of the 1960s and 1970s.[19]

Neither phrenologists, nor astrologers, nor psychologists could predict with certainty the course of a life. It therefore remained the job of parents to promote good morals, encourage proper character development, and cultivate a pleasing personality in their infants. Perhaps if babies grew up to be less than wealthy and wise, then the various predictive tools used earlier would allow parents to understand that their infants' potential had been limited or corrupted at birth and that they did not need to assume the blame for their offspring's problems.

Educational and medical authorities helped disseminate emerging ideas about infant development. In 1921, the Children's Bureau published *Child Care and Child Welfare: Outlines for Study* with source material for vocational teachers of home economics. A section on child mentality and management underscored the importance of the first year of life and outlined week by week and then month by month the motor, sensory, mental, and emotional development that babies demonstrated. The bulletin's reference list included the work of Millicent Washburn Shinn and John B. Watson, an early leader in the field of behavioral psychology. Commercial publishers also produced materials for parents interested in furthering the development of their babies. In 1929 *Parents' Magazine* ran an advertisement for "The University Plan for Character Building," a volume intended to help parents prepare their babies mentally, physically, and socially. The image illustrating the advertisement showed a baby preparing to crawl up steps beginning with ones labeled obedience, cheerfulness, and self-control, and culminating at the top step with leadership. *Parents' Magazine*, founded three years earlier to promote parent education in the new psychology and science of childrearing, featured a distinguished board of advisors. It quickly built a large circulation and reached millions of households.[20]

One of the best-known proponents of infant training, psychologist John B. Watson, investigated the emotional and motor development of babies under one year to determine what was instinctual and what developed as a habit. Watson believed that infants' emotional responses could be conditioned and he became notorious for an experiment teaching a baby he called "Little Albert" to fear rats. Contending that the science of psychology would yield through experimentation the methods for shaping human behavior, Watson believed that knowledge could then be carefully applied to improving society. His writings on childrearing appeared in popular magazines, such as a 1928 article in *Cosmopolitan* entitled "What about Your Child?" That same year, he published *Behaviorism* and four years later *The Psychological Care of Infant and Child*, in which he advised mothers to never hug and kiss their children or let them sit on their laps. The problem was not, as other experts argued, that kissing conveyed germs, but rather that it led to the creation of unhappy children. Having little faith in the abilities of mothers to rear children or to manage their own lives, Watson believed they needed scientific instruction in the psychological care of children. He viewed his book as the equivalent of Holt's 1894 manual *The Care and Feeding of Children*, but it had far less influence on actual nursery practices and a personal scandal (an affair with a graduate student he later married) forced him out of academia. His status eclipsed, he moved on to a career in advertising.[21]

Watson's ideas appeared in a a baby book distributed by the S.S. Kresge Department Store Infants' Department in 1939. It included inquiries about the awakening of intelligence and the development of self-help, as well as places for listing measures taken against diseases. Several years earlier, in 1931, an article in *Publishers Weekly* directed at the sellers of baby record books suggested that customers did not like the books that asked for too many firsts or entry places "to record the temperamental as well as unpleasant sides of a baby's character." Perhaps a growing popular interest in psychological development and the notion that behavioral flaws could be corrected by proper training dampened mothers', publishers', and baby book retailers' fears.[22]

Few infants seemed to endure the harsh conditioning Watson favored, but many of them experienced some physical discipline. One infant, a mother explained in her journal, had to be stopped from sucking his thumb and so wore gloves on his hands and had his arms pinned in place at night. The battle over thumb sucking, described as a "vicious habit," continued for several years. Baby books held descriptions of spankings, sometimes detailed on pages with prompts for recording "discipline." A 1907 baby book contained the poem "The Spanking," while a 1908 baby book had an account of a month-old infant that began: "Baby received some discipline this morning. She refused to go to sleep before breakfast and also refused to be good." A query about "My first discipline" in a baby book led a mother to write in the voice of her infant, "Mamma smacked me for taking my ring off." What psychologists formally labeled "negative reinforcement" and behaviorist Watson endorsed as necessary to healthy development appeared to be a familiar practice.[23]

Parental training in infant development theory could be passive – when it came by way of printed material – or active – when taught by nurses or by caseworkers observing how parents treated their babies. When visiting a ten-month-old baby and his indigent family in New York City in 1938, a public health nurse discovered to her shock that the parents held and entertained the baby for hours at a time. Their misguided behavior defied the then current norms of proper infant care, which required parents to refrain from indulging babies. As the nurse explained, coddling prevented the baby from depending upon himself. If the parents failed to get the situation under control, she warned, they would be faced with a new challenge: "food fads." During the nurse's visit, the baby began to cry and when she observed the father starting to pick him up, she directed him to put the infant in another room and close the door. After a few weeks, she promised, the baby would be trained. An earlier generation of nurses making rounds might have given strict instructions about feeding schedules and routines for sunbathing with an explanation how they protected the infant's health. As psychological theories infused baby care regimens, nurses assumed responsibility for teaching parents how to nurture babies' personalities.[24]

Modern concepts of infant development began appearing in fancy baby books in the 1920s. *Our Baby's First Seven Years*, published in 1928 by the Mother's Aid of the Chicago Lying-In Hospital, included places for noting "awakening intelligence," along with multiple pages for entries on physical development. *The Modern Baby and Child Development Record: From Birth to Sixteen Years* appeared the following year. Written by John E. Anderson and Florence L. Goodenough and published by *Parents' Magazine*, its advertising come-on began "Doctors, educators, and physicians urge you to Keep a Scientific Record of Your Child." Anderson and Goodenough, professors at the Institute of Child Development at the University of Minnesota, disparaged what they called "old-fashioned Baby Books containing merely a heterogeneous collection of snapshots, 'cute sayings,' locks of hair, and whatnot" and offered a modern substitute that called for "running accounts of developmental inventories at stated periods." The volume's 398 pages included detailed questions about heredity, as well as physical and mental development. The inventory for a three-month-old baby included queries about motor and language development such as "Does the child turn head to mother's voice when previously unaware of her presence?" The authors also asked about intellectual development with questions like "Does child grope adaptively on loss of nipple? Describe" and they inquired about personality and character development, and interests and activities. For three-month-old babies, the questions included, "If the open hand is brought suddenly within a few inches of the child's eyes, does he blink?" A typical question for a nine-month-old baby was, "Does he look for familiar objects in accustomed places?" Conscientious mothers, the authors made explicit, needed to assess each change in an infant's life from the introduction of a new food to the acquisition of a new word.[25]

The age-related inventory of development implied the existence of a set of universal standards against which infants could be measured. As developmental psychologist and prolific author Elizabeth B. Hurlock explained, parents no longer had to "judge their babies' advancements according to the ages at which certain traits appeared in the babies of their friends," but instead they could make use of "standards made from the records of thousands of babies based on the results of carefully planned experimental studies." Modern mothers, Hurlock made clear, needed to follow data-driven infant care advice and perform their own rituals of data collection. She produced a 128-page baby book, *Baby's Early Years*, in 1952 that provided information about how to "Test Your Baby" along with places to "Record your baby's speech," "Your baby's intelligence," "Your baby's emotions," and "Your baby's play." The unexamined infant life, it seemed, was not a modern infant life, even if worth living.[26]

In 1949, Hurlock published *Fashions for Babies*, a booklet distributed by the F. W. Woolworth stores, a nationwide retail chain. While the text aimed to encourage the purchase of diapers, bibs, and clothes, paragraphs scattered throughout the volume appeared under the heading "A Thought for Mothers." Here, Hurlock offered words of wisdom about infant care. She made a simple pitch: be modern and know what psychologists have to say about babies. "Specialists of today agree that trying to hide your love for your baby is one of the worst things you can do for him. Being cold and self-restrained is old fashioned. Be modern and love your baby as much as you like." Being modern did not, however, mean being undisciplined, she reminded mothers a few pages later. "No matter how much you love your baby, do not make the mistake of giving him too much of your time and attention," lest he "become so accustomed to the limelight that he will be unhappy if other people, too, do not give him the center of the stage." Hurlock did not mean to convey to mothers that all you need is love; they also needed to provide their infants with material goods. After one year of age, she explained, babies became clothes conscious, learning that they "make people notice him and this he enjoys." Pity the poor child whose garments did not make the grade.[27]

Public health advice about infants' mental and emotional development lacked the uniformity of health instructions, with their unwavering support for germ avoidance and daily scheduling. A South Dakota State Board of Health pamphlet commanded, "Babies should play," explaining they "like to romp and play on the floor." Nevertheless, hygiene concerns led to the caution, "Be sure to spread a sheet or washable rug on the carpet, for carpets hold dirt and germs tracked in by dogs, cats, and human feet." The Better Babies Bureau of *Women's Home Companion* disagreed, instructing readers, "Do not encourage your baby to play before the second year." Taking the middle ground, the baby book *Memories of Baby Days*, published in 1923, presented a date certain for inaugurating play and a rationale for restraint: "Never play with a baby till over six months – then seldom, '*Excitement Harms.*'" The 1930 edition of the *Book of Baby Mine* offered a more detailed explanation: "All young infants are extremely nervous," and parents therefore needed to "avoid exciting them, playing with them, or handling them too much." Was the curse of neurasthenia – a late nineteenth- and early twentieth-century diagnosis of a nervous disorder applied to those grappling with the stresses of modern life – to be found among the youngest Americans? Or were warnings about nervousness meant to prevent episodes of crying that might follow play periods and upset mothers? The contradictory claims about play and other habits suggested that while many experts agreed that infants needed to be guided in their cognitive and emotional development, the precise methods for doing so had yet to be determined. As experts broadcast new ideas about infant life, mothers faced new demands and had to meet a Goldilocks standard of parenting – not too rigid, not too yielding, but just right.[28]

Despite the perils of overstimulation, families took their babies on trips to visit relatives, they took them to church, and let them play with other children and with animals. "Most babies suffer because they are used to amuse older people, and are forced to laugh or are tossed about and excited when they need to be resting quietly," a brochure from the Louisville, Kentucky, Babies' Milk Fund Association warned. Yet baby books recounted frequent family visits during which grandparents and other relatives held babies. Undoubtedly some kissing occurred. Baby books reveal that many infants relished the company of siblings, cousins, and neighborhood children. They interacted with pets, and enjoyed situations that exposed them to germs. The baby book of a young girl born in St. Charles, Illinois, in 1921 described how she played with her pet collie, Lady Jane XII, and with Lady Jane's puppies as well as with chickens. Noting her intellectual growth, her mother recorded that by the age of one she said the word "chickie."[29]

Sales of rattles and other toys along with baby book accounts of patty-cake and other games make clear that the expert prohibitions on play did not dissuade parents from violating the "laws" of proper childrearing. The contest between psychologists urging calm and marketers selling toys resulted in a clear and overwhelming victory for the latter. Manufacturers produced toys, people bought them, and babies played with them. Leroy Gregory of Denair, California, born in 1918, owned rattles, a teddy bear, balls, a rubber kitty, a rag kitty, blocks, a train, and a little auto. The baby book of Nell, born in 1922, contained a notation that she sat alone on the floor and in the bathtub, knew how to wave bye-bye, play patty-cake, and hum three notes of "Smile Awhile" by age one, suggesting frequent opportunities to play and lots of stimulation. In recording their babies' amusements, mothers followed the dictates of experts who taught them to observe their infants' burgeoning intellectual growth, but they ignored the advice not to overtax babies' nervous systems.[30]

Modern scholars surveyed women's magazines and other printed material to uncover the connection between infants and the spread of psychology. A study of magazines published in the 1930s and 1940s described how an emphasis on the dangers of the overstimulation of babies and instructions about their need for strict schedules slowly gave way to pieces about intellectual growth and discussions of accommodating their needs. Another scholarly work pointed to the 1940s as the decade in which this transition in messaging took place. Studies of successive editions of *Infant Care* similarly showed a shift in emphasis from health promotion to supporting personality development through an appreciation of babies' cognitive and emotional growth.[31]

Students being prepared for the job of mothering learned about the psychological growth of infants and children from reading home economics textbooks. On some college campuses, women acquired the requisite skills by tending to actual infants. They lived in practice houses for several weeks, collectively rearing practice babies and toddlers obtained from orphanages and social welfare agencies. The babies acquired new "mothers" every few weeks. An article about the first practice babies – being reared at the University of Minnesota – appeared in *Ladies Home* in 1920 under the title "The Baby with Forty Mothers." In 1952, *Life* magazine profiled the babies reared in Cornell University's practice house; all of them received the last name Domecon – for Domestic Economy. According to a 1954 *Look* magazine article, at least forty-one schools had student mother programs, some of them in place for twenty-five years. No discussion occurred regarding the psychological effects on infants of having a shifting and large group of caretakers. Instead, the babies' experiences – having been well fed and carefully tended – reportedly made them prized candidates for adoption.[32]

Research underscored the importance of providing loving attention to infants as well as meeting their physical needs. An investigation at the Iowa Child Welfare Research Station in the 1930s demonstrated that orphaned babies tended by women living in a facility for the mentally retarded experienced more mental growth than babies left to lie alone and ignored in their orphanage cribs. The latter group, with no stimulation, declined in its mental abilities. A follow-up study conducted thirty years later confirmed the initial findings. The study author also concluded that predicting the IQ of an infant was not possible because babies interacted with their environments; they did not "passively absorb its impact." As data appeared to give support for infant stimulation over depravation, changes would follow in institutional practices and adoption procedures.[33]

Psychologists turned babies into research subjects, examining them, watching them, filming them, and conducting experiments on them in university laboratories and hospitals, as well as in their homes. Investigators observed infants' achievements, such as locomotion, and assessed babies' adaptive behavior and personalities in an attempt to turn close observations into quantitative measurements. Psychologists hoped to use their findings both to establish norms and to explain individual variations. Gesell undertook much of this work, producing both popular and professional books and articles, along with members of his research team. They addressed topics such as the development of children and adolescents, the behavior and growth of twins, and the indications that particular infants and children were "exceptional." Gesell's work with Couney's incubator infants was a small part of a large research program.[34]

Gesell and his colleagues analyzed several thousand babies at the Yale Clinic of Child Development in order to determine whether and how they grew according to a pattern of natural laws. Babies' development, he concluded, "conforms to certain orders of succession … They constitute the mechanics or laws of growth." In a 1932 Science Service Radio Talk broadcast over the Columbia Broadcasting System, he promised that if scientific progress in studying the child continued at the current rate, it would be possible to detect individual variations at a very early age, leading to "prevention and cure of many behavioral disorders." In a further effort to share his findings with the public, Gesell directed a 1934 movie, *Life Begins*. It opened with him explaining that babies have intelligence, feeling, will, and an inborn personality, all of which are governed by natural laws. The next scenes showed infants at different ages as their development advanced; they wriggled, rolled over, crept, and then walked alone.[35]

Parents could not make babies walk or talk until they were ready, Gesell concluded – something most parents likely figured out on their own. Despite their native understanding of babies, curious parents purchased and consulted Gesell's books and read his articles in popular magazines that explained infants' cognitive growth. Inspired by his work, some mothers wrote to Gesell to ask about making their own records and to inquire about the methods for conducting developmental tests at home. "My baby (boy) is 10½ months of age and I would like some way of testing his reactions periodically to measure his progress," a woman wrote after learning about Gesell's work from an article in the *New York Herald Tribune* in 1938. The same article, printed in the *Chicago Daily News*, inspired a registered nurse from Pharr, Texas, to write about her boy, who "appears normal in every way," but, she explained, she would "enjoy checking him." Gesell replied to these correspondents and others that he did not give advice by mail and suggested they consult his publications. Many did. His book on the first five years of life, followed by works on ages five to ten and then ten to sixteen, sold extremely well,

Figure 7.1 Dr. Gesell studying a baby, 1947
Credit: Yale University, Harvey Cushing/John Hay Whitney Medical Library

appeared in translation, and made him into a public figure. He became so well known that a 1956 *New Yorker* cartoon depicted two matrons looking at a bookstore shop sign announcing his book on youth, with one remarking, "What I want is one on husbands from forty to fifty."[36]

Studies of infant and child development attracted private funders and led to the creation of university-based research centers beginning in 1917 with the opening of the Child Welfare Research Station at the University of Iowa. The Institute of Child Development at the University of Minnesota followed in 1925 with funding from the Laura Spelman Rockefeller Foundation, which underwrote other children's research institutes, including those at Teachers College Columbia University, the University of California Berkeley, and the University of Toronto. By 1933, professionals in the now-established discipline founded the Society for Research in Child Development.[37]

Child development grew up with the new funding, as scholars produced more research and publications. Yet a core question remained without a definitive answer. How, precisely, and to what degree did heredity and environment, together and separately, determine the development of infant minds? For all their efforts at precision, the researchers' accounts reveal that their observations sometimes differed little in form and value from the notations made in baby books. Professor Mary M. Shirley began the Minnesota Infant Study in 1925, investigating twenty-five infants in their first two years of life. She wrote monographs on their postural and locomotor development, their intellectual growth, and their personalities, describing the experimental devices and measuring tools used to chart the data. Shirley reported that Renie May batted a paper-wrapped roll of cotton at five or six weeks and that at eleven weeks Quentin grasped his mother's hand. His development continued apace. "At 41 weeks Quentin stood up in his crib and pulled his blanket and stocking off the railing." On and on went the observations and notations. "At 45 weeks Patty held the lid of the can over one eye and smiled at the examiners as she did so."[38]

Babies sometimes frustrated the work of researchers by acting predictably. While conducting a study of the hunger reaction in newborn infants, an investigator watched the tiny subjects writhe and throw themselves about, "kicking, slashing, howling, and expending an amount of energy which almost taxes the capacity of the recording device." The self-described "impassive experimenter" had a difficult time refraining from trying to quiet the infant in a "truly motherly or fatherly sense," but eventually learned to become "more passive during the hunger reaction." The report concluded that picking up the baby and attempting to pacify her or him worked only for a brief time because the hunger remained – a finding that would have surprised no one who had experience with a hungry infant and might have led some to question the reason for the study. As psychologists continued their quest for knowledge, their experiments sometimes journeyed beyond the relatively benign observational studies. An investigation of emotional responses to pain, involving twelve tiny experimental subjects, concluded they did not enjoy being pricked with needles by investigators. Mothers who had inadvertently stabbed babies with diaper pins could have told them that. Other studies found answers without meaning. In their quest to find racial and gender differences in newborns, investigators found differences they could measure, but they could not demonstrate the significance of their findings. The questions investigators posed revealed more about the social and cultural milieu in which they worked than it did about the babies. Race and gender differences mattered because people agreed that they did.[39]

As intellectually futile and unkind as some of the psychological experiments seemed, they were far less harmful than some of the studies of orphaned infants and other babies (and children) undertaken by medical researchers. Non-therapeutic experiments on orphaned babies included withholding orange juice until they developed scurvy, obtaining spinal fluid from African American infants at an Atlanta hospital without obtaining consent for the risky procedure, performing a skin graft on at least one infant following thymectomy (removal of the thymus gland), and subjecting forty-eight-hour-old infants to x-rays of their bladders. Although ostensibly conducted for the purpose of uncovering useful scientific knowledge, these and other ethically insupportable, cruel studies constituted assaults on babies' physical and emotional well-being and made clear how race and orphanhood made infants vulnerable to experimentation.[40]

Developmental researchers, undeterred by their unclear findings, continued on in their quest to make psychology into a predictive science. Their detailed and careful observations of large numbers of infants yielded data about their personalities and potential that they hoped would be predictive of their adult characteristics. The longitudinal study conducted at the Institute of Child Development at the University of Minnesota followed individuals for twenty-eight years and failed to find early measures that explained the babies' subsequent development. The research did, however, show that what were called "care factors" and the child's own capabilities mattered. In 1939, Gesell and his colleagues, having seen 10,000 infants in their Yale clinic, published *Biographies of Child Development: The Mental Growth Careers of Eighty-Four Infants and Children*. The authors selected a diverse group of cases to report, including those demonstrating that some of their predictions did not pan out. Ida B., labeled retarded at one year, tested as superior at age five. B. C., born to a fifteen-year-old mother he never saw, tested as low average at three months, spent his first year in an institution in a supine position, and suffered from rickets and possibly megacolon (a dilation of the large intestine often causing bowel problems). After he was adopted by a young couple, his IQ rose from between 80 and 85 to 115 by age twelve. Some babies, of course, never deviated in their development; they began as intellectually limited and remained so through their lives. A critical finding for all of the infants studied was that each had a distinct personality.[41]

Once codified, this commonsense observation would be used to develop new ideas about proper parenting. Rather than raising all babies on the same precise schedule developed by experts, mothers had a new mandate: understanding and adapting to their infants' distinct characteristics and needs. Infants once thought to learn by conditioning came to be seen as able to develop via a natural inclination to self-mastery. Ironically, as medical advice began to stress accommodation to babies' needs, growing numbers of infants were born in hospitals, which kept them isolated from parents and on strict feeding schedules. Even a successful experiment in rooming-in failed to convert the doctors and nurses working in hospitals to practicing what other professionals had begun to preach.[42]

Babies' futures defied prediction – whether one attempted to discern them using traditional folk practices or via laboratory experiments in psychology. Nevertheless, psychology assumed an increasingly powerful place in American life in the twentieth century in higher education, in professional practices such as social work, and in popular culture. Its ascendancy resulted in no small part from curiosity about babies and profound concern about their futures. Understanding infants came to be seen as providing a pathway for enhancing their individual and collective well-being. Experts hoped their studies would yield useful knowledge and that parents would learn to construct babies' inner lives in the same way they learned to defend them from disease.

The writings of physician Josephine Hemenway Kenyon reveal the kinds of instructions parents received. In 1934, Kenyon published the first edition of the popular and often updated *Healthy Babies Are Happy Babies: A Complete Handbook for Modern Mothers*, written in response to the letters she received from readers of her column in *Good Housekeeping* magazine. By the time the third edition of her book appeared in 1943, she reported having received 287,000 letters sent to the *Good Housekeeping* "Health and Happiness Club" from "anxious mothers." Kenyon believed in careful record keeping. In a 1940 magazine column titled "How to Keep a Baby's Record," she listed the observations mothers needed to make. It began, of course, with height and weight, followed by a section on nursing (breast or bottle) and then one on development and firsts. Next came health habits (food, toilet, sleep, and clothing), a list of illnesses, dates of inoculations, and, finally, behavior notes. Mothers, Kenyon explained, needed to take the record to the doctor on a "first birthday visit" in order to discuss the baby's "month-by month development." She told readers to "check those points in which the child excels, learn the weak spots in your regimen, and find out how to remedy them." In some ways, her suggestions echoed the early twentieth-century practices espoused by adherents of the child study movement. But, unlike that program, which voluntarily engaged a small group of well-off women, modern infant care now demanded psychological study and record keeping by all mothers.[43]

In the post–World War II years, amidst a baby boom and the Cold War, the stakes in infant development grew even higher. In 1950, experts convened in Washington, DC, for the fifth White House Conference on Children and Youth. Participants explored the means for helping children develop healthy personalities and the "mental, emotional, and spiritual qualities essential to individual happiness and responsible citizenship." Discussants acknowledged both the influence of developmental psychology and a growing belief in individualism as modernism. The fate of the nation, their comments suggested, could be linked to infants' healthy psychological development.[44]

In the postwar years, many babies avoided the rigid discipline imposed on an earlier generation as experts reversed course. Babies, parents learned, needed to "self-regulate" and to enjoy a loving, supportive nursery life. A powerful example of the shift can be seen in the life of Benjamin Spock, born in 1903. His mother brought him up according to the rules laid down by infant care expert Luther Emmett Holt, a champion of scheduling. Raised in a rule-driven household, he rejected its tenets as an adult. Spock became a world-famous pediatrician and the best-known proponent of what some called permissive parenting – more accurately described as affectionate, democratic parenting. Modern infants brought psychology into the home and into American life. While the advice changed over the twentieth century, the underlying principle, that infants and indeed all individuals had complex inner lives that might be discerned and shaped, became part of American culture.[45]

8

BABIES' CHANGING TIMES
Depression, War, Peace

66 **I**'M GOOD AND MAD!" DECLARED AN angry-faced baby. "I've been hearing a lot about a couple of guys called Hitler and Hirohito." Just what was a baby going to do about that? "I'm telling my Mommy and Daddy to really get going and buy Bonds and Stamps," a "real investment for my future." The angry baby advertisement appeared in a 1944 issue of *Congratulations: A Magazine for Mothers*, which had a baby in a blanket on the cover along with a $100 Series E War Bond. Elsewhere a war bond advertisement from the Aluminum Company of America featured a mother with a baby in her arms asking, "Isn't he worth it?" Babies and war bonds share a long history. During World War I, when Liberty Bonds financed the American Expeditionary Force sent to Europe, a lucky infant born in Red Lake, Minnesota, received a $100 Liberty Bond from her parents and recorded in her baby book. The World War II campaign to sell war bonds proved larger and longer, involving a kind of saturation advertising bombardment using all available media as well as face-to-face encounters at work and at leisure sites. Uncle Sam conscripted salesbabies in the cause and numerous companies deployed baby faces in their World War II advertising arsenal.[1]

Wartime issues of *Congratulations* included a full-page advertisement from Mennen's antiseptic baby oil – "Special Wartime Rules for Baby Care" – reminding readers about the shortage of doctors and nurses because of battlefield demands. Between 40,000 and 45,000 physicians and about 59,000 nurses reported for active duty during the war. With medical personnel stretched thin on the home front, babies had to put up with long waits for care and families needed to manage on their own. Other conditions during wartime, from rationing to the shortage of various materials, also changed babies' lives.[2]

Figure 8.1 "For Baby's Future Buy War Bonds," 1941–1945
Credit: US Office for Emergency Management, Office of War Information

The expansion of the federal government, first with New Deal programs in the Great Depression and then during World War II, presented some babies with new resources. Government efforts included programs to care for the infants and children of mothers working in defense industries and payments to health care providers supplying obstetric and pediatric services to the wives and babies of servicemen. The former aimed at supporting the production of war matériel and the latter endeavored to boost the morale of America's fighting forces. Never intended as permanent expansions of federal social welfare funding, the measures lasted only for the duration. "Uncle Sam" stepped back after the war, assuming a respectful distance from the nursery, continuing to send money to the states for needy infants and children, and voicing concern for their development, but without any direct meddling. The partnership between parents and the federal government inaugurated by the Children's Bureau reached a rapid peak in wartime and declined equally swiftly in peacetime.

In the lean years of the Great Depression, Americans young and old lived by the slogan "use it up, wear it out, make it do, do without." With millions unemployed and struggling, thrift became a necessity and families had to stretch their resources. Baby clothes made at home, an Aunt Sammy radio script suggested, needed to be "large enough at the start to fit the baby for a few months," as many families could not afford to buy or make new ones. Some infants and their families lived through the depression with help from government programs. The *Book of Baby Mine* for Ronald Temple, born in 1937, gave an account of his birth at home – before the doctor arrived: "My big brother saved my life by covering me with a warm blanket." His family appeared to be quite comfortable at the time of his birth. He received many gifts, had an account at the Toledo Trust Company, and enjoyed a beach vacation in his early years. But later he attended a Works Progress Administration nursery school, suggesting a decline in his family's fortunes.[3]

Under President Franklin D. Roosevelt, the federal government expanded in both size and scope. New agencies provided citizens with emergency relief, farm support, and jobs programs. Regulation of industry, agriculture, and banking increased with the inauguration of New Deal programs aimed at reviving the economy. However, consumer spending remained low. Following the United States' entry into World War II the economy recovered and employment increased as industrial and agricultural output grew to meet the needs of the armed forces. Families once again acquired savings, in part by purchasing war bonds out of patriotism and in part because there was not much to buy. Factories turned out planes and tanks rather than consumer goods. Other economic shifts resulted because the National War Labor Board froze wages in national industries. Employers responded to worker shortages as men were called up to military service and to the wage limits by offering benefits, including health insurance, which helped move births from home to hospital. Despite the wage freeze, per capita wartime income rose faster than the cost of living and low-income households experienced the greatest economic advancement. Household savings grew and the peacetime that followed brought a new round of consumer purchasing.[4]

During the war, babies, like all citizens, received ration books from the federal government's Office of Price Administration. They contained stamps used for acquiring rationed goods, including certain foodstuffs, as well as tires, fuel, and clothing. Purchases required cash as well as the stamps and, despite the overall growth in income, some families continued to struggle to put food on the table. Mrs. Border, a mother of six children receiving aid from the Charity Organization Society in New York City, reported having trouble getting the provisions she needed for her infants born in 1943 and 1945, although the family obtained milk from the Free Milk Fund for Babies and the youngest baby did receive his orange juice.[5]

The birth of a baby entitled the family to obtain an additional ration book by visiting the local rationing board with a statement from a physician or hospital, or with an official birth certificate. The Pet Milk Company provided this handy information in its 1943 baby book as part of a strategic effort to maintain its customer base. Once babies received their ration books, their families had sixteen points a week to spend on canned milk, which many infant formulas required. Like all other canned products, canned milk required ration points because the military needed the tin. (With the supply of tin interrupted, other products used for babies such as diaper pins ceased being manufactured, as did consumer items used in the nursery such as bottle warmers and electric fans.) Fluid milk did not require ration stamps, making fresh milk formulas attractive, if families owned either an icebox or a mechanical refrigerator. Fortunately for canned milk producers, many families had neither, especially in the South, where farmers and sharecroppers often relied on springs, cellars, and wells to keep their babies' milk cold or used canned milk.[6]

Shortages and rationing changed babies' material lives, though probably not in ways they noticed. The war emergency placed limits on civilian use of rubber because most of it came from Southeast Asian nations occupied by the Japanese and the armed forces needed all available rubber for tires and other products. Adult citizens did their part by turning in old tires for recycling and made limited purchases of new ones using ration points. Babies went without new rubber bottle caps, rubber sheets, rubber pants, and rubber toys. They continued to have access to new rubber nipples, however, because there was no substitute. Physician Dorothy Whipple, who worked for the Children's Bureau for a time and wrote the 1945 edition of *Infant Care*, explained this in her wartime baby manual, *Our American Babies*, published in 1944.[7]

War needs also led to restrictions on babies' wardrobes. The diversion of looms for the production of textiles needed by the military meant a temporary shortage of diaper fabric, undoubtedly burdening those who had to wash available diapers more frequently than they might have liked. Clothing rationing limited babies to only three new pairs of shoes a year, which Whipple declared insufficient for their rapidly growing feet. She suggested cutting the toes off the old pairs. Or, family members could donate their own clothing ration points to the baby. As an infant shoe company advertisement in *Congratulations* reminded mothers, babies needed five types of shoes: the kicker, the creeper, the crawler, the trainer, and the walker. It seems unlikely that many babies acquired them all. When rationing ended in 1946, family larders and closets filled once again. Some unused pages from a sugar ration booklet ended up preserved in the baby book of a boy born after the war, on Independence Day, July 4, 1948. Perhaps his mother hoped to memorialize his wartime sacrifice, or her own.[8]

Children's Bureau officials advised the War Production Board regarding the production of infant care items such as baby carriages and strollers and on matters such as milk rationing and the amount of infant formula to be produced. The inevitable shortages led to inquiries and complaints. A woman working in a defense plant near Wichita, Kansas, wrote to the Bureau protesting that families living outside the city could only purchase Grade C milk because Grade A milk required a prescription and was reserved for city dwellers. Another mother complained about the difficulty buying mild soap needed by babies. A serviceman from Oak Ridge, Tennessee, inquired where to buy a child's metal cup, while another serviceman, stationed at Buckingham Army Air Field in Ft. Myers, Florida, reported that oranges "grew like grass," but his neighbors told him not to feed the juice to his baby for fear of acidosis. The reply from the Children's Bureau expert let him know his baby would be able to enjoy a little diluted orange juice. In his letter, the man explained that he finally understood the meaning of the phrase "Fathers worry too."[9]

The long tradition of parent education continued through the war years. After hostilities broke out, the Blue Network began airing a weekly radio program, *The Baby Institute*, featuring early child development educator Jessie Stanton. The Blue Network consisted of 155 stations and reached more than 23 million homes. *The Baby Institute* broadcast reportedly received letters from thousands of listeners. Parents who tuned in heard from physicians and educators, and received timely information about topics such as "Feeding Babies in Wartime" and "Milk in Wartime." On January 17, 1943, as American forces made their first bombing raids on Germany, pediatrician Benjamin Spock appeared on the show to discuss thumb sucking. Other episodes presented up-to-date information on expectant motherhood, telling women that smoking in moderation and occasional drinking presented no problems.[10]

Like other radio broadcasts about infant care, the Baby Institute covered popular subjects such as toilet training, food schedules, and clothing. But, unlike "Aunt Sammy," a government broadcast, *The Baby Institute* had a corporate sponsor, Heinz. According to a brief article in *Broadcasting*, an industry news journal, Heinz had begun producing baby food in the 1930s and sponsored the wartime shows to keep "its famous name before the public." Other radio programming also provided information about infant and childcare in the war years, including *Parents' Magazine of the Air*, which went into syndication in 1944. After the war, in 1954, infants got their own radio show, *Two a.m. Feeding*, broadcast from a New York City station. It coupled information to parents with commercials for appropriate products and signed off with a lullaby to help the baby fall asleep.[11]

The product babies might have wanted to give up for the duration (and beyond) was foul-tasting cod liver oil. They were out of luck. While imports ceased to arrive from Norway, much had been stockpiled and both American and Canadian factories stepped up their production or began making and marketing substitutes, such as salmon oil and whale oil. Thanks to these measures and to cost controls imposed by the Office of Price Administration in April 1942, babies continued to be dosed with fish oils during the war and tussles over this despised substance continued to appear in baby books.[12]

The war presented enormous challenges to one group of babies – those born and raised in wartime internment camps housing Japanese Americans. Executive Order 9066 signed by President Roosevelt in early

1942 and upheld by the Supreme Court led to the removal of more than 120,000 Japanese-American citizens from the West Coast. They first entered Temporary Assembly Centers and went from there to ten camps administered by the federal government's War Relocation Authority. Mass incarceration caused numerous hardships for infants and their families. Some babies received care from interned physicians and nurses in hastily erected and undersupplied hospital facilities, but others went without needed medical attention. Camps often lacked needed drugs and equipment and had a shortage of professional personnel. In some instances, camp residents received care from quickly trained internee helpers. In oral histories, former internees recalled difficult living conditions in badly heated, tiny rooms, and the challenges to baby care posed by poor camp sanitation, harsh climates, and insufficient food supplies. One woman remembered lining up at the communal laundry early in the morning to get hot water to be used in scrubbing dirty diapers on washboards. Another detainee recalled how she and her siblings gave up their milk for their baby brother.

> Dan was just two weeks old and my mother's milk was drying up and so she needed to heat up milk. And what we did as a family, the three of us kids, we would go eat at the mess hall and at each meal one of us would bring our milk back to the apartment or place so my mother could heat it up and feed Dan.

One woman recollected the rules against baby pictures because the authorities forbade cameras in the camps. She managed to obtain a picture when an outside photographer came to the camp to take a wedding photograph.[13]

Camp newspapers, understandably, did not report on problems or did so only to assure residents they would soon be solved. The Tule Lake (California) camp paper printed a story in 1942 reporting that feeding the camp's babies required 450 bottles of formula to be prepared daily under the supervision of a registered nurse and eleven formula aides. At the Tulare Assembly Center (California), the newspaper stated, the babies received SMA formula, but that the camp had yet to receive a sufficient amount of baby food. Both newspapers implied that camp authorities subscribed to and attempted to follow the modern principles of infant feeding, especially in regards to formula preparation. At the

Figure 8.2 Special food formula is prepared for babies at the Manzanar
Reception Center for Evacuees of Japanese Ancestry, Manzanar
Relocation Center, Manzanar, California, 1942
Photographer: Clem Albers
Credit: US Department of the Interior, War Relocation Authority

Fresno Assembly Center (California), a county fairground where families
lived until permanent camps were erected, a newspaper headline made
this clear: "Babies Fed Scientifically." Living up to that promise proved
difficult for both camp authorities and families. A woman recalled her
infant daughter's suffering because she was allergic to the powdered
milk provided by the camp. "She was hospitalized in the camp, went in
and out, in and out, with stomach disorders," she explained, because the
family could not afford to buy canned milk from the outside.[14]

In some respects, internment camp life for babies mirrored life in
communities on the other side of the barbed wire. Births took place

in hospitals and infants received postnatal care at home. Mothers took infants to camp well-baby clinics and families displayed their infants at camp baby shows. At the Rohwer Camp (Arkansas), parents had the opportunity to attend "Better Children's Day" and learn all about infant development by viewing the 1934 film *Life Begins* by Arnold Gesell. Camp newspapers printed birth announcements, recording, for example, six births over one weekend in August 1942 at the Manzanar (California) camp. Infant deaths occurred as well. Difficult camp living conditions and excessive summer heat in particular led to preventable infant mortality, something acknowledged in some of the official records and described in interviews with former residents. Mass internment meant that the federal government became a provider of health care for infants and their families and it did not always do a successful or even an adequate job.[15]

Another group of babies received health care thanks to the federal government – those born to the wives of servicemen in the four lowest pay grades of the US armed forces, a group that included 87 percent of all enlisted men. With a special appropriation from Congress each year, beginning in March 1943, the Children's Bureau distributed funds to state health agencies to pay for prenatal, delivery, and hospital care, as well as care for sick children under one year of age. The funding came via the Emergency Maternity and Infant Care Act (EMIC). Federal dollars ultimately supported more than 1.2 million births without regard for the parents' income, race, or length of residence in the community. The funding covered the wives and babies of servicemen missing, killed in action, or honorably discharged as well as the babies of unmarried parents, if paternity was acknowledged. Medical supervision continued until the infant reached one year of age. Under EMIC, the federal government established the fee schedule for the doctors and hospitals and determined the standards they had to meet in terms of services and facilities. Women giving birth at home also received subsidized maternity care. With so many men in uniform, the EMIC program underwrote the care of one out of every seven babies born in the United States during its brief existence.[16]

EMIC met a genuine need. Military hospitals reported difficulties serving the wives of servicemen who came to reside in nearby communities. Congress responded with funding not as a duty to citizen babies and their mothers but to ease the worries of men in uniform. As an article from the Children's Bureau explained, "The nation has sent its men around the world to guard and protect the land and lives of its people. In their absence, our country is honor bound to guard and protect the life and health of the wives and babies who are left behind." By describing EMIC as a way of supporting the military, the Children's Bureau leaders undermined their ultimate goal – making it the model for broader government-supported health care programs to be inaugurated after the war ended.[17]

Even if the Bureau's leaders' strategy for expanding health care had been more overt from the outset, the results would likely have been the same. Many physicians and their representative organizations tolerated EMIC during wartime but viewed it with trepidation precisely because they feared it would lead to a national health program. They bristled at its government-mandated cost controls and standards and they used their political clout to make sure that the EMIC program ended at the conclusion of hostilities. In peacetime, care for service members and their dependents continued at military facilities and when these institutions proved unable to address all their needs, Congress enacted an insurance program providing access to civilian hospitals and services – the Dependents Medical Care Program of 1956.[18]

Other federal programs shaping infant lives during World War II included day care and home care (then termed foster family care) services for working mothers. Limited in funding and designed primarily for children aged two to six, mostly to provide after-school services, the federal dollars assisted few infants, despite the need. A notable private program, the childcare centers of the Kaiser Company shipyards, only accepted children at age eighteen months or older. A study by the War Manpower Commission in the Los Angeles area submitted to the Senate Committee on Education and Labor in 1943 documented the need for infant care for those up to age two, counting 9,391 infants in need of services in February of that year and 46,391 by December of that year. However, the cultural bias against mothers of babies in the workforce coupled with the expense of providing adequate infant care limited the number of spots for infants. Martha May Eliot, associate chief of the Children's Bureau, testified before a Senate committee that the Bureau preferred that mothers of children under two not be employed in war jobs. If they needed to work, she explained, the best accommodation was day care in small groups of two or three. Other individuals speaking at the hearing suggested that most infants under two received care from relatives or foster family day care or via some other privately managed arrangement.[19]

An account of a wartime infant's care appeared in a 1943 article in *Parent's Magazine* describing how Billy, a war baby, received care in shifts from his mother and his mother's friend Sue. A military wife, Sue boarded in Billy's home and cared for him while his mother worked the graveyard shift at an aircraft factory. Sue worked the day shift and traded off care of the infant. Billy's daily routine had an order to it that would have impressed the factory managers. With military-like precision, it ended each night at 5:30 PM with cod liver oil and orange juice, dinner, a bath, and lights out at 8:00 PM. It missed only the playing of taps.[20]

Baby book entries from the war years hint at EMIC-supported births and detail babies' other wartime experiences. Diane Deene, an African-American baby born in October 1944 at Henry Ford Hospital in Detroit while her father served in the army, was a likely EMIC baby. So too was Edward J. Maloney III, born at a Newport, Rhode Island, hospital in 1945. His baby book mentioned a substitute godfather, Lieutenant Commander John Smith. Many baby books contained pictures of fathers and relatives in uniform and the *Log-o'-Life* book included entries for both "Military Service" and "Citations for Heroism." Well-kept baby books also revealed the experiences of infants who grew up to serve their country. The last words inscribed in the baby book of Charlie Flood (whose numerous accidents in infancy and childhood were recounted in the introduction of this book) recounted his death at age thirty. His loving mother described how he was killed in action in Europe six weeks before the end of World War II.[21]

The percentage of babies born in hospitals increased substantially from the mid-1930s through the end of World War II thanks to EMIC and to growing enrollment in health insurance plans. At the same time, infant mortality rates continued their decline, decreasing by 26 percent from 1930 to 1939, and by 33 percent from 1940 to 1949. New Deal programs appear to have helped to lower infant death rates in the

South, and seem to have been particularly effective in improving the lives of African American infants. Vaccines also helped infants to avoid sickness and death. Leslie Hope, born in Corvallis, Oregon, in 1944, received her smallpox, diphtheria, and tetanus shots as recommended. She avoided those illnesses, but did experience colds, measles, and tonsillitis, recovering from all of them. The improved health of the nation's young reflected both specific developments in the medical arena, an expanding economy, and the decreasing rate of poverty in the war and postwar years. Within a short time, the discovery and widespread use of new antibacterial drugs would further lower rates of sickness and death.[22]

Infant mortality rates fell; challenges remained. In a 1940 report on "The Health Situation of Negro Mothers and Babies in the United States," a Children's Bureau investigator documented high death rates among both infants and mothers, and the fact that 55 percent of births involved nonmedical personnel, defined as "untrained or poorly trained midwives." Poverty accounted for much of the mortality problem, as did rural isolation, a lack of prenatal care, and poor maternal health. Four-fifths of the babies in the study were born in the Southern states, and two-fifths of them in rural areas. Urban infants fared better. In Northern cities, life chances for African American babies increased as compared to their rural counterparts, perhaps because of greater access to and greater use of health services including prenatal, delivery, and postpartum care. A study of African American women migrating to Pittsburgh before and after World War I found they transitioned quickly from midwife births at home to hospital births and proved more accepting of available medical services than white migrants to the city. The pattern continued for some time. A study of indigent white Southern migrants to Detroit in the early 1960s found they avoided using health care facilities while African Americans, who had migrated north decades earlier, took advantage of available medical services. Local conditions varied, of course, but the national picture showed continuing racial and class disparities in infant mortality.[23]

Birth rates in the United States reached their lowest point during the Great Depression, falling to 18.4 per 1,000 in 1933 (by way of comparison, in 2016, the birth rate stood at an estimated 12.5). America's entrance into the war led to a short spike in births as marriage rates climbed and "goodbye" babies followed, but the birth rate declined again as draft calls rose and men went overseas. Examining the demographic data, a leading American sociologist and statistician from the University of Chicago, William Fielding Ogburn, observed that 1942 would likely show a record of 3 million births, the largest in American history. But, he lamented, "while war brides have babies, war widows do not." Ogburn predicted a dearth of future citizens even if the war ended and marriage rates picked up. Looking ahead, he saw, "first, a shortage of pupils in the elementary school, then afterward fewer in the high schools. Still later there will be fewer students in college and fewer workers." Retailers too worried about postwar conditions, fearing the middle class would shrink, diminishing the public's buying power as families in the lowest income groups lacked the financial wherewithal to sustain consumer demand. Countering the gloomy predictions, some forecasters painted a rosier picture of the world to come and they proved correct. Peacetime inaugurated a baby boom; in 1957, the peak year, the birth rate reached 25.3 per 1,000 and the demand for hospital cribs and the market for nursery items exploded amid a consumer revolution.[24]

Also exploding in the postwar years: nuclear weapons being tested above ground and stockpiled for use in future conflicts. By the late 1940s, a dark cloud hung over the nation's cribs as the Cold War between the Soviets and Americans heated up and as they competed along with their respective allies for global dominance. In the new era of atomic weaponry, citizens and professionals began preparing for the next conflict. At the 1950 White House Conference on Children and Youth, Stanford psychologist Lois Meek Stolz, who had directed the Kaiser Child Service centers during World War II, presented four principles of a war program for infants, should a new conflict begin. First, she explained, babies should not be evacuated from emergency areas without their mothers. Second, mothers with infants should be the last source of manpower in wartime. Third, if mothers needed to undertake war work, then provision for substitute care needed to be arranged following the best principles of mental hygiene. Finally, Stoltz, reflecting the role of psychology in American life, stated that there needed to be counseling to help mothers understand their own and their babies' needs in wartime. Other health professionals also readied their colleagues in case the Cold

War turned hot. A 1951 nursing journal article, "Bomb Born Babies," gave instructions for supervising deliveries during a national defense emergency.[25]

Parents worried. In August 1961, a mother from Rhode Island wrote to ask pediatrician Benjamin Spock about the two-week supply of food she needed to keep in a fallout shelter in order to feed her infant son in case of atomic attack. In her letter, she observed that she was one of many women who "must be thinking along the same lines – and, if they're not, they should be." Across the nation families and communities prepared for possible nuclear war by building underground fortifications designed to protect them from radioactive debris following a nuclear explosion. They filled their shelters with food, water, and other goods in case of a lengthy stay. In his reply to the worried mother, Spock gave a vague answer, suggesting a supply of the foods normally given to the baby needed to be set aside. Nuclear anxiety appeared in a different form in another letter to Spock. A mother wrote to ask if her baby's death from a malformed heart resulted from the fallout from atomic bomb tests. He explained that it was not the cause.[26]

Bomb testing led some scientists to issue warnings about fallout, including both direct effects on individuals from radiation exposure and threats to future generations in the form of mutations caused by genetic damage. In 1958, a "Baby Tooth Survey" began in St. Louis to gauge the degree of exposure to the radioactive isotope Strontium 90, a product of nuclear testing. The baby teeth collected (amounting to nearly 300,000 by 1970) demonstrated increased levels of the isotope from the tests. Once kept in baby books as innocent ephemera, infants' teeth became scientific material in the Cold War era, tiny signs of a troubling, weapon-filled world. Similarly, milk, a substance identified with and vital for babies, became a marker of radiation exposure. In 1959, *Consumer Reports* revealed that its tests of milk samples from fifty cities found contamination with Strontium 90. Like invisible germs a generation earlier, invisible enemies, now in the form of radioactive isotopes, threatened the nation's babies. Worried members of the public found a new ally when, in 1962, less than a year after he replied to the worried mother about stocking her fallout shelter, Spock became a spokesman for SANE, the National Committee for a Sane Nuclear

Policy, a group working for disarmament. A Cleveland, Ohio, father wrote to Spock in the wake of his announced opposition to nuclear testing to ask what kind of milk to give his daughter when she stopped drinking formula. Spock answered powdered or evaporated milk and mentioned the fallout risk.[27]

Americans trusted Spock, the baby expert whose best-selling book, *Common Sense Book of Baby and Child Care*, published in 1946, quickly became the bible of infant care. Costing only ten cents in paperback and translated into many languages, it garnered a huge worldwide audience because of its accessible style, helpful organization and index, and reassuring message that parents should trust themselves (even as Spock told them what to do). As mothers and fathers consulted the book for advice about babies, they absorbed the modern gospel of psychology; Spock had undertaken psychoanalytic training and its influence appeared in his writings.

Following the book's publication, Spock's public's career soared. By 1954, he was writing a regular advice column for *Ladies Home Journal* and the following year he landed his own half-hour television show on NBC on Sunday afternoons. He remained in the limelight as the baby expert in the decades that followed, even as his political beliefs began to alienate (and attract) those with whom he interacted in person and in print.

Each article Spock wrote for *Ladies Home Journal* prompted letters with questions, confessions, and advice. When he touched on aspects of infant care, mothers responded with requests for help and often their letters resembled those written to the Children's Bureau by an earlier generation. Mothers sent queries about feeding, colic, toilet training, and sleeping. In 1960, a woman from Ohio wrote about her five-month-old baby who wouldn't go to sleep without crying for hours. A year later, a mother from Burbank, California, asked him what foods she should give her two-month-old baby, having received conflicting advice from the doctors in her medical group. Spock replied that starting solids "is a matter of style more than scientific knowledge," a statement that might have offended his peers even as it served to ease the worries of parents. The letters covered new topics as well as traditional ones. A column on PKU (phenylketonuria), a rare inherited disorder for which screening tests had recently been developed, resulted in several letters.[28]

With large sales and tremendous staying power, the *Common Sense Book of Baby and Child Care* toppled manuals calling for rigid parenting from many family bookshelves. The parenting advice Spock dispensed countered the prescriptions of behaviorist John B. Watson and challenged others who continued to espouse rigidity, conditioning, and emotional detachment. The new recommendations urged parents to forgo regimentation and treat their infants as individuals, observing their developmental stages rather than impressing a pattern of development upon them. Spock's work reflected the older ideas of Freud and the more recent influence of Arnold Gesell, whose work he recommended to readers. Social historians as well as political supporters and opponents would note Spock's influence on American culture. Baby books reveal that many, but not all, babies experienced the new style of parenting that followed from putting contemporary theories into practice.

The Cold War years saw the flowering of modern psychology with new infant care practices building on studies of infant and child development begun in earlier decades. The language of personality and self-regulation seeded the cultural terrain with new perceptions of individuals and their inner lives, which in turn enabled what one scholar termed psychology's expanding jurisdiction. In the nursery, this meant that middle-class mothers and fathers began offering their infants and children more affection and greater latitude in behavior than previous generations had provided. And, when faced with rebellion on the home front, many parents often substituted psychological techniques for physical discipline.[29]

Well before Spock put pen to paper, other writers and medical experts endorsed what came to be called modern infant care. Along with his wife, Mary M. Aldrich, pediatrician C. Anderson Aldrich published *Babies Are Human Beings: An Interpretation of Growth* in 1938. Influenced by Gesell, the Aldriches explained that infants followed an orderly sequence of physical and mental development, while also expressing their individual personalities and responses to their environments. The Aldriches endorsed affectionate baby care, taking direct aim at Watson's claims that kissing, hugging, and rocking babies produced spoiled children. They explained:

> Conscientious mothers often ask the doctor whether it is proper to fondle the baby. They have a vague feeling that it is wrong for babies to be mothered, loved or rocked, and that it is their forlorn duty to raise their children in splendid isolation "untouched by human hands" so to speak, and wrapped in cellophane like boxes of crackers we buy. This idea is particularly at variance with the growth plan.

In an obituary for C. Anderson Aldrich, his mentor during the period he worked at the Mayo Clinic, Spock lauded his response to the "inflexible rules" laid down for babies "without regard for their individual differences and developmental readiness." He added that Aldrich was twenty years ahead of his time in his thinking. Stella B. Applebaum, a freelance writer, produced *Baby: A Mother's Manual* in 1944 and similarly endorsed the new style of parenting. She echoed the advice of the Aldriches with her statement: "You will never spoil a baby by attending to his needs." Her book included introductions by a pediatrician and a psychiatrist.[30]

With their attention to the ways in which infant experiences became the foundation of personality development, Spock and his peers helped inaugurate what a historian called a "permissive turn" in American cultural life. In the nursery and elsewhere, psychology infiltrated many aspects of national life and commanded both resources and social power, helping to shape ideas about military readiness and public responses to the Cold War. Government spending to investigate and promote mental health increased and attention turned to new subjects such as the psychological impact of racial discrimination on children and the psychological makeup of women demanding equality and greater opportunity to participate in the economy and in the political arena. At the same time, the psychology of infant development continued to be taught to parents because, experts believed, children reared with the proper emotional guidance would have the individual personalities and collective consciousness needed to shape a healthy society and to sustain democracy amid the continuing tensions of the Cold War.[31]

When Spock addressed the White House Conference on Children and Youth in 1950 on "What We Know about the Development of Healthy

Personalities in Children," his talk ranged over nearly every subject related to infant and child development as he recounted the needs of youngsters living in families and institutions. He reminded the audience an infant is "clearly intended to love and to evoke love, from the beginning." Spock crystallized his beliefs into the pithy and reassuring statement: "Don't be afraid to kiss your baby when you feel like it." His words exemplified the remarkable change in infant care advice that occurred in a single generation.

The triumph of modern psychology did not entirely lay waste to old ideas. A rear guard continued to express concerns about overindulgence, challenging the new cadre of experts who proclaimed that a less severe style of parenting produced well-adjusted infants, children, and adults. The conservative disciples of what might be called Holtian or Watsonian parenting practices espoused long-standing doctrines about the inculcation of proper habits and the necessity for strict discipline as vital to healthy development. Widely published etiquette expert Emily Post broadcast this message in her 1940 *Children Are People and Ideal Parents Are Comrades*. Despite the use of the term *comrade*, Post was not promoting Bolshevik childcare ideals, but those of a previous generation of physicians. She explained, "As early as the first months – possibly weeks – of his life, the child whose training is to proceed along the smoothest road learns that each day's schedule turns on the wheel of time, which neither hurries nor halts." Sleeping, eating, bathing, and exercising at "exact times" produces a "healthy and tranquil and therefore well-behaved child." Allan Roy Dafoe, the famed Dionne quintuplets' doctor, delivered the same message in his 1942 *How to Raise Your Baby*: "Don't put off the bowel control routine for more than the first month of a child's life." Douglas Bruce, whose mother used Dafoe's baby book, apparently had a late start, with bowel training at eight months and bladder training at ten, but nonetheless had a more regimented life than Spock adherents would endorse. Physician Josephine Hemenway Kenyon, an actual student of Holt's, endorsed in her book "a fixed routine" and acknowledged what few other advisors admitted, a daily schedule afforded mothers and fathers as well as babies "the greatest comfort."[32]

Late twentieth-century scholars pointed out that the triumph of Spock meant more work for mothers as they attended to the spontaneous demands of infants. However, routines preached in early decades, involving such things as bowel training month-old infants and early conditioning of bladder control, also imposed a cost in time, even if they ultimately reduced the number of hours spent laundering diapers. For the most part, debates over parenting styles proved largely academic. Neither the advocates of strict scheduling nor the proponents of self-regulation ultimately determined what happened in the nursery. Baby books, casework reports, and community studies reveal that many mothers treated babies with affection and ignored scheduling long before it became the modern way. Conversely, the sources show that even when the new style of affectionate parenting dominated public discussions, some mothers stuck to tried-and-true regimentation. Attempts to make mothers conform to particular parenting styles, like attempts to make babies meet the expectations of parents, did not always succeed. Yet, postwar parents learned about and paid attention to modern ideas about infant development.[33]

Citizen babies did their part in war and in peace. They coped with rationing, served as symbols of the nation to help sell war bonds, and donated their teeth for fallout testing. They enjoyed government benefits when born to the wives of servicemen and endured hardships living under government-controlled internment camps. Their peacetime dividend came in the form of an acknowledgment of their individual needs and temperaments. Mustered out of programs begun as a wartime necessity, the public citizen babies who merited the attention and funds of the national government became, in the baby boom years, private citizen babies, whose welfare was first and foremost the responsibility of their families and whose value soared or descended depending on their race, health, and intellectual potential.

9

BABY BOOM BABIES

I N 1944, AN ADMIRAL RADIO ADVERTISEMENT acknowledged wartime shortages and promised prosperity in the years to come with the headline "No … Your post-war Admiral Radio won't bathe the baby!" In the postwar years, readers might have been tempted to ask, why not? Mass-produced consumer products seemed ready to answer any household need, promising convenience, practicality, and style. Why couldn't they also bathe the baby or change a few diapers? And there were so many to bathe and change! Between 1946 and 1964, more than 76 million babies entered the nation's homes.[1]

Baby boom babies grew up in extraordinarily prosperous times. The economy returned to growing through consumption. In addition to buying big items – homes, cars, appliances, and other durable goods – middle-class parents bought more small items for their babies. They outfitted nurseries with new cribs, dressed their babies in new clothes, served them store-bought baby foods, spent more on their medical services, and purchased toys designed to promote babies' physical and mental development. Ironically and perhaps predictably, as babies' lives and futures became measurably better in the baby boom years, public interest in their collective welfare eased.

Baby boom babies lived in a material world, a medical world, a cultural world, and a political world. It was also, increasingly, a private world. Thanks to a significant decline in rates of illness and death in the postwar decades and to the growing interest in protecting private family life, infants' well-being ceased to be a federal government priority. Infants remained "citizen babies," as political rhetoric still claimed their collective futures were the nation's future, but, for the most part, responsibility for ensuring those futures rested with their families. Federal efforts on behalf of babies (and children) increasingly came via means-tested programs rather than those focused on all of America's young.

As in the early part of the century, people prized some babies and not others. The value of healthy white infants rose as families competed to adopt them and sometimes spent large sums to acquire them. At the same time, the publicly appraised value of other infants, such as those declared disabled or members of racial minorities, remained low. Babies without families sometimes languished in under-resourced institutions. Other infants faced challenges such as poverty, discrimination, means-tested social programs, and the lack of a national health system, which limited their lives by denying them the resources they needed to survive and thrive.

Many postwar babies grew up in new, expanding suburbs. The exodus from cities and the purchase of new homes, supported by government loan programs, set off what *Forbes* called a stampede, as "appliance mania" set in. The increase in the production of electricity and growing incomes meant families owned more appliances than ever before – refrigerators for keeping milk and baby food fresh, and washers and dryers for laundering diapers and baby clothes. While economic surveys did not report on purchases of nursery items, it seems clear from both advertising and baby book gift lists that buying for babies increased. Advertisements for baby foods, infant formulas, clothes, toiletries, toys, furniture, and household products such as detergents designed for washing infant clothes and diapers filled newspapers, magazines, and, increasingly, television. Even commercial air carriers began advertising the services they provided to flying babies.[2]

Hospital deliveries became standard in the baby boom years, increasing from 56 percent of all births in 1940 to 97 percent by 1965. With the passage of the Hill-Burton Act, the government provided funds for the expansion and modernization of health care facilities and required that they provide a reasonable amount of free services in return. In the years that followed, both the number of hospital beds and the percentage of the population with health insurance grew. Babies born in hospitals went home with gifts from marketers. In 1955, Massachusetts's Waltham Hospital distributed a "nursery kit." It contained a mailing card from the Boston Diaper Service for a free copy of Dr. Spock's *Baby and*

Child Care, a sample packet of Dennison diaper liners, and the Beech-Nut pamphlet *Happy Mealtimes for Your Baby*. Signing up for the diaper service brought another gift: free use of a Detecto Baby Scale for three months. An expanding economy knit consumer culture and nursery life into an ever-tighter union and the hospital nursery served as a connecting link.[3]

Where families once wrote in baby books the names of the doctor and nurse who helped with the delivery, they now memorialized their infants' arrivals by tucking hospital identification bracelets and infant footprints into the pages. Some states began mandating the use of a newborn identification system in hospitals, while other hospitals simply adopted the practice voluntarily. Carol Pence, born to a military family in Albuquerque, New Mexico, in 1948, had both her handprints and her footprints in her baby book. The book of a baby born in Fort Worth, Texas, in 1957 included his hospital identification bracelet and, more prosaically, the bill.[4]

In saving birth ephemera, families amassed evidence of postwar advances in biomedicine. Karen Scott, an African American baby born in New York City in 1948, had a bottle-feeding pamphlet, her hospital admission card, and a Mt. Morris Park Child Health Station Appointment Book with a vaccination and immunization record tucked inside her baby book. The baby book of a boy born in Peoria, Illinois, in 1948 contained the handwritten reports of his pediatrician; he saw the doctor thirteen times in his first two years. Sally Ann Griffith started receiving her shots at the age of six months. "Took them very well. Some fever," her mother wrote. Born in Lusk, Wyoming, in 1952, Sally's fact-filled baby book related the highs and lows of her early months. Her mother made notes on her smiles, vocabulary, locomotion, diet, and her first Christmas. In a health record, her mother reported she endured her first hospitalization (for the flu) at the age of four months and her first cold at seven months. Many postwar baby books contained similar collections of medical records, most often formula prescriptions, diet advice, reports from regular checkups, and vaccine charts. Vaccination became so common that an advertisement in *Congratulations* began, "As careful parents you wouldn't think of not immunizing your new baby against dangerous diseases, but have you overlooked financial immunization?"[5]

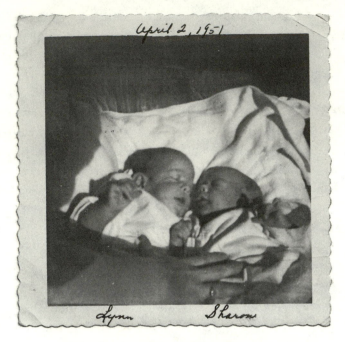

Figure 9.1 Twins Lynn and Sharon Weiner, 1951
Photographer: Charles Weiner
Credit: Private collection of Lynn Weiner

Vaccines and antibiotics transformed the lives of postwar American babies by dramatically decreasing the risk of death, the incidence of disease, and episodes of serious, life-threatening illnesses. The production and widespread distribution of penicillin in the late 1940s inaugurated a new era in medicine, and other antibiotic compounds soon joined the roster of agents capable of killing the bacteria responsible for many deadly infectious diseases. Infant deaths from pneumonia and meningitis as well as other common illnesses declined thanks to antibiotics, which also prevented the transmission of congenital syphilis when used to treat infected mothers. The heralded introduction of the Salk inactivated polio vaccine in 1955 prevented new cases of the viral disease that once left some victims paralyzed and roused public anxiety. A tremendous scientific achievement, the creation of an inactivated polio vaccine and its successor, a live virus vaccine, cemented the public's faith in American science during the 1950s. The measles vaccine licensed in 1963 received far less public acclaim than the polio vaccine, but had a more powerful effect on rates of illness and death. Prior to its development, annual cases of measles numbered half-a-million a year and measles-related deaths numbered about 500 a year. After the vaccine appeared the incidence of measles declined by 95 percent.[6]

Parents welcomed the new vaccines and kept up their babies' immunizations, welcoming each new addition to the arsenal. The advent of a combined vaccine for diphtheria, tetanus, and pertussis (whooping cough), sometimes called the three-in-one shot, and subsequent production of a four-in-one shot that incorporated the polio vaccine, made it easier to fully immunize infants. The combined doses also raised concerns among a few parents. Letters to pediatrician Benjamin Spock inquired about the advisability of giving a baby a four-in-one shot rather than the three-in-one and to report troublesome reactions after vaccine administration. Spock's first edition of *The Common Sense Book of Baby and Child Care* included information about the whooping cough, diphtheria, and tetanus inoculations and warnings about reactions (fever and crankiness) that he regarded as mild. Spock consistently reiterated his support for vaccines when replying to letters from anxious mothers in the 1960s, and he updated the information in later editions of his book as new vaccines became available. Baby books often did double duty as immunization ledgers. Randall Smalls's baby book reported on his vaccines and his illnesses. Born in 1954 in Washington, Pennsylvania, he received the polio vaccine shortly after it became available; by then he had already survived measles at the age of seven months, as well as chicken pox.[7]

A booming economy and a boom in babies meant that baby books continued to be an effective way to reach consumers. As they had in previous decades, businesses bought pages printed for area customers. The 1950 *Our Baby Album* contained advertisements from local merchants in Oklahoma City, including the bank, the supermarket, and the drive-in movie theater. Manufacturers also continued to give away advertisement-filled baby books, as infants continued to serve as conduits between the marketplace and the private household. Nitey Nite Sleepers offered *Life with Baby* in 1946. The 1951 edition of *Our Baby Book* from Norton, Kansas, incorporated both advertisements from nearby enterprises, among them the bank and pharmacy, and a coupon for Gerber's Strained Meat.[8]

With competition heating up in the baby food industry and baby food sales moving from the drug store to the grocery store, producers sought to establish customer loyalty at an early age. Thanks to their aggressive marketing, the convenience of feeding babies from a can or jar, and rising household income, sales of baby foods soared. As a scholar recently observed, the baby food industry proved so influential that doctors followed its lead and began recommending the introduction of solid foods at younger and younger ages. Gerber, Heinz, and Beech-Nut (a company that began as a seller of ham and bacon) dominated the market. The companies expanded their product lines and marketing and by 1948, according to a food historian, "baby food was the most commonly purchased processed item in ten large American cities." The Gerber Company, which began processing food for babies in 1927, initially reached customers through advertisements in medical journals and women's magazines while its core business remained canned fruits and vegetables. Its success with young consumers led it to abandon its initial production and trademark the slogan, "Babies Are Our Business ... Our Only Business" in 1956. If infant food makers pleased the palate of the first baby in a family, their efforts would be rewarded with continuing sales when younger siblings arrived in the household.[9]

Gerber's early advertising made use of expanding popular knowledge regarding the psychology of infant care. In 1939, the company produced "Foods for Baby: Vegetables, Fruits, Cereals, Soups and Mealtime Psychology." Among the insights presented in this small volume was the impressive manipulative skills of infants: "The baby of only a few weeks of age very soon learns that your concern and anxiety are an effective way for him to secure more attention." Babies, evidently quick studies of human nature, challenged their elders, but their moves could be countered when mothers learned a little strategy: "Let him think this is something he is doing himself, not something you are forcing him to do," the text advised. The mealtime *pas de deux* portrayed in Gerber's booklet suggested that while babies had inborn psychological skills, mothers needed to develop their manipulative talents through practice.[10]

The 1955 edition of *Infant Care* instructed parents to ask the doctor about starting solid foods and observed that "Some start giving these extra foods when a baby is only a few weeks old, others wait until babies

are about 3 to 4 months old." One year earlier, an article in *Look* magazine observed that some doctors started babies on strained meats before
they turned two weeks old, while others waited two months. With about
4 million new consumers arriving the previous year, the article observed,
"America's baby-food bill topped $200 million," not including milk.[11]

Once babies started eating solid food, a vast menu awaited them.
Companies developed extensive product lines, promising purchasers
that the new foodstuffs passed muster with a large panel of infant testers.
Baby food manufacturers presented infants with options for a complete
meal, not soup to nuts, but a first course of meat and vegetables followed
by a sweet. Beech-Nut, for instance, developed and sold the "surprise
baby dessert of the year! Natural Fruit Gel." The company's come-ons
included store coupons and promotions featuring giveaway items such
as tablemats. Helping to sell Beech-Nut foods were the cute Brecker
quadruplets, three girls and a boy born in Queens, New York, in 1963.[12]

A rapidly growing customer base lured new entrants to the infant food
industry in the baby boom years. Swift, a meatpacking company, introduced strained meat for babies in 1947, following research conducted
at the Nebraska Experiment Station on six-week-old infants living in
adoption institutions. According to the nurses' reports, the eighteen
babies not only enjoyed the meat, they avoided anemia and "slept better"
than the fifteen babies in the control group. Birds Eye, a frozen food
company, attempted to break into the baby food business a few years
later with an instant food consisting of dry frozen crystals. Mothers only
had to add water and serve. An advertisement in the *Buffalo Courier-
Express Pictorial* from 1961 explained, "No wait for food to heat, no
handling problems or breakage with handy boxes. Now in your grocer's
frozen food cabinet." The product failed. Perhaps mothers preferred
the recently introduced glass jars or the traditional cans, or maybe their
babies failed to appreciate the taste of reconstituted crystallized food. In
addition to newspaper and magazine advertisements and store coupons,
baby food companies promoted their wares with commercials on both
children's and adults' television shows. And they got an extra boost as
Americans ventured into the final frontier: astronaut John Glenn consumed Gerber's applesauce from a feeding tube during a 1962 earth-
orbiting space flight.[13]

Baby books from the postwar years not only recorded changes in infants' diets, they contained notes on babies' "progress" and "accomplishments," as if at birth infants set forth on a path to success and each obstacle they traversed needed recording. The drumbeat of psychological assessment pounded into public consciousness by a previous generation of baby care experts continued to sound. The updated eighth edition of *Your Child Year by Year,* published in 1945, promised its development record would be useful for the child's doctors and teachers, a reminder that babies' progress would be monitored outside as well as inside the family. The magazine *Better Homes and Gardens* produced an equally extensive baby book in 1946 with places to record "physical and mental growth, personality, interest, [and] abilities" beginning with the prenatal period and ending with the sixth year. The revised edition of the purposefully named *Our Baby's First Seven Years: A Baby Record Book Including Scientific Charts Which Will Prove of Practical Service to the Mother and Growing,* published in 1958 (by then having sold 1.5 million copies of its various editions), had places for more medical information and more developmental record keeping than earlier editions. Following the latest advice from its panel of experts, the text emphasized treating infants and children as individuals and so, for example, removed the exact prescription on hours of sleep. The new edition also excised the previous command about teaching emotional control.[14]

Postwar babies experienced psychologically focused scrutiny; their activities did not change, but the meaning of certain behaviors transformed. Babbling, once enjoyed by parents as the precursor to speech, became, in the eyes of experts, a mark of intellectual growth. A baby's first "words" such as "goo" and "da," first laugh, first crawling, and first standing alone became events to record as evidence of development. The expanding cultural power of modern psychology meant that each new activity observed in a baby came to be seen as a milestone or, if seen at a particularly youthful age, as an achievement. The number of pages devoted to infant development distinguished postwar baby books from their predecessors, even as traditional entry places, for things like horoscope charts and gift lists, remained in the volumes. Reading numerous baby books makes clear that infants introduced new patterns of consumption, medical oversight, and psychological investigation to their families, and each family documented the results in its own way. As in the past, the economic situation of a family became evident in the notes kept in baby books. The family of Jane Smith, an African American woman born in Southern California in 1945, kept a *Log-o'-Life* memory book for her. It opened with details of her early months, included notes about the champagne brunch following her christening, and contained, from eighteen years later, a newspaper clipping about her return to college at UCLA after a summer spent in Mexico in 1963.[15]

A paradox of postwar infant care lay in the fact that as babies' lives became less rigidly scheduled, they became, ideally, more scrutinized. Testing of infants no longer went on just in university laboratories; it now occurred at home. Babies had exams to pass. The marking period began early, but the opportunity to earn a good grade lasted a long time. For example, with the turn to permissive parenting and a focus on "readiness," toilet training that once began by holding six-week-old babies over a bowl instead commenced in the second half of the first year. Barbara Arrow, born in Los Angeles in 1949, began her training at eight-and-a-half months. Her mother reported on her slow but steady progress in *Our Baby's First Seven Years*, detailing the various steps her daughter mastered (while using her Up-See-Daisy toilet seat), until finishing the job by the time she turned three. Along the way Barbara acquired a bathroom vocabulary, enabling her to indicate when she needed to void and these words were noted in her baby book as well. Another infant was nearly two when the training ended, and by then, his mother wrote, he could say, "bap-room." Where once notations in baby books simply recorded the age when a child attained mastery, if the mothers bothered to record the end of training at all, in the baby boom era they sometimes included exquisite details about each step forward. Barbara's mother not only chronicled her toilet training she kept notes on nearly every other aspect of her baby's development. And, in addition to her formal baby book, Barbara had a *Your Baby's Diary and Calendar* from H. J. Heinz in which her mother pasted a diet slip from the doctor.[16]

Diets received careful study, perhaps made necessary by the need to chart infants' reactions to the vast array of commercial foods presented to them. James Walton, born in Evanston, Illinois, in 1946, started on carrots at three months, squash, green beans, beef, lamb, and vegetable soup at four months, and sweet potatoes, applesauce, prunes, apricots, and bananas at six months. Each addition appeared in his copy of *Our Baby's First Seven Years*. He also got regular doses of Vi-Pente cod liver oil in ten ounces of juice every day between 9:00 and 9:30 AM. The instructions came on an "Infant Diet Schedule" from his doctor that his mother kept in his baby book. The slip advised "Beechnut or Heinz canned vegetables are satisfactory to start. Later we prefer to use home-cooked fresh vegetables," followed by instructions for their preparation. The instruction sheet commanded: "DON'T FORCE FOOD. Your attitude should be – 'Take it or leave it!'" In addition to his expanding diet, James's mother kept careful notes of his physical and mental development and his budding vocabulary.[17]

Physicians sometimes handed out precise food preparation instructions. The slip inside Barbara Arrow's baby book gave detailed orders: "Boil egg 10 minutes; peel off white and mash yolk, add salt and milk. Serve at breakfast feeding." Barbara's mother noted each addition to her diet as well as the foods she refused, evidently following the "take it or leave it" plan. Was food refusal an instance of the limited but seemingly effective example of infant agency? Was it self-expression? Or were infants "diapered dictators," as an article in *Congratulations* dubbed them, who expressed their preferences by clamping their mouths shut or spitting out distasteful items? Once seen as a dangerous accommodation to infant will, acquiescence to food refusal became, in the baby boom years, an indication that parents knew how to bring up babies the modern way. Mothers acknowledged and recorded their infants' preferences. Joe Shapiro's 1947 baby book included places to answer questions about "what I like" and "what I hate." Baby books from the prewar years did not inquire about such things. As for Joe, his mother reported he hated spinach.[18]

The characteristics of individual babies received particular scrutiny when they awaited professional placement in adoptive homes. In the early decades of the twentieth century, adoption seemed to many people a risky and unscientific way to form a family. As psychologist Henry H. Goddard warned in 1911, families of good stock should not be taking in children of poor pedigree. But starting around the 1920s, childless couples began to seek infants for adoption, although toddlers and even older children remained a more popular choice. Experts, led by Arnold Gesell, believed that babies needed to undergo an observation period of several months before being placed. Developmental tests could then be administered to reveal the baby's intellectual potential and personality and the baby could then be matched with an appropriate family. Adoption, he argued, could not be "intrusted [*sic*] altogether to good will or to intuitive impulse"; it required the "combined critical judgment of the social investigator, the court, the physician, and the mental examiner." Gesell developed and taught others to use normative scales of development and pushed to delay adoptions until babies could be assessed using the scales.[19]

People considering adoption sometimes wrote to Gesell for advice. A 1933 letter from a couple, both university graduates, asked about the mental testing of a baby boy to be placed with them in a few months, explaining, "we feel that for our protection, particularly with a daughter of our own, some estimate of the adopted baby's mentality should be arrived at before the probationary period of a year is over." Gesell referred them to his book on the mental growth of the preschool child. Another letter in 1940 asked about adopting a baby with a poor background, referring to the birth mother's "immorality" and the emotional instability of the deceased alleged birth father, who came from "a family of roving preachers." Gesell replied that while he did not take "an exaggerated view of the harmful influence of a 'poor background,'" in that particular instance it was a deterrent and he would "hesitate to proceed with the suggested adoption." His hard-and-fast hereditarian views may have softened a bit, but Gesell clung to pieces of them even as he recognized the potential of a loving home. So did ordinary Americans who maneuvered between the old religion of inheritance and the new faith in environment when they attempted to form families by adoption.[20]

Writing for the general circulation magazine *Saturday Evening Post* in 1943, Gesell explained that gifted parents needed babies that wouldn't disappoint and babies of "obscure" background needed testing to see if they were "normal." Beyond matching for intelligence, many adoption authorities believed that babies and parents should be matched on physical characteristics, religion, race, and temperament. With so many expectations to meet, the quest for the right infant to adopt could be perilous. An anonymous account in *Atlantic Monthly* in 1940 described one family's search for a baby. After discussing a couple that had lost their blond Anglo-Saxon boy and adopted a "Slavic-looking child," who they did not love, the author described her own expectations. "We didn't want a doorstep baby of unknown parentage … We wanted the best material available." Some babies, the author explained, came from married couples experiencing hard times and too proud to beg, evidently a sign that they produced top-flight "material." As a historian of adoption noted, the professional interest in synchronizing the mentality of children and parents could be thwarted because of class differences between the families of infants available for adoption and the families able to overcome the economic hurdles to adoption. The author of the *Atlantic* article concluded her piece telling about her adoption of a baby of "good stock" with a college graduate father, an unusually intelligent mother, and a certified IQ marking her "brighter than average." Threaded through the article was a suggestion of a kind of elastic popular eugenics, with a woman's first illegitimate offspring having less of a hereditary taint than subsequent children. As the author explained, she investigated placement agencies and found many of the babies they placed were a first child born out of wedlock because "no one … would be eager to raise a mother's second or third illegitimate child, even though biologists claim that the germ plasm of the offspring is in no way affected."[21]

Gesell's ideas about carefully observing and monitoring infants continued to hold sway among professionals, even as early adoption became more popular in the postwar years. Child placement experts worked hard to make adoption "modern," meaning both rational and scientific, and they met with some success. The Child Welfare League proposed adoption standards and some states passed laws and undertook investigations of facilities placing children. In addition, the Children's Bureau made numerous studies of adoption and answered letters from prospective adoptive parents. However, the federal government never gained control or even oversight of the adoption process; it remained with the states and in some cases was only lightly overseen or regulated.[22]

Well explored by historians, adoption practices reveal many profound cultural shifts in the United States over the course of the twentieth century. Pregnancy outside of marriage slowly became less stigmatized, leading to fewer infants to adopt as single women chose to raise their infants. Theories of eugenics faced challenges thanks to new findings about environmental influences. For infants, the great transformation was in their value. In her 1947 book *Adopting a Child*, Frances Lockridge provided a brief history of adoption recounting how, in the first part of the twentieth century, abandoned babies turned up in theaters and rooming houses. In the postwar period, adoptable babies brought high prices. One family, she reported, paid $2,000 while another gave $500 for a baby from a maternity home only to watch it die. Lockridge presented the examples to support her demand that proper investigations of babies and families take place before completing an adoption. She pointed out that licensed adoption agencies used the Gesell system to test infant development – checking to see if the baby followed a moving object with his eyes and noticed the ringing of a bell, for example. The tests, emblematic of the effort to place adoption on a scientific footing, began several decades earlier, but picked up steam as developmental psychology captured the imagination of professionals overseeing adoptions.[23]

Despite his support for many of Gesell's theories, Benjamin Spock disagreed with him about delaying adoption, acknowledging the risks but concluding "the younger the better." "The only disadvantage of a very young adoption is that it's harder to tell what kind of child it is going to be," he wrote. Spock's psychoanalytic training taught him to question the emotional needs of adopting families as well as infants and to suggest that that adoptive parents provide the baby with the proper environment. Using psychological explanations, he wrote that both parents must want the adoption, that it not be undertaken to shore up a troubled marriage, that single people should not adopt, that adoptions should not take place to give a lonely child a companion, and that it should not be done in order to replace a child who died.[24]

Demand for newborn infants to adopt grew in the baby boom years, particularly as childless couples looked to expand their households. Determinist arguments about heredity lost much of their scientific allure with revelations of how Nazi racial hygiene theories were used to justify genocide; no longer would one's biological inheritance be seen entirely as one's destiny. Increasingly, social scientists and developmental experts found evidence that a good loving home could overcome many hereditary deficits and that early placement offered advantages to babies. Keeping infants in institutions until their intellectual potential revealed itself came to be understood as detrimental to both their cognitive and their emotional development. The months of observation suggested by Gesell no longer seemed useful if parents had the ability to make a happy home and a happy baby starting right after birth. Lockridge summed up the new orthodoxy in a condensed version of her book: "The studies prove the fundamental soundness of human nature. It has the capacity to blossom when given the right soil." Increasingly, experts and families rejected older theories and came to believe that babies needed to be planted as early as possible.[25]

Parents seeking to adopt babies from licensed facilities underwent psychological assessments as well as evaluations of their incomes and homes. Even those who passed the tests might not be able to obtain an infant because of the limited domestic supply. Some families looked to foreign adoption as orphaned infants and children came to the United States after World War II under the Displaced Persons Act of 1948 and subsequent amendments extending the legislation. Following the end of hostilities in the Korean War, black-Korean mixed-raced babies and other Korean babies began to be adopted as well under the Refugee Relief Act of 1953. In the years that followed, transnational and transracial domestic and foreign adoptions became more common.[26]

Approximately half of all infants adopted in the United States went to family members; of the remaining adoptions, half involved private arrangements and the other half took place under the auspices of licensed agencies. Run by social work professionals who applied standards for placing children with prospective parents, licensed agencies and their allies in the Children's Bureau worked to regulate both individual adoptions and the overall process. The agencies placed babies – most of them born to single mothers – with carefully selected families and paid strict attention to matching the characteristics of infants and families. Writing to her mother in 1962, biology professor Jolane Solomon described what the adoption agency told her about the boy she waited to adopt, including details of his parents' educational background and religion and their height and complexion, all of which matched hers and those of her husband. As she explained, "They gave us these physical details and chose him for us so that we'd know that he will grow up to be similar to us in looks."[27]

Successful adoptions required patience. In 1942, the Chicago Foundlings' Home reported that it required a six-month waiting period while the superintendent completed the study of the home and certified the arrangement. While waiting, families could visit the institution on a monthly basis, a typical arrangement. Some would-be adoptive parents avoided licensed placement agencies because of the long wait or shunned them because their request for a baby seemed unlikely to be fulfilled. Other would-be adoptive parents met with rejection, turned away after failing to win the approval of the social workers who acted as gatekeepers. In those situations, families might respond by seeking out private arrangements through intermediaries, mostly doctors, lawyers, and the proprietors of independent maternity homes. Private adoptions could be completed quickly and with little interference. They accounted for the other half of non-family adoptions. National adoption data, not broken down by age, showed that approximately 72,000 adoptions took place in 1951, and the number grew to 135,000 by 1964 and continued to rise thereafter. Adoptions by family members and some private arrangements may not have been included in these figures.[28]

In the nineteenth century, reformers believed that so-called illegitimate infants needed to remain with their mothers in order to morally uplift them from their "fallen" state. In the twentieth century, babies took on a new role: cleansing their mothers and themselves from the stain of illegitimacy by entering adoptive homes. Maternity homes, where single women frequently gave birth, became way stations on the path to respectability. Philanthropic and religious groups ran some of the establishments, most prominently the National Florence Crittenton Mission homes. They opened in the late nineteenth century to provide care to unmarried pregnant women and through the twentieth century placed infants in adoptive homes.[29]

Other babies passed into adoptive homes from the hands of private boarding home operators who worked independently and avoided professional oversight. They found clients by reaching out to pregnant women and offering them free maternity care and in some cases financial support in exchange for the opportunity to place their babies. The unregulated transactions, sometimes frankly illegal, proved highly lucrative for the homes' proprietors and business partners. Couples paid for the costs of the care provided by maternity home operators and for the fees charged by various intermediaries, including doctors, lawyers, and judges. Independent placements involved as many as 50,000 to 60,000 children each year, according to estimates presented in Senate hearings in 1955.[30]

Revelations about interstate and international baby selling that breached ethical barriers received periodic media attention. A notorious Memphis branch of the Tennessee Children's Home Society raked in approximately $1,000,000 arranging adoptions, according to a *New York Times* article in 1950. The Tennessee facility arranged at least 424 adoptions in California and 308 in New York while operating with no legal or medical oversight. But New Yorkers did not have to go south for a baby. In 1951, a front-page story in the *New York Times* detailed the arrest of a local ring of baby brokers with the headline, "4 Doctors among 9 Indicted Here in $500,000 Baby Black Market." Stories about baby brokers appeared in numerous other newspapers. The *Times-Union* of Hendersonville, North Carolina, printed an article in 1953 about the Children's Bureau report on adoption under the headline "Baby Black Market with Disregard to Boundaries Flourishes as Price Varies from $3500 to Medic Fee." The prices paid left little doubt that within the consumer culture of the postwar United States, babies could be highly sought after, expensive items.[31]

Sustained attention to baby buying came in 1955 when the Senate Subcommittee to Investigate Juvenile Delinquency held four days of hearings to investigate what the press called the "adoption racket." Tennessee Senator Estes Kefauver, an adoptive parent whose son came from the Cradle Society, a well-known Illinois adoption agency, led the hearings. In an irony unremarked upon at the time, the Cradle Society served a well-off clientele and engaged in some questionable practices that raised concerns among adoption professionals. A 1944 letter from Katherine Lenroot, chief of the Children's Bureau, to First Lady Eleanor Roosevelt reported on the case of a family paying $1,000 for a child from the Cradle Society. The Cradle Society operated with a set of ironclad rules about religious matching and the quality of babies it placed. The Cradle Society found a half-Jewish, half-Catholic baby for its clients Al Jolson and Ruby Keeler, both well-known film stars. Even while satisfying would-be parents, the agency maintained strict barriers of admission. It rejected handicapped infants with physical defects or brain injuries and those whose parents were chronic alcoholics.[32]

The rationale for the Juvenile Delinquency subcommittee's work lay in theories of infant psychology. "Improperly placed children," Senator Kefauver observed at the opening of the hearings, could become mal-adjusted and possibly delinquent. The subcommittee held two days of hearings each in Miami and Chicago. Witnesses described the problems of unregulated adoption and spoke on behalf of established social wel-fare organizations, which, along with the Children's Bureau, hoped to place all adoptions under professional control and strict legal regulation. The hearings delved into the motives of all parties: adoptive parents, the various professionals who eased them through the adoption process, and the authorities attempting to shut down the baby trade.[33]

Testimony before the Senate subcommittee revealed little about the lives of babies prior to or after adoption, but made clear that families wanted only physically healthy and developmentally sound infants. A father from New Jersey, speaking anonymously, explained to the sub-committee how, after two frustrating years of trying to adopt a baby through various agencies, he and his wife learned of a Montreal mater-nity home and flew to Canada to be introduced to adoptive babies. They rejected a two- or three-month-old baby with defective eyes that appeared malnourished. They then flew their pediatrician to Canada and he conducted a complete physical and serological examination (presumably for syphilis) on another baby and on the baby's mother. Once satisfied, the couple completed the adoption. In his testimony, after listing all the health problems he believed that the infant might yet display, including blindness, epilepsy, mental deficiency, and hereditary diseases, the man admitted, "we were taking a heavy, calculated, and per-haps stupid risk." Yet they went ahead with the adoption. It was a sellers' market and while the buyers had to beware, they couldn't be too picky.[34]

At the conclusion of the hearings, Kefauver introduced a bill to outlaw the commercial sale of children and the coercion or enticement of women to give up babies for adoption. Despite the fact that thirty-four of forty-eight states had no laws regarding the sale of babies and despite the support of the Children's Bureau and other welfare organizations, no legislation passed. An amended version of the Kefauver legislation introduced in 1965 followed another round of hearings, and it too did not become law. Adoption remained the responsibility of the states; national protection of vulnerable infants, perhaps the ultimate expression of citizen babyhood, was not to be.[35]

Possibly inspired by the hearings, in 1956, the Kraft Television Theater aired "Babies for Sale," a melodramatic account of an illegally arranged adoption that ended with the couple surrendering their adopted baby to the birth mother. One scene involves a bit of haggling between the prospective father and the broker who says, "I understand you want our merchandise but you don't want to pay our price," and a few moments later, "I'm doing business in a seller's market." It was an accurate assessment.[36]

Babies were not cheap. Newspaper exposés listed prices as high as $10,000. Anecdotal accounts in the Kefauver hearings reported payments ranging from $1,500 to $5,000 or more. In one instance, a baby seller received $1,700 for a baby boy and only $1,500 for a baby girl, but no testimony or articles explained whether the gender difference in pricing was typical or a reflection of demand. The Kefauver hearings and newspaper tales of black market arrangements succeeded in keeping the story of baby brokers before the public. However, a frank discussion of babies as commodities to be bought and sold did not take place. Economists might discuss what it cost to bear an infant and rear her or him to adulthood, but assessing the fair market value of an infant was anathema. Nevertheless, dollars changed hands.

Even with media attention to the illegal baby trade resulting from the Kefauver hearings and the periodic arrests of baby brokers, the deal making continued, undoubtedly because it was so lucrative. New York City authorities uncovered a million-dollar adoption racket operating in 1959 that included a side business in loan sharking and gambling. Baby dealing, it appeared, offered a greater return on investment than traditional illegal activities. The prices paid for babies suggest that, though often born to poor single women, many grew up in the homes of the well-off. In 1956, the year after the hearings, the average (median) family income in the United States was estimated to be $4,800; clearly, families pursuing private adoptions needed substantial resources to complete the process.[37]

The precise economics of baby selling remained opaque. Expenses claimed by participants included stipends to the birth mothers, room and board payments to maternity home operators, fees to doctors for delivering the babies, payments to lawyers for arranging the adoptions, and sometimes payoffs to judges approving the adoptions. Minor sums also went to cover court-filing fees, preparation of paperwork including obtaining and notarizing birth certificates, and the expense incurred placing newspaper advertisements seeking babies for adoption. The hearings did not make clear the profits accruing to each party after they covered their expenses, but they did suggest that attorneys reaped the greatest reward. While one lawyer said he arranged only six or seven a year as a small part of his business, others revealed working on sixty or more cases annually.

In acquiring babies through questionable procedures, families resisted the expertise and judgments of psychologists and social workers, professionals who believed that they alone possessed the ability to make proper investigations of all parties and to determine appropriate placements. The families turning to the grey or the black market to quench their desire for parenthood refused to have their plans stifled by the judgments of experts or blocked by marketplace competition for a scarce commodity. The cultural authority of modern psychology proved no match for families seeking babies. Yet, even though they followed a shady or illegal path to adoption, the families shared with the professionals whose advice they eschewed a belief in environmentalism, but with a critical caveat. They did not want disabled infants; there was very little room for what some people saw as "damaged goods" in a consumer society.[38]

Both the popular press and the Kefauver hearings reported on families returning babies after adoption if they discovered the infants to be "defective" or part African-American. Minority and mixed-race infants proved difficult to place, while disabled and disfigured babies had an even harder time finding a home. In an unusual case reported in the Kefauver hearings, a family desperate for children accepted "afflicted" infants – one without a nose who had to be fed with a medicine dropper and another with a harelip, an opening in the upper lip that may extend to the nose. Undoubtedly other families welcomed disabled infants. Most often disabled babies given up by their birth mothers and fathers who did not get adopted went into public care. Occasionally mothers left behind so-called boarder babies when they exited hospital maternity wards, reenacting a pattern of desertion that previously took place on the steps of asylums. The infants' stays in hospitals sometimes lasted many months, resulting in significant risks to their emotional and physical health. In 1964, an article in the *Chicago Tribune* reporting on boarder babies in Cook County Hospital observed that the infants often became ill because of their proximity to sick children.[39]

Even when parents did not give up their disabled infants for adoption, professionals advised them to send the babies away for special care when they reached an appropriate age. The rationales for separation included meeting the needs of the child and sustaining the emotional health of the family by avoiding psychological difficulties thought to arise from caring for a disabled child at home. A couple from Cleveland, Ohio, wrote to Gesell in 1935 after their pediatrician informed them their six-month-old baby was a "Mongolian type," a common reference at the time to individuals with Down syndrome, a highly visible condition linked to physical differences and intellectual deficits. Answering for Gesell, his colleague physician Catherine Strunk Amatruda told them the infant's condition was not their fault and was not hereditary, but that they needed to find an institution for him where he would be better off. She cautioned against seeking quick cures, faith healing, or running from doctor to doctor seeking a different diagnosis.[40]

Institutionalization of disabled infants and children would remain the standard recommendation for decades. Spock's first edition of *Common Sense Book of Baby and Child Care* offered much the same advice as Amatruda. He described the difficulties of caring for very young handicapped children at home and their need for special schooling or placement in institutions when they grew older, explaining that most public placement facilities did not accept children under age five. In the specific case of babies with what he termed Mongolism, Spock suggested

sending the infant to a special care home right after birth. He reasoned: "Then the parents will not become too wrapped up in a child who
will never develop very far, and they will have more attention to give to
their normal children who need it – either the children that they already
have or the ones that they should have afterwards." Several mothers with
institutionalized infants wrote to Spock about their disabled babies. One
woman described the seven-month-old brain-damaged daughter she
placed in an institution for the mentally retarded. Another woman won-
dered what to tell her older children, who had looked forward to the
birth of the baby, about the decision to send the newborn with Down
syndrome to a private facility.[41]

Public conversations about disabled infants slowly began to shift in the
baby boom years. Families became advocates for their disabled infants
and children, founding the National Association for Retarded Children
in 1950, and lobbying to make support for those with intellectual disabilities a public priority. Repeated exposés of the horrific conditions
in institutions warehousing disabled children reinforced their calls
for community support and home care for infants and children, more
funding for their education, and training, and increased access to medical and social services. Even Spock revised his thinking, shifting away
from advising that babies diagnosed with Down Syndrome be placed into
care as quickly as possible. He began to advise families to get counseling
from social service agencies or a psychiatrist if they were uncertain about
what to do.

The federal government played a limited but sustained role in assisting
disabled infants and babies without families; they received assistance
from funds channeled to the states under Title V of the Social Security
Act. After President John F. Kennedy took office in 1961, he convened
a group of experts to study mental retardation and subsequently signed
into law in 1962 the measure creating the National Institute of Child
Health and Human Development within the National Institutes of
Health. The following year, Congress enacted two other pieces of legislation: the Maternal and Child Health and Mental Retardation Planning
Amendment to the Social Security Act and the Mental Retardation
Facilities and Community Mental Health Construction Act. The legislation aimed to assist all those with intellectual disabilities and mental

illness, not just the young. The amendment to the Social Security Act did, however, contain prevention funds through maternity and infant care.

Two episodes increased attention to infant disabilities in the 1960s. First, the births of babies with missing or foreshortened limbs from prenatal exposure to thalidomide, most of whom were born overseas, brought attention to the need to study teratogens – agents, including drugs, chemicals, infections, and radiation – that can damage an embryo or a fetus. Second, an epidemic of rubella in 1964–1965 left thousands of infants who were exposed in utero blind, deaf, mentally handicapped, and suffering from heart defects. Both events led to changes in law and social policy, with the births of babies with Rubella syndrome playing a critical role in loosening abortion restrictions first in the states and then nationally and the births of thalidomide-damaged infants changing drug licensing and testing laws. After the baby boom ended, some infants received help from new means-tested programs including Medicaid – begun in 1965 to provide health insurance to low-income families – and the Special Supplemental Program for Women, Infants, and Children – begun in 1972 to provide nutritional support.[42]

Writing babies into history deepens our knowledge of fundamental developments in American life and reminds us of the diversity of the nation and the diversity of experiences that together shape our households, communities, and culture. Babies ushered their families into the modern world of consumer culture, medical science, and psychology. Babies moved local, state, and federal government officials to act on their behalf because of their high mortality rate and their need for protection. As their risks of death and their need for civic investment in their futures appeared to decline, public citizen babies became private citizen babies. Uncle Sam continued to write checks; but he no longer had an open invitation to visit the nursery and tell parents how to raise their infants. In less than a century, "our babies" became "my babies" and "their babies," an arc of social change that marked the beginning and end of a social welfare ethos inspired by the nation's most vulnerable citizens.

CODA

Kissing and Dismissing Babies: American Exceptionalism

ISTORIANS OF THE UNITED STATES REPEATEDLY raise the
question of American exceptionalism, the idea that the nation
has a special character shaped by its natural resources, democratic government, and honoring of personal liberty. Together, some
argue, these qualities add up to a culture in which upward mobility,
manifest destiny, wealth accumulation, and idealism flourish and
hope for future opportunities triumphs over immediate injustices and
stirrings of rebellion. Other historians look at different aspects of the
American story, including inequality, violence, and racism, and they see
private corporate interests trampling civic and collective needs and creating a pyramid of wealth that fewer and fewer families can hope to
scale. Historians engaged in global and comparative history consider
the topic of exceptionalism as well, questioning whether American
identity consists of a set of stories that elevate patriotism while undermining collective investments in the public good. Babies are not part
of these debates, but their histories and their current situation offer an
interesting perspective on the subject.

Consider the demographic data about infant mortality. The massive
decline in infant death rates over the course of the twentieth century
is a profound example of how government programs large and small
delivered life itself. In 1900, 100 infants out of 1,000 died before their
first birthday, and while advantages of class and ethnicity appeared to
protect some infants more than others, death stalked the nation's nurseries. In 2016, the estimated infant mortality rate in the United States,
according to the Central Intelligence Agency, stood at 5.8 per 1,000 live
births, an achievement won by an infrastructure program supporting
safe drinking water and effective sewage disposal, and by public health

education, food safety laws, prenatal and maternal health services, vaccination campaigns, housing reform, and income growth.[1]

Yet, compared to other nations, the American story looks less than triumphant. In 2016, the infant mortality rate stood just below that of Serbia and just above that of Bosnia and Herzegovina. When compared to the wealthiest countries in the world, the United States had the highest rate of infant deaths. There were of course, regional, ethnic, and racial differences in those mortality figures. Worth noting is that the United States spends more on health care than the other nations, but is the only nation on the list of wealthy countries that fails to require paid maternity leave or give health care to all its citizens. The missing support structures are distressing examples of exceptionalism.[2]

The same biomedical knowledge is applied in all the wealthy countries and the global consumer economy is at work in all of them as well. In accounting for the gaps – chasms, really – between the death rates of infants in the United States and other nations, and among different communities and ethnic groups within the United States, attention must turn to the public realm – with the absence of programs to alleviate poverty by providing quality education and good jobs with fair wages, to provide access to quality health care, and to support healthy communities free of environmental threats.

In terms of poverty, the data show how life in the United States has gotten markedly better over the course of the twentieth and twenty-first centuries. Taking this long view provides a sense of progress and optimism. But reports about our present situation serve as a reminder of how far there is to go. According to the US Census Bureau, in 2015, 13.5 percent of Americans lived in poverty and nearly half of them, 6.1 percent, amounting to 19.4 million people, lived in what is defined as deep poverty, meaning 50 percent below the poverty threshold. A disproportionate number of people living in deep poverty are young, African American, and Hispanic. We don't have a precise count of the number of infants living in those families, but we know they are there and we know the long-term consequences of poverty on infants' development and health. We also know from public policy research and from the examples of other nations that solutions to the linked problems of infant mortality and deep poverty exist. Enacting them takes political will.[3]

Big government will not save all babies; it has no single set of answers to the question of how to ensure their emotional well-being or protect them against diseases, accidents, and other types of harm. Nurturing babies requires families and communities – a social infrastructure. It also requires a physical infrastructure and economic resources – the foundation upon which communities are built and families are supported.

Baby kissing is a grand historic American tradition, beloved by political candidates and by officeholders as well. It reportedly began with President Andrew Jackson in 1833. In the twenty-first century, baby kissing continues. All too often it masks baby dismissing – having babies' fortunes, their very lives, largely determined by the economic and social status of the families into which they were born rather than reflecting a public as well as a private commitment to their well-being. Baby kissing and baby dismissing are both examples of American exceptionalism and the latter is a blight on our nation.[4]

NOTES

INTRODUCTION

1 I am using the term *modern* to refer to the United States after the late nineteenth and early twentieth centuries' rise of large-scale industries, rapid urbanization, and increasing immigrant and migrant populations. On the larger question of the debate over the existence and meaning of modernity as an intellectual construct, see Bruno Latour, *We Have Never Been Modern* (Harvard University Press, 1993).

2 G. Stanley Hall, *Adolescence: Its Psychology and Its Relations to Physiology, Anthropology, Sociology, Sex, Crime, Religion and Education* (D. Appleton & Company, 1904).

3 On children's agency, see, for example, Daniel Thomas Cook, "Agency, Children's Consumer Culture and the Fetal Subject: Historical Trajectories, Contemporary Connections," *Consumptions, Markets and Culture* 6 (2003): 115–32.

4 The history of children, childhood, and parenting is voluminous. For two recent examples, see Steven Mintz, *Huck's Raft: A History of American Childhood* (Belknap Press of Harvard University, 2004); and Paula S. Fass, *The End of American Childhood: A History of Parenting from Life on the Frontier to the Managed Child* (Princeton University Press, 2016). On parental worries, see Peter N. Stearns, *Anxious Parents: A History of Modern Childrearing in America* (New York University Press, 2003).

5 Frank Hobbs and Nicole Stoops, *Demographic Trends in the 20th Century: Census 2000 Special Reports*, US Bureau of the Census, November 2002, www.census.gov/prod/2002pubs/censr-4.pdf.

6 Frances Brundage, *Our Baby* (Raphael Tuck & Sons, 1914) UCLA HQ 779. B8940 copy 2; and Palache Family Papers, 1839–2004; Jeannette Palache Baby Book, 1900–20, MC 528, Box 10, Folder 16, SLRI.

7 *All about Me: Baby's Record* (Saalfield Publishing Company, 1918) UCLA HQ 779.A416 1918b; and Janet Laura Scott, *Baby's First Five Years* (Whitman Publishing Company, 1941) UCLA HQ 779.S429ba 1941.

8 *Book of Baby Mine* (Baby Mine Company, 1935) UCLA HQ779.B724 1935 copy 18, Decatur, Illinois; and *Book of Baby Mine* (Baby Mine Company, 1940) UCLA HQ779.B724 1940 Copy 65, Augusta, Maine.

1 INFANT LIVES AND DEATHS

1 Jess R. Peterson, *Omaha's Trans-Mississippi Exposition (Images of America)* (Arcadia Publishing Company, 2003); John Wakefield, *A History of the Trans-Mississippi and International Exposition* (1903), www.omaha.lib.ne.us/transmiss/secretary/table .html. See also "A Western Creation: The Trans-Mississippi Exposition at Omaha, Nebraska," *Frank Leslie's Popular Monthly* 46 (1898): 442–46, https://babel .hathitrust.org/cgi/pt?id=inu.32000000494502;view=1up;seq=464; and Robert W. Rydell, "The Trans-Mississippi and International Exposition: 'To Work Out the Problem of Universal Civilization,'" *American Quarterly* 33 (1981): 587–607.

2 "One More Little Injun Boy," *Omaha Daily Bee*, August 9, 1898, http:// chroniclingamerica.loc.gov/lccn/sn99021999/1898-08-09/ed-1/seq-1/#words= Spotted+Little+Back. See also Peter Bolz, "More Questions than Answers: Frank A. Rinehart's Photographs of American Indians," *Native American Studies* 8 (1994): 35–42. For Rinehart's images, see www.omahapubliclibrary.org/trnasmiss/.

3 Mary Alice Harriman, "The Congress of American Aborigines at the Omaha Exposition," *Overland Monthly and Out West Magazine* 33 (1899): 504–12, https://babel.hathitrust.org/cgi/pt?id=iau.31858036877037;view=1up ;seq=521; Russell Thornton, *American Indian Holocaust and Survival: A Population History since 1492* (University of Oklahoma Press, 1987); and Josh Clough, "'Vanishing' Indians? Cultural Persistence on Display at the Omaha World's Fair of 1898," *Great Plains Quarterly* 25 (2005): 67–86.

4 Patrice Kay Beam, "The Last Victorian Fair: The Trans-Mississippi Exposition," *Journal of the West* 33 (1994): 10–23; US Census Bureau, "Table 13. Population of the 100 Largest Urban Places: 1900," www.census.gov/population/www/ documentation/twps0027/tab13.txt; James W. Trent Jr., "Defectives at the World's Fair: Constructing Disability in 1904," *Remedial and Special Education* 19 (1998): 201–11; and Peterson, *Omaha's Trans-Mississippi Exposition*.

5 Jeffrey P. Baker, *The Machine in the Nursery: Incubator Technology and the Origins of Newborn Intensive Care* (Johns Hopkins University Press, 1996); and Susan J. Pearson, "'Infantile Specimens': Showing Babies in Nineteenth-Century America," *Journal of Social History* 42 (2008): 341–70.

6 "Dr. Martin Arthur Couney," Neonatology on the Web, www.neonatology .org/pinups/couney.html; and Baker, *Machine in the Nursery*.

7 Baker, *Machine in the Nursery*; William A. Silverman, "Incubator-Baby Side Shows," *Pediatrics* 64 (1979): 127–41; "From Birth to Death at the

Pan-American Exposition," Neonatology on the Web, http://ublib.buffalo
.edu/libraries/exhibits/panam/hsl/incubators.html; Arthur Brisbane, "The
Incubator Baby and Niagara Falls," *Cosmopolitan* 31 (1901): 509–16; and John
Zahorsky, "The Baby Incubator on the 'Pike'," *St. Louis Courier of Medicine*
31 (1904): 345–58, Neonatology on the Web, www.neonatology.org/classics/
zahorsky/zahorsky1.html.

8 "Panama-Pacific International Exposition, San Francisco, California,"
Neonatology on the Web, www.neonatology.org/pinups/ppie1915.html;
"Incubator Babies at Wonderland Park," *Minneapolis Journal,* May 20, 1905, www
.neonatology.org/classics/wonderland2.html; "Premature Babies at Lake Street
Amusement Park," www.friendsofthecemetery.org/history/alley_articles/
wonderland_babies_july2004.shtml; and Gary R. Brown, "The Coney Island
Baby Laboratory," *American Heritage of Invention and Technology* 10 (1994): 24–31.

9 Edward J. Brown, "A New Baby Incubator," *Medical Record* 41 (1892):
446–47; and John D. Stoeckle and George Abbott White, *Plain Pictures of Plain
Doctoring: Vernacular Expression in New Deal Medicine and Photography* (MIT Press,
1985) pp. 63–64.

10 Judith Walzer Leavitt, *Brought to Bed: Childbearing in America, 1750–1950*
(Oxford University Press, 1988); Charles E. Rosenberg, *The Care of Strangers:
The Rise of America's Hospital System* (Johns Hopkins University Press, 1995);
"Series B. 313–330 Hospitals and Beds, by Type of Hospital: 1909–1953,"
Bicentennial Edition: Historical Statistics of the United States; Colonial Times to 1970,
p. 79, www2.census.gov/library/publications/1975/compendia/hist_stats_
colonial-1970/hist_stats_colonial-1970p1-chB.pdf; and "Historical Notes
on Milk Commission of Chicago and Infant Welfare Society of Chicago,"
Infant Welfare Society of Chicago Records, 1903–76, Box 1, Chicago History
Museum (hereafter CHM).

11 Sydney A. Halpern, *American Pediatrics: The Social Dynamics of Professionalism,
1880–1980* (University of California Press, 1988).

12 Baker, *Machine in the Nursery*; Joseph B. De Lee, "Infant Incubation, with
the Presentation of a New Incubator and a Description of the System at
the Chicago Lying-In Hospital," *Chicago Medical Recorder* 22 (1902): 22–40;
"Watching Premature Babies," (undated typescript) Julius Hays Hess Papers,
1935–55 (hereafter Hess Papers) Crear Ms 51, Box 2, Folders 7, 10, 12, 14,
16, 18, SCRC; and Elizabeth A. Reedy, "From Weakling to Fighter: Changing
the Image of Premature Infants," *Nursing History Review* 11 (2003): 109–27.

13 Leona Baumgartner, "'Incubator Babies' Claiming Special Care of the
City," *New York Times,* January 15, 1939, p. D5; and Katherine Shedd Bradley,
1908–82 Papers, NL; and http://files.library.northwestern.edu/findingaids/
david_bradley.pdf.

14 Ansley J. Coale and Marvin Zelnik, *New Estimates of Fertility and Population in the United States* (Princeton University Press, 1963) p. 22; Frank Hobbs and Nicole Stoops, *Demographic Trends in the 20th Century: Census 2000 Special Reports* (US Bureau of the Census, November 2002), www.census.gov/prod/2002pubs/censr-4.pdf; and Virginia Yans-McLaughlin, *Family and Community: Italian Immigrants in Buffalo, 1880–1930* (Cornell University Press, 1977) p. 106.

15 Samuel H. Preston and Michael R. Haines, *Fatal Years, Child Mortality in Late-Nineteenth Century America* (Princeton University Press, 1991).

16 Henry Horace Hibbs Jr., "The Present Position of Infant Mortality: Its Recent Decline in the United States," *Publications of the American Statistical Association* 14 (1915): 817; and Michael Haines, "Fertility and Mortality in the United States," http://eh.net/encyclopedia/fertility-and-mortality-in-the-united-states/. I am using race as a social not a biological construct; I use the language of racial categorization employed during the period under discussion.

17 Bernadine Courtwright Barr, "Entertaining and Instructing the Public: John Zahorsky's 1904 Incubator Institute," *Social History of Medicine* 8 (1995): 17–36.

18 Brown, "Coney Island Baby Laboratory"; and Elizabeth Walker, "Saving the Babies Who Arrive Too Soon," *Everyweek Magazine, Utica New York Observer*, September 10, 1933, Hess Papers, Box 16 Oversize, SCRC.

19 "Incubator Graduates Hold a Reunion; Forty Healthy Babies Meet at Coney Island, Their Photographs Taken, Greatest Interest in the Triplets – Low Death Rate among the Infants," *New York Times*, August 1, 1904, p. 7.

20 "Infant Incubator Homecoming," typed transcript, Box 3, Hess Papers, SCRC.

21 Ellis Parker Butler, *The Incubator Baby* (Funk & Wagnalls, 1906) p. 6.

22 Laflin Family Papers, 1830–1974, Diaries, Josephine K. Laflin, October 24, 1898, Box 3, CHM; and www.lakeforest.edu/library/archives/indexes/Laflin_biography.php.

23 Jay Ruby, *Secure the Shadow: Death and Photography in America* (MIT Press, 1995); and Josephine Gear, "The Baby's Picture: Woman as Image Maker in Small-Town America," *Feminist Studies* 13 (1987): 419–42.

2 VALUING BABIES

1 Box 276, Case Files, Community Service Society Records, 1842–1995, CUA; and Emily K. Abel, *Hearts of Wisdom: American Women Caring for Kin, 1850–1940* (Harvard University Press, 2000) pp. 150–76.

2 Box 282, Case Files, Community Service Society Records, 1842–1995, CUA.

3 Box 265 and Box 249, Case Files, Community Service Society Records, 1842–1995, CUA.

4 Molly Ladd-Taylor, *Mother-Work: Women, Child Welfare, and the State, 1890–1930* (University of Illinois Press, 1994); Maureen A. Flanagan, *America Reformed: Progressives and Progressivisms, 1890s–1920s* (Oxford University Press, 2007); Jackson Lears, *Rebirth of a Nation: The Making of Modern America, 1870–1920* (Harper, 2009); Meckel, *Save the Babies*; Samuel H. Preston and Michael R. Haines, *Fatal Years: Child Mortality in Late Nineteenth-Century America* (Princeton University Press, 1991); Cynthia A. Connolly, *Saving Sickly Children: The Tuberculosis Preventorium in American Life, 1909–1970* (Rutgers University Press, 2008); Kwang-Sun Lee, "Infant Mortality Decline in the Late 19th and Early 20th Centuries: The Role of Market Milk," *Perspectives in Biology and Medicine* 50 (2007): 585–602; Julie Miller, "To Stop the Slaughter of Babies: Nathan Straus and the Drive for Pasteurized Milk, 1893–1920," *New York History* 74 (1993): 159–84.

5 Molly Ladd-Taylor and Lurie Umansky, "Introduction," *"Bad" Mothers: The Politics of Blame in Twentieth-Century America* (New York University Press, 1998) pp. 1–28; and James Marten, "'No Beer for Babies': The Child Welfare Exhibit," *Chicago History* 33 (2005): 36–51.

6 Seth Koven and Sonya Michel, eds. *Mothers of a New World: Maternalist Politics and the Origins of the Welfare State* (Routledge, 1993); Ronald D. Cohen, "Child-Saving and Progressivism, 1885–1915," in Joseph M. Hawes and N. Ray Hiner, eds. *American Childhood: A Research Guide and Historical Handbook* (Greenwood Press, 1985) pp. 274–309; and Hamilton Cravens, "Child-Saving in the Age of Professionalism, 1915–1930," in Hawes and Hiner, *American Childhood*, pp. 415–88.

7 Constance Kirby, "Bargains in Babies," *Harper's Bazaar* 46 (June 1912): 46.

8 Viviana A. Zelizer, *Pricing the Priceless Child: The Changing Social Value of Children* (Princeton University Press, 1994).

9 Robert D. Plotnick et al., "The Twentieth-Century Record of Inequality and Poverty in the United States," in Stanley L. Engerman and Robert E. Gallman, eds. *Cambridge Economic History of the United States*. Cambridge Histories online, http://dx.doi.org/10.1017/CHOL9780521553087.005; Richard A. Meckel, *Save the Babies: American Public Health Reform and the Prevention of Infant Mortality, 1850–1929* (Johns Hopkins University Press, 1990); and Jeffrey P. Brosco, "The Early History of the Infant Mortality Rate in America: A Reflection upon the Past and a Prophecy of the Future," *Pediatrics* 103 (1999): 478–85.

10 "Will Sell One Baby to Save the Others: Husband Going Blind and Mrs. Monteque Fears Starvation for the Whole Family," *New York Times*, April 15, 1911 p. 20; and "Baby Not for Sale, Luck's Turned: Monteque Family to Stay

United Thanks to Kind-Hearted Times Readers," *New York Times*, April 16, 1911, p. 7.

11 Audrey B. Davis, "With Love and Money: Visiting Nurses in Buffalo, New York, 1885–1915," *New York History* 71 (1990): 45–67; and Robert Coit Chapin, *The Standard of Living among Workingmen's Families in New York City* (Russell Sage Foundation, 1909).

12 Jacob A. Riis, *How the Other Half Lives: Studies among the Tenements of New York* (1890 [reprint, Penguin, 1997]) pp. 166–67; "56 Infants Die in Seven Days," *Washington Post*, July 12, 1906, p. 2; and "Combats Infant Mortality," *Washington Post*, July 3, 1908, p. 14; Chicago, *Report of the Department of Health of the City of Chicago for the Years 1907, 1908, 1909, 1910* (Chicago, 1911) p. 117, cited in Paul A. Buelow, *Health and Illness in Chicago's River Wards and the Near West Neighborhood*, http://tigger.uic.edu/depts/hist/hull-maxwell/vicinity/nws1/intimate/essays/healthandillness.pdf; Rochester, NY Health Bureau, "How to Take Care of Babies during Hot Weather," 190? Box 640, Item 37829, NYAM; Rose A. Cheney, "Seasonal Aspects of Infant and Child Mortality: Philadelphia, 1865–1920," *Journal of Interdisciplinary History* 14 (1984): 561–85; and Thomas Neville Bonner, *Medicine in Chicago, 1850–1950*, 2nd edn. (University of Illinois Press, 1991) p. 99.

13 Jacqueline H. Wolf, *Don't Kill Your Baby: Public Health and the Decline of Breastfeeding in the 19th and 20th Centuries* (Ohio State University Press, 2001).

14 Meckel, *Save the Babies*.

15 Table Aa145-184 Population by Sex and Race, 1790–1990; and Table Aa1896-1921-Foreign-Born Population by Sex and Race: 1850–1990, *Historical Statistics of the United States, Millennial Edition Online*, http://hsus.cambridge.org.proxy.libraries.rutgers.edu/HSUSWeb/search/searchTable.do?id=Aa145-184; http://hsus.cambridge.org.proxy.libraries.rutgers.edu/HSUSWeb/search/searchTable.do?id=Aa1896-1921.

16 Geoffrey Warner, "Black Infant Health: Where to in the 21st Century?" *Review of Black Political Economy* 26 (1999): 29–54; and Table Ab912-927 – Fetal Death Ratio, Neonatal Mortality Rate, Infant Mortality Rate, and Maternal Mortality Rate, by Race: 1850–1998, *Historical Statistics of the United States, Millennial Edition Online*; Preston and Haines, *Fatal Years*; and Meckel, *Save the Babies*.

17 Marilyn Irvin Holt, *Linoleum, Better Babies and the Modern Farm Woman, 1890–1930* (University of New Mexico Press, 1995); and John Spargo, *The Bitter Cry of Children*, reprint edn. (Quadrangle Books, 1968) p. 40.

18 S. Josephine Baker, *Fighting for Life* (Macmillan, 1939).

19 "Find Abandoned Baby," *Evening Times-Republican*, August 8, 1916, http://chroniclingamerica.loc.gov/lccn/sn85049554/1916-08-08/ed-1/seg-9/; "Baby Is Left on Priest's Doorstep," *The Mitchell Capital*, August 22, 1912,

http://chroniclingamerica.loc.gov/lccn/sn2001063112/1912-08-22/ed-1/ seg-9; and "In the News and out of the Ordinary," *Alma Record*, October 29, 1914, http://chroniclingamerica.loc.gov/lccn/sn850338709/1914-10-29/ ed-1/seg-3/.

20 Amos G. Warner, *American Charities*, rev. edn. (New York, 1908) p. 267; "Death Rate 96 Per Cent," *New York Times*, December 29, 1897, p. 5; Elna C. Green, "Infanticide and Infant Abandonment in the New South: Richmond, Virginia, 1865–1915," *Journal of Family History* 24 (1999): 187–211; and Julie Miller, *Abandoned: Foundlings in Nineteenth-Century New York City* (New York University Press, 2008).

21 George Walker, *The Traffic in Babies: An Analysis of the Conditions Discovered during an Investigation Conducted in the Year 1914* (Norman Remington Company, 1918).

22 Russell Sage Foundation, "A Concrete Suggestion on the Care of Babies" (Russell Sage Foundation, ca. 1905) Box 652, Item 45206, NYAM; Lillian D. Wald, "Boarded-Out Babies," New York Association of Neighborhood Workers of the City of New York, 1907, Box 63, Item 89102, NYAM; and Zelizer, *Pricing the Priceless Child*, pp. 169–207.

23 "Johnson Jury Out; Fate of Alleged Baby Farmer Is Still Undecided," *Minneapolis Journal*, November 1, 1905, p. 6, http://chroniclingamerica .loc.gov/lccn/sn83045366/1905-11-01/ed-1/seg-7/; and "Light Sentence for Baby Farmer," *Pensacola Journal*, December 22, 1906, p. 1; http:// chroniclingamerica.loc.gov/lccn/sn87062268/1906-12-22/ed-1/seg-1/.

24 Arthur Alden Guild, *Baby Farms in Chicago: An Investigation Made for the Juvenile Protection Association, 1917* (Chicago, 1918); and Sherri Broder, *Tramps, Unfit Mothers, and Neglected Children: Negotiating the Family in Late Nineteenth Century Philadelphia* (University of Pennsylvania, 2002) pp. 157–200.

25 Linda Gordon, *Heroes of Their Own Lives: The Politics and History of Family Violence*, (Viking, 1988) pp. 43–45; and Edward MacGaffey, "A Pattern for Progress: The Minnesota Children's Code," *Minnesota History* 41 (1969): 234–36.

26 Walker, *Traffic in Babies*; and Guild, *Baby Farms*, p. 24.

27 Elizabeth Rose, *A Mother's Job: The History of Day Care, 1890–1960* (Oxford University Press, 1999); and Susan Porter Benson, *Household Accounts: Working-Class Family Economics in the Interwar United States* (Cornell University Press, 2007).

28 Anne Durst "'Of Women, By Women, and for Women': The Day Nursery Movement in the Progressive-Era United States," *Journal of Social History* 39 (2005): 141–59; and US Dept. of Labor, Women's Bureau, *Womanpower Committees during World War II: United States and British Experience*, Bull. No. 244 (GPO, 1953) p. 31.

29 Jane Addams, *Twenty Years at Hull House: With Autobiographical Notes* (Macmillan, 1912) p. 169; Deborah A. Skok, *More Than Neighbors: Catholic Settlements and Day Nurseries in Chicago, 1893–1930* (Northern Illinois University Press, 2007) pp. 149, 151; DePaul Settlement and Day Nursery, Folder 10, Welfare Council of Metropolitan Chicago Records, 1914–78, CHM; Bertha Payne Newell, "Social Work of Women's Organizations in the Churches: Methodist Episcopal Church South," *Journal of Social Forces* 1 (1923): 310–14; Emily D. Cahan, *Past Caring: A History of U.S. Preschool Care and Education for the Poor, 1820–1965* (National Center for Children in Poverty, 1989); Sonya Michel, *Children's Interests/Mothers' Rights: The Shaping of America's Child Care Policy* (Yale University Press, 1999); Rose, *A Mother's Job*; and Gwendolyn Salisbury Hughes, *Mothers in Industry: Wage-Earning Mothers in Philadelphia* (New Republic Incorporated, 1925) p. 197.

30 "Report of Study of the Chicago Nursery and Half Orphan Asylum Made for the Council of Social Agencies of Chicago," Box 19, Welfare Council of Metropolitan Chicago Records, 1914–78, CHM.

3 HELPING CITIZEN BABY

1 Letter to and from Mrs. Lyle S. Davis, May 1932, Box 381, Folder 4-8-1-2-1, USCB Central File, 1929–32 RG 102, NARA II.

2 Gretchen A. Condran and Samuel H. Preston, "Child Mortality Differences, Personal Health Care Practices, and Medical Technology: The United States, 1900–1939," in Lincoln C. Chen, Arthur Kleinman, and Norma C. Ware, eds. *Health and Social Change in International Perspective* (Harvard School of Public Health, 1994) pp. 171–224.

3 Letter from S. J. Crumbine (undated), Mabel Alice Taylor Collection, B. IX, f. Letters, KCK; "Mothers' Baby Books: Instruction for Mothers in the Care of Infants," *Public Health Reports* 29 (1914): 677; and Dorothy E. Bradbury and Martha M. Eliot, *Four Decades of Action for Children: A Short History of the Children's Bureau* (GPO, 1956).

4 Rima D. Apple, *Perfect Motherhood: Science and Childrearing in America* (Rutgers University Press, 2006).

5 Annette K. Vance Dorey, *Better Baby Contests: The Scientific Quest for Perfect Childhood in the Early Twentieth Century* (McFarland & Company, 1999); and Better Babies Bureau, Women's Home Companion, "Hints to Mothers Who Want Better Babies" (Better Babies Bureau, 191?) Box 783, Item 127992, NYAM.

6 Marilyn Irvin Holt, "Children's Health and the Campaign for Better Babies," *Kansas History: A Journal of the Central Plains* 28 (2005): 174–87; Mary A.

Whedon, "What They Mean to Women: Today State Fairs Are Milestones of Rural Progress," *The Farmer's Wife* 18 (1915); A. M. Stern, "Beauty Is Not Always Better: Perfect Babies and the Tyranny of Paediatric Norms," *Patterns of Prejudice* 36 (2010): 68–78; http://dx.doi.org/10.1080/00313220218811367; Martin S. Pernick, "Taking Better Baby Contests Seriously," *American Journal of Public Health* 92 (2002): 707–08; and Anna Steese Richardson, "The Better Babies Bureau and What It Is Doing for American Babies," *Women's Home Companion* 40 (1913): 22, 29.

7 *Baby Days* (Reilly & Britton, 1908) UCLA HQ779.B1157 1908b; and *Biography of a Better Baby* (Commercial Milling Company, not after 1927) UCLA HQ779. B11245 1927.

8 Steven Seldin, "Transforming Better Babies into Fitter Families: Archival Resources and the History of the Eugenics Movement, 1908–1930," *Proceedings of the American Philosophical Society* 149 (2005): 199–225; Erica Bicchieri Boudreau, "'Yea, I Have a Goodly Heritage': Health versus Heredity in the Fitter Family Contests, 1920–1928," *Journal of Family History* 30 (2005): 366–87; and Laura L. Lovett, "Fitter Families for Future Firesides: Florence Sherborn and Popular Eugenics," *Public Historian* 29 (2007): 69–85.

9 Martin S. Pernick, *The Black Stork: Eugenics and the Death of "Defective" Babies in American Medicine and Motion Pictures since 1915* (Oxford University Press, 1996).

10 Lawrence L. Foley and Chas. D. McMillin, *Log-o'-Life: A Monument to the Faithful Co-operative Spirit and Parental Interest of Our Father and Mothers*, rev. edn. (McMillin-Foley Publishing Company, 1946) UCLA HQ779.L831 1946.

11 Nannie Helen Burroughs Papers, 1900–63, Box 62, Folder 4, LOC; and Video, Office for Emergency Management, Office of War Information, Overseas Operations Branch, "Allied Patrols in Action on Anzio Beach, [etc.] 1944 National Archives Catalog," http://research.archives.gov/description/39009.

12 Henry H. Hibb Jr., *Infant Mortality: Its Relation to Social and Industrial Conditions* (Russell Sage Foundation 1916); and Theda Skocpol, *Protecting Soldiers and Mothers: The Political Origins of Social Policy in the United States* (Harvard University Press, 1992).

13 Paul A. Lombardo, *A Century of Eugenics in America: From the Indiana Experiment to the Human Genome Era* (Indiana University Press, 2011); Martin S. Pernick, "Eugenics and Public Health in American History," *American Journal of Public Health* 87 (1997): 1767–72; and Clinch Calkins, *Some Folks Won't Work* (Harcourt, Brace & Company, 1930) p. 28.

14 Illinois State Board of Health, "Our Babies: How to Keep Them Well and Happy, a Booklet for Mothers" (1916) p. 6. Box 445, Item 115604, NYAM.

15 Kriste Lindenmeyer, *A Right to Childhood: The U.S. Children's Bureau and Child Welfare, 1912–1946* (University of Illinois Press, 1997); and Skocpol, *Protecting Soldiers and Mothers*, pp. 480–524.

16 Anna Louise Strong, "Child-Welfare Exhibits, Types and Preparations," US Dept. of Labor, Children's Bureau (GPO, 1915) p. 9.

17 *Baby's Record: Interesting Happenings during the "Baby Age" of ...* (1929) UCLA HQ779.B12 1929; "Children's Year Working Program," Children's Year Leaflet No. 3. US Dept. of Labor, Children's Bureau (GPO, 1918) p. 9.

18 Cressy L. Wilbur, "Some of the Measures Most Urgently Needed for the Prevention of Infant Mortality in the United States," in *American Association for Study and Prevention of Infant Mortality, Transactions of the Third Annual Meeting 1912* (Franklin Printing, 1913) p. 27; US Children's Bureau, *Birth Registration: An Aid in Protecting the Lives and Rights of Children* (GPO, 1914); and S. Shapiro, "Development of Birth Registration and Birth Statistics in the United States," *Population Studies* 4 (1950): 86–111.

19 "Save 100,000 Babies; Get a Square Deal for Children," Children's Year Leaflet No. 1 Prepared in Collaboration with the Department of Child Welfare of the Woman's Committee Council of National Defense (GPO, 1918); "Save the Baby; Hope of the Nation! Slogan Sounded," *Chicago Tribune*, May 29, 1918, p. 1; and Richard A. Meckel, *Save the Babies: American Public Health Reform and the Prevention of Infant Mortality, 1850–1929* (Johns Hopkins University Press, 1990).

20 Meckel, *Save the Babies*; "Summary of Report of Infant Welfare Society of Chicago for the Years 1921 and 1926," Box 78, Welfare Council of Metropolitan Chicago Records, CHM; Samuel J. Crumbine, *Frontier Doctor* (Dorrance Company, 1948) p. 212; Edmond Souchon, "Original Contributions of Louisiana to Medical Science," *Publications of the Louisiana Historical Society*, vol. 8 (Louisiana Historical Society, 1916) p. 82; and Jennifer Lisa Koslow, *Cultivating Health: Los Angeles Women and Public Health Reform* (Rutgers University Press, 2009).

21 *Children's Year: A Brief Summary of Work Done and Suggestions for Follow-up Work*, US Dept. of Labor (GPO, 1920).

22 Meckel, *Save the Babies;* Lindenmeyer, *A Right to Childhood*; Skocpol, *Protecting Soldiers and Mothers*; Molly Ladd-Taylor, *Mother-Work: Women, Child Welfare, and the State, 1890–1930* (University of Illinois Press, 1994); Kriste Lindenmeyer, "Saving Mothers and Babies: The Sheppard-Towner Act in Ohio, 1921–1929," *Ohio History* 99 (1990): 105–34; Carolyn M. Moehling and Melissa A. Thomasson, "Saving Babies: The Contribution of Sheppard-Towner to the Decline in Infant Mortality in the 1920s," NBER Working Papers Series Working Paper 17996, National Bureau of Economic Research, April, 2012,

www.nber.org/papers/w17996; and Gunnar Almgren, Susan P. Kemp, and Alison Eisinger, "The Legacy of Hull House and the Children's Bureau in the American Mortality Transition," *Social Service Review* 74 (2000): 1–27.

23 Ray Lyman Wilbur, "A Survey and a Challenge," *White House Conference 1930: Addresses and Abstracts of Committee Reports* (Century, 1931) pp. 16, 25.

24 Box 127, Folder 11,410, USCB Central File, 1914–20, RG 102, NARA II.

25 Emma Duke, *Infant Mortality: The Results of a Field Study in Johnstown, Pa., Based on Births in One Calendar Year* (GPO, 1915).

26 US Children's Bureau, *Infant Mortality, Montclair, N.J.: A Study of Infant Mortality in a Suburban Community* (GPO, 1915); and "Memorandum to Miss Lathrop," Box 125, Folder 11,100, USCB Central File, 1914–20, RG 102, NARA II.

27 Glenn Steele, "Maternity and Infant Care in a Mountain County in Georgia," US Children's Bureau Publication No. 120 (GPO, 1923) p. 24.

28 Films are on the website https://cb100.acf.hhs.gov/videos.

29 Anna Rochester, *Infant Mortality: Results of a Field Study in Baltimore, MD. Based on Births in One Year*, US Children's Bureau Publication No. 119 (GPO, 1923) p. 33; and J. H. Mason Knox Jr. and Paul Zentai, "The Health Problem of the Negro Child," *American Journal of Public Health* 16 (1926): 805–09.

30 "The Fourth Annual Conference of the National Association for the Advancement of Colored People," *The Crisis* 4 (1912): 80; Mary B. Talbert, "Women and Colored Women," *The Crisis* 10 (1915): 184; and "National Urban League," *The Crisis* 23 (1921): 85. For the letters exchanged between Terrell and the Coolidge administration, see Letters to and from Mary Church Terrell, 1924–25, Calvin Coolidge Papers, LOC, http://memory.loc .gov/cgi-bin/query/r?ammem/cool:@field(NUMBER+@band(mc22)).

31 Elizabeth C. Tandy, *Infant and Maternal Mortality among Negroes*, US Children's Bureau Publication No. 243 (GPO, 1937) 3, 24; Keith Wailoo, *Dying in the City of the Blues: Sickle Cell Anemia and the Politics of Race and Health* (University of North Carolina Press, 2001) pp. 69–83.

32 Sandra Crouse Quinn and Stephen B. Thomas, "The National Negro Health Week 1915 to 1951: A Descriptive Account," *Minority Health Today* 2 (2001): 44–49; "National Negro Health Week," *Public Health Reports* 36 (1921): 559–61; and Roscoe C. Brown, "The National Negro Health Week Movement," *Journal of Negro Education* 18 (1949): 377–87.

33 Susan L. Smith, *Sick and Tired of Being Sick and Tired: Black Women's Health Activism in America, 1890–1950* (University of Pennsylvania Press, 1995); Darlene Clark Hine, "The Ethel Johns Report: Black Women in Nursing, 1925," *Journal of Negro History* 67 (1982): 212–28; Thomas J. Ward Jr., *Black Physicians in the Jim Crow South* (University of Arkansas Press, 2010); and

Vanessa Northington Gamble, *Making a Place for Ourselves: The Black Hospital Movement, 1920–1945* (Oxford University Press, 1995).

34 Second Report on Child Welfare Conditions in Cumberland County, North Carolina, Box 31 Folder 4-11-2-7, USCB Central File, 1914–20, RG 102, NARA II; and Memorandum of Fourth Month's Work in Cumberland County, North Carolina, Box 31, Folder 4-11-2-7, USCB Central File 1914–20, RG 102, NARA II.

35 US Children's Bureau, *The Story of Infant* Care (GPO, 1965) p. 1; and "Care of the Baby," Supplement No. 10, *Public Health Reports*, December 13, 1913 (GPO, 1914), www.hrsa.gov/ourstories/mchb75th/mchbcaringinfants.pdf.

36 Nancy Pottisham Weiss, "Mother, the Invention of Necessity: Dr. Benjamin Spock's Baby and Child Care," *American Quarterly* 29 (Winter 1977): 519–46; Mrs. Oswald Stein, *A Baby's Day* (Lake View Press, 1917) p. 7.

37 Rima D. Apple, *Perfect Motherhood: Science and Childrearing in America* (Rutgers University Press, 2006); US Children's Bureau, Chart No. 14 (revised February 1930), "First Four Months, Baby's Daily Time Card" (GPO, 1930); and E. P. Thompson, "Time, Work-Discipline, and Industrial Capitalism," *Past and Present* 38 (1967): 56–97.

38 Jacquelyn Litt, "Mothering, Medicalization, and Jewish Identity, 1928–1940," *Gender and Society* 10 (1996): 190; and Jacquelyn Litt, "American Medicine and Divided Motherhood: Three Case Studies from the 1930s and 1940s," *Sociological Quarterly* 38 (1997): 293.

39 USDA Radio Service, "Housekeepers' Chat: Why Fruit Juice for the Baby," June 19, 1935; https://archive.org/details/whyfruitjuicefor1935unit; USDA Radio Service, "Housekeepers' Chat: Taking Baby to the Country," May 28, 1930, https://archive.org/stream/takingbabytocoun1930unit#page/n1/mode/2up; USDA Radio Service, "Housekeepers' Chat: The Well-Behaved Baby," February 26, 1930, https://archive.org/details/wellbehavedbaby1930unit; USDA Radio Service, "Housekeepers' Chat: A Sunshine Package for the New Baby," November 19, 1930, https://archive.org/details/CAT31163398_0; and Susan Smulyan, "Radio Advertising to Women in Twenties America: 'A Latchkey to Every Home,'" *Historical Journal of Film, Radio & Television* 13 (1993): 299–314.

40 David Goodman, *Radio's Civic Ambition: American Broadcasting and Democracy in the 1930s* (Oxford University Press, 2011); Daniel J. Czitrom, *Media and the American Mind: From Morse to McLuhan* (University of North Carolina Press, 1982); and Elizabeth A. Toon, "Managing the Conduct of Individual Life: Public Health Education and American Public Health, 1910 to 1940" (PhD dissertation, University of Pennsylvania, 1988).

41 White House Conference on Child Health and Protection, *The Young Child in the Home: A Survey of Three Thousand American Families: Report of the Committee on the Infant and Preschool Child* (Appleton-Century, 1936).

42 Eva Lucile Bascom and Dorothy Reed Mendenhall, "Child Welfare: Selected List of Books and Pamphlets, comp. by Elva L. Bascom … and Dorothy Reed Mendenhall … Publ. By the Council on Health and Public Instruction of the American Medical Association" (AMA, 1918), Box 110 Item 75028, NYAM; and Chicago Department of Health, "What Must We Do to Be Saved …" Chicago: The Department, ca. 1920 Box 264 Item 114205, NYAM.

43 Jacqueline H. Wolf, *Don't Kill Your Baby: The Decline of Breast Feeding in the 19th and 20th Centuries* (Ohio State University Press, 2001) and Rima D. Apple, *Mothers and Medicine: A Social History of Infant Feeding, 1890–1950* (University of Wisconsin Press, 1987).

44 Molly-Ladd Taylor, *Raising a Baby the Government Way: Mothers' Letters to the Children's Bureau 1915–1932* (Rutgers University Press, 1986).

45 Letter from Mrs. Ernest Curit, 1937, Box 756, Folder 4-8-4-1-0, USCB, Central File, 1937–40, RG 102, NARA II; Letter from Mrs. Emalen Steward, August, 1937, Box 756, Folder 4-8-4-1-0, USCB Central File, 1937–40, RG 102, NARA II; Letter from Pauline Mozzar to Eleanor Roosevelt, May, 1942, Box 109, Folder 4-9-1-1, USCB Central File, 1941–44, RG 102, NARA II; and Letter to the Children's Bureau, October 22, 1941, Box 109, Folder 4-9-1-1, USCB Central File 1941–44, RG 102, NARA II.

46 Gallup Poll (AIPO) June 1937. Retrieved May 16, 2014 from the iPoll Databank, Roper Center for Public Opinion Research, University of Connecticut. www.ropercenter.uconn.edu.prox.libraries.rutgers.edu/data-access/ipoll/ipoll.html.

4 BRINGING UP BABIES I

1 Bigger and Scholotte baby books in author's possession; and Annie F. Cox, *Baby's Kingdom* (Lea and Shopard, 1891) UCLA HQ779.c887b 1891.

2 A. O. Kaplan, *Baby's Biography* (Brentano's, 1891) UCLA, HQ779.K14b 1891 copy 2; and A. O. Kaplan, *Baby's Biography* (Brentano's, 1891) UCLA HQ77. K14b 1891 copy 6.

3 Susan Strasser, *Satisfaction Guaranteed: The Making of the American Mass Market* (Pantheon, 1989); Peter N. Stearns, "Stages of Consumerism: Recent Work on the Issues of Periodization," *Journal of Modern History* 69 (1997): 102–17; and Gary Cross, *An All-Consuming Century: Why Commercialism Won in America* (Columbia University Press, 2000).

4 Martha L. Olney, *Buy Now, Pay Later: Advertising, Credit, and Consumer Durables in the 1920s* (University of North Carolina Press, 1991); and Penne Rested, "The Third Sex: Historians, Consumer Society, and the Idea of the American Consumer," *Journal of Social History* 47 (2014): 769–86.

5 Jessica Helfand, *Scrapbooks: An American History* (Yale University Press, 2008); and Ellen Gruber Garvey, *Writing with Scissors: American Scrapbooks from the Civil War to the Harlem Renaissance* (Oxford University Press, 2013).

6 Strasser, *Satisfaction Guaranteed*, pp. 102–05; C. H. Claudy, *The Kodak Baby Book* (Eastman Kodak Company, ca. 1908) UCLA TR146.C615k 1908; *Our Baby* (S.l., not after 1918) UCLA HQ779.O9211 1918; *Our Baby's Book* (Geo. W. Parker Art Company, 1915) UCLA HQ779.O9222 1915; and Evelynn von Hartmann, *Baby's Life* (Barse & Hopkins, 1913) UCLA HQ 779.H333b 1913 copy 4.

7 Maud Humphrey, *Baby's Record* (Frederick A. Stokes Company, 1898); *The Babyhood Journal: A Record of Baby's Doings from the Day of Its Birth* (Contemporary Publishing Company, ca. 1899) UCLA HQ779.B11384 1899 copy 1l; and Frances Brundage and May Sandheim, *Our Baby* (Raphael Tuck & Sons, 1914) UCLA HQ779.B894o 1914. See also Shawn Michelle Smith, *American Archives: Gender, Race and Class in Visual Culture* (Princeton University Press, 1999).

8 *Baby* (Reilly & Lee, 1914) UCLA HQ779 B112 1914; US Census Bureau, Statistical Abstract of the United States, 1999, Table 1439, "Transportation Indicators for Motor Vehicles and Airlines: 1900 to 1998," www.census.gov/prod/99pubs/99statab/sec31.pdf; Evelyn von Hartman, *Baby's Life* (New York, 1913) UCLA HQ779.H333b 1913 copy 2; Paul F. Brissenden, "Earnings of Factory Workers, 1899–1927," Census Monograph X, Bureau of the Census (GPO, 1929), Part IV Table B, "Number of Average Wage Earners ..." p. 383.

9 Nancy Tomes, *The Gospel of Germs: Men, Women, and the Microbe in American Life* (Harvard University Press, 1989); Nancy J. Tomes, "Merchants of Health: Medicine and Consumer Culture in the United States, 1900–1940," *Journal of American History* 88 (2001): 519–47; *Coke Dandruff Cure and Hair Tonic Baby Book* (Kaufmann & Straus, ca. 1903) UCLA HQ779.C682 1903; *A Record of Our Baby's Life* (Record Publishing Company, 1913) UCLA HQ779.R313 1913; Carl J. Ward, *The Baby* (Published By the Progressive Merchants Whose Announcements Appear on the Following Pages, 1915) UCLA HQ779.B1122 1915; Alice L. Muncaster, Ellen Sawyer, and Ken Kapson, *The Baby Made Me Buy It! A Treasury of Babies Who Sold Yesterday's Products* (Crown Publishers, 1991); Daniel Delis Hill, *Advertising to the American Woman 1900–1999* (Ohio State University Press, 2002); and "Castle Hall Twins Cigars," Duke University Libraries Digital Collections, http://library.duke.edu/digitalcollections/eaa_D0293/#info.

10 Baby books for Catherine Ellen Frost, Ms. Coll. No 501.030, UCLA; and *Baby's Health: A Practical Handbook for the Young Mother* (Merval Corporation, ca. 1916) UCLA HQ779.B1158 1916b.

11 William E. Harris, "Baby Record Books," *Publishers Weekly* 119 (April 11, 1931): 1916–18.

12 Amelia Earhart Papers, 1835–1977, Baby Book, Series II, SLRI; *Baby record of …* (not after 1925) UCLA HQ 779.B1139 1925 copy 2; Arthur Laurents Papers, 1900–2011, Box 128, Folder 6, Music Division, LOC.

13 Maud Humphrey, *Baby's Record* (Frederick L. Stokes Company, ca. 1898) UCLA HQ779.H926b 1898 copy 3; L. Emmett Holt Patient Records, Box 1, Folder 3, CHSL; Kathleen W. Jones, "Sentiment and Science: The Late Nineteenth Century Pediatrician as Mother's Advisor," *Journal of Social History* 17 (1983): 79–86; Sterling Morton Papers, 1891–1961, Letters, Box 1 and Box 2, CHM; and *Cute Things the Baby Says* (S.l.: s.n. not after 1913) UCLA HQ 779.C988 1919.

14 *The Best Baby* (Compliments of the Borden Company, ca. 1918) UCLA HQ779.B561 1918, copy 2.

15 Lawrence Clark Powell Papers (Collection 229) Household Account Book, Box 13, Folder 1, CYUCLA.

16 Stuart Chase, "A Budget for Three," *Good Housekeeping* 62 (1916): 124–26; Voluntary Parenthood League (NY), "Babies and the High Cost of Living: What Is to Be Done about It?" Box 759 Item 77404, NYAM.

17 US Dept. of Labor, *100 Years of U.S. Consumer Spending, Data for the Nation, New York City, and Boston* (May 2006), www.bls.gov/opub/uscs/; Frank Stricker, "Affluence for Whom? Another Look at Prosperity and the Working Classes in the 1920s," *Labor History* 24 (1983): 5–33; William Leach, *Land of Desire: Merchants, Power, and the Rise of a New American Culture* (Pantheon, 1992) pp. 85–90; Clair Brown, *American Standards of Living* (Blackwell, 1994) p. 139; and Cross, *An All-Consuming Century*, pp. 17–23.

18 Natalie Kneeland, *Infants' and Children's Wear* (A. W. Shaw Company, 1925) p. 93; Daniel Thomas Cook, "Agency, Children's Consumer Culture and the Fetal Subject: Historical Trajectories, Contemporary Connections," *Consumption, Markets & Culture* 6 (2003): 115–32; Daniel Thomas Cook, *The Commodification of Childhood: The Children's Clothing Industry and the Rise of the Child Consumer* (Duke University Press, 2004).

19 Albertine Randall Wheelan, *Mother Stork's Baby Book* (Dodge Publishing Company, 1904) UCLA HQ779.W561m 1904; Nelson Dickerman Papers, 1880–1965, Baby book of Delight Dickerman, NMAH; *Little Baby's Big Day* (S.l., ca. 1916?) UCLA HQ779 L777 1916; *Babyhood* (S.l., ca. 1911) UCLA HQ779 B1138 1911; *Baby* (Reilly & Lee Company, 1914) UCLA HQ779.B112 1914b; and Gary Cross, *Kids' Stuff: Toys and the Changing World of American Childhood* (Harvard University Press, 1997).

20 Jessie Wilcox Smith, *Baby's Red Letter Days* (Just's Food Company, 1901) CCLP; *Our Baby's Own Book* (John Carle and Sons, 1914) CCLP; and *How to Care for Baby: Dedicated to the Mothers of America* (Smith, Kline and French, 1907) UCLA WS 113.S642h 1907.

21 Helen Woodward, *Through Many Windows* (Harper & Brothers, 1926) p. 204; Roland Marchand, *Advertising the American Dream: Making Way for Modernity, 1920–1940* (University of California Press, 1986).

22 *Our Baby's Book* (Osborn Company, ca. 1908) UCLA HQ779.0922 1908; and *Our Baby's Book* (Osborn Company, ca. 1938) UCLA HQ779.0922 1938.

23 Melcena Burns Denny, *Book of Baby Mine* (Baby Mine Company, 1915) UCLA HQ779.B724 1915b copy 14; and Melcena Burns Denny, *Book of Baby Mine* (Baby Mine Company, 1930) in author's possession.

24 Melcena Burns Denny, *Book of Baby Mine* (Book of Baby Mine Company, 1915) UCLA HQ779.B724 1915f; and Melcena Burns Denny, *Book of Baby Mine* (Book of Baby Mine Company, 1935) in author's possession.

25 Merode pamphlet is in *Baby's First Book of Jingles* (S.l.; 1925) CCL; *Life*, February 27, 1939, p. 42; and Tomes, *Gospel of Germs*.

26 *My Diary* (Gerlach-Barklow Company, ca. 1936) UCLA HQ779.M995; *My Baby's Book* (Brown & Bigelow, not after 1939) UCLA HQ779.M9945 1939; and US Children's Bureau, *Infant Care*, 2nd edn. (GPO, 1921).

27 George Bryan Pitts II Baby Book; Box 1, Folder 21, Lee-Morgan-Pitts Family Papers, 1798–1955, LOV; Jo B. Paoletti, "Clothing and Gender in America: Children's Fashions, 1890–1920," *Signs* 12 (1987): 136–43; and Richard S. Tedlow, *New and Improved: The Story of Mass Marketing in America* (Basic Books, 1990).

28 *Our Baby's Book* (Osborne Company, 1925) UCLA HQ779.0922 1925; Letter to Miss Reno, June 9, 1941, USCB Central File 1939–44, RG 102, Folder 4-8-4-1-0, NARA II; Edna Mason Kaula, *All His Life* (Richard Krueger, ca. 1944) UCLA HQ779.K21a 1944; Edna Mason Kaula, *All Her Life* (Richard Krueger, ca. 1944) UCLA HQ779.K21ha 1944; Baby Book of Linda Jane Laubenstein, v. 3, Linda J. Laubenstein Papers, 1947–93, SLRI; Elizabeth B. Hurlock, *Baby's Early Years* (C. R. Gibson & Company, 1952) UCLA HQ779.H965b 1952; Hochschild, Kohn & Co. Department Store for Babies (Hochschild, Kohn & Co., 1951) Ms. Coll. No 502.011 BIOUCLA; Jo B. Paoletti, *Pink and Blue: Telling Boys from Girls in America* (Indiana University Press, 2012).

29 [The County Health Nurse] Folklife Project, Life Histories, 1936–39, LOC, www.loc.gov/item/wpalh002096/; [Mrs. Nannie Carson] Folklife Project, Life Histories, 1936–39, LOC, www.loc.gov/item/wpalh001898/; [In-Laws and T.B.'s] Folklife Project, Life Histories, 1936–39, LOC, www.loc.gov/item/wpalh002074/.

30 *1897 Sears Roebuck & Co. Catalog* (facsimile edition) (Chelsea House, 1993); Sears, Roebuck & Co., *The Baby Book* (Sears, Roebuck & Co., ca. 1914) Ms. Coll. No 502.010 UCLA; and Sears, Roebuck & Co., *Catalog, Fall–Winter*,

1936–1937, Hathi Trust Digital Library, http://catalog.hathitrust.org/Record/001738159.

31 Cheryl Lemus, "Save Your Baby, Save Ten Percent: National Baby Week, the Infants' Department, and the Modern Pregnant Woman, 1905–1925," *Journal of Women's History* 25 (2013): 165–87; and Jan Whitaker, *Service and Style: How the American Department Store Fashioned the Middle Class* (St. Martin's Press, 2006) pp. 245–53.

32 "His Majesty, the Baby, Rules Chicago," *Chicago Tribune*, April 19, 1914; U.S.C.B. *Baby-Week Campaigns*, rev edn. (GPO, 1917); and Letter from Mrs. J. S. Levin, March, 1929, Box 381 Folder 4-8-1-2, USCB Central File 1929–32, RG 102, NARA II.

33 Letter to Janette Townsend, Executive Secretary, Infant Welfare Society, January 31, 1933, CHM; and Letter to Dr. Edwin Dailey, US Children's Bureau, from Mrs. Hermien D. Nusbaum, May 18, 1936, Box 756 Folder 4-8-4-1-0, USCB Central File 1937–44, RG 102, NARA II.

34 Box 29, file "Macy's Infant's and Children's Department," file, "Macy's Scrapbook," and Box OV6, file "Advertising, Macy's Infants and Children's Departments, 1930–32 and undated," Margaret Fishback Papers, 1863–1978 and undated, bulk 1920–73, HART.

35 Benjamin J. Klebaner, *American Commercial Banking: A History* (Twayne, 1990) pp. 102, 132; and Jesse Stiller, "The Thrift Movement in America, 1909–1920," *Financial History* 90 (2008): 28–31.

36 Joshua J. Yates and James Davison Hunter, "Introduction: The Question of Thrift," in Joshua J. Yates and James Davison Hunter, eds., *Thrift and Thriving in America: Capitalism and Moral Order from the Puritans to the Present* (Oxford University Press, 2011) pp. 3–33; *Our Baby's Book* (Osborne Company, 1925) UCLA HQ779.O922 1925; *Baby's Own Book* (S.l., 1940) UCLA HQ779.D1184 1940b; *Your Friend the Merchant* (S.l., not before 1917) UCLA HQ779.Y82 1917b, Donald Goodall Papers 1938–42, Box 1, AAA; Corinne Wogener and Karal Ann Marling, *Money in the Bank: The Katherine Kierland Herberger Collection* (University of Minnesota Press, 2006).

37 Claudia Goldin and Lawrence F. Katz, "Human Capital and Social Capital: The Rise of Secondary Schooling in America, 1910–1940, *Journal of Interdisciplinary History* 29 (1999): 683–723; *Baby's Bank and Record Book* (Banker's Thrift Book Company, ca. 1926) UCLA HQ779.B114 1926; and *Baby's Savings Book* (Farmers and Mechanics' Savings Bank, not before 1933) Ms. Coll. No 502.003 UCLA.

38 Melcena Burns Denny, *Book of Baby Mine* (Simplicity Company, 1915) HQ779.B724 1915b; and Melcena Burns Denny, *Book of Baby Mine* (Simplicity Company, 1915) HQ779.B724 1915b copy 10.

39 Viviana A. Zelizer, "The Price and Value of Children: The Case of Children's Insurance," *American Journal of Sociology* 86 (1981): 1036–56; Viviana Zelizer, *Pricing the Priceless Child: The Changing Social Value of Children* (Princeton University Press, 1985); and *Baby: A Budding Life* (Shield Man of the National Life and Insurance Company, not after 1937) UCLA HQ779.B1123 1937.

40 Lila Houghteling, *The Income and Standard of Living of Unskilled Laborers in Chicago* (University of Chicago Press, 1927); Robert Coit Chapin, *The Standard of Living among Workingmen's Families in New York City* (Russell Sage Foundation, 1909) pp. 191–94; Lizabeth Cohen, *Making a New Deal: Industrial Workers in Chicago, 1919–1939* (Cambridge University Press, 2008); Prudential Life Insurance Company of America, "The Baby, Useful Information as to Its Care and Feeding and Training" (Prudential Life Insurance Company, ca. 1934) Box 621 Item 115234, NYAM; *Our Baby's Souvenir Book* (Western & Southern Life Insurance Company, not before 1908) UCLA HQ779.O96 1908; *Our Baby* (Rio Grande Life Insurance Company, not after 1941); and *Baby Days* (Equitable Life Insurance Company, ca. 1920) UCLA HQ779B.113 1920.

41 Melcena Burns Denny, *Book of Baby Mine* (Simplicity Company, 1915) UCLA HQ779.B724 1915b copy 7; and Mary V. Dempsey, *Infant Mortality: Results of a Field Study in Brockton, Mass. Based on Births in One Year* (GPO, 1919) p. 27.

42 *Baby's Health and Record* (Merval Corporation, ca. 1923) UCLA HQ779.B116 1923.

43 Industrial Research Department, Wharton School of Finance and Commerce, University of Pennsylvania, *Research Studies XII*, Case Studies of Unemployment Compiled by the Unemployment Committee of the National Federation of Settlements (University of Pennsylvania Press, 1931) pp. 70, 137–8; [Mother Heart] American Life Histories: Manuscripts from the Federal Writers' Project, 1936–40, LOC, www.loc.gov/item/wpalh002177/; *Such as Us: Southern Voices of the Thirties*, Tom E. Terrill and Jerrold Hirsch, eds. (W.W. Norton & Company, 1979) p. 252.

44 Christine Frederick, *Selling Mrs. Consumer* (Business Bourse, 1929) pp. 18, 104.

45 *My Diary* (Gerlach-Barklow Company, 1936) UCLA HQ779.M995 1936; *Babyhood* (S.l., not after 1911) UCLA HQ 779.B1138 1911; Hermien D. Nusbaum, *Our Baby's First Seven Years* (Mother's Aid of the Chicago Lying-In Hospital, 1928) UCLA HQ779.O928 1928b; Lawrence L. Foley, *Log-o'-Life: A Monument to the Faithful Co-operative Spirit and Parental Interest of Our Mothers and Fathers Book* (McMillan-Foley Publishing Company, 1933) UCLA HQ779.L831 1933; *Our Baby's Own Book* (John Carle & Sons, 1914) UCLA HQ779.O93 1914b copy 2; *Nursery Log* (Lutheran Brotherhood, ca. 1920) UCLA HQ779.N974 1920; Theresa Howland Shute, *A Book for the Cradle-Roll Baby*

(Abington-Cokesbury Press, 1920) UCLA HQ779.S562b 1929; Janet Robson, *A Catholic Baby's Record* (Catholic Manufacturing Company, 1945) HQ779. R667c 1945; Sadie Rose Weilerstein, *Our Baby: A Record Book for the Jewish Child Covering the First Five Years* (National Women's League of the United Synagogue of America, 1950) UCLA HQ779.W422o 1964.

46 Fanny Y. Cory, *Our Baby Book* (Bobbs-Merrill Company, 1907) UCLA HQ779. C8330 1907; *All about Me: Baby's Record* (Sig. Schwartz Company, ca. 1918) UCLA HQ779.A416 1918b; Thresa Shute Howlad, *A Book for the Cradle Roll Baby* (Abington-Cokesbury Press, 1929) UCLA HQ779.S562b 1929; *Our Dear Baby: A Record for Mothers to Keep* (S.l., not after 1928) UCLA HQ779.O965 1928; and Figure Bg-D. Church and congregation membership as a percentage of population: 1890–1989; *Historical Statistics of the United States,* http://hsus .cambridge.org.proxy.libraries.rutgers.edu/HSUSWeb/essay/ showessayimage.do?imgId=Bg.ESS.01-Img-R,&essayId=Bg.ESS.01&imgIdx=0.

47 Karal Ann Marling, *Merry Christmas!: Celebrating America's Greatest Holiday* (Harvard University Press, 2000); Leigh Eric Schmidt, *Consumer Rites: The Buying and Selling of American Holidays* (Princeton University Press, 1995); and Mabel Betsy Hill, *Our Baby* (Richard G. Krueger, not after 1927) UCLA HQ779.H645o 1927.

48 Margaret Ann Meta Morris Grimball, *Baby* (S.l., ca. 1915) UCLA HQ779. G861b 1915; and Baby Book, 1914, Folder 1, Box 1, Catherine Nicholson Papers, 1897–2005, DURL.

5 BRINGING UP BABIES II

1 Diary, 1896–1902, Folder, G6545, Goodrich Family Papers, SLRI; Louis Starr, *Hygiene of the Nursery* (Blakiston, 1888); Letter from Mabel Hubbard Bell to Alexander Graham Bell, September 2, 1906, Alexander Graham Bell Family Papers, 1834–1074, LOC, www.loc.gov/resource/magbell.042; Letter from Katherine Kerr Moore to May Walden, October 5, 1917, Box 2, May Walden Papers, Correspondence 1884–1957, NLC.

2 Alisa Klaus, *Every Child a Lion: The Origins of Infant and Health Policy in the United States and France, 1890–1920* (Cornell University Press, 1993); J. B. Fonssagrives, *The Mother's Register: Current Notes of the Health of Children (Boys)* (Nation Press, John Ross & Company, 1872) UCLA HQ 779.F676m 1872; Catherine Rollet, "History of the Health Notebook in France: A Stake for Mothers, Doctors, and State," *Dynamis* 23 (2003): 143–66; Ralph Oakley Clock, *Our Baby* (D. Appleton & Company, 1912) 94–95.

3 Baby Book of James Harper Jr., Box 5 Folder 5 Series III; James Harper Family Papers, 1800–1925, CUA; Dorothy Kirchwey Brown papers, Carton 4, Folder

92 and Folder 72, and Carton 5, Folder 95, SLRI; and Edith Lowe, *Story of Our Baby* (Edith Kovar, 1929) UCLA HQ779.L913s.

4 Frances M. Wold, ed. "The Letters of Effie Hansen, 1917–1923: Farm Life in Troubled Times," *North Dakota History* 48 (1981): 20–43.

5 Children's Bureau, "April and May Weighing and Measuring Test, Part I, Suggestions to Local Committees" (GPO, 1918); Elizabeth Robinson Scovil, *How to Bring Up a Baby: A Handbook for Mothers* (Proctor & Gamble Company, 1906) UCLA HQ779.432h 1906; Lawrence T. Weaver, "In the Balance: Weighing Babies and the Birth of the Infant Welfare Clinic," *Bulletin of the History of Medicine* 84 (2010): 30–57; Jeffrey P. Brosco, "Weight Charts and Well Child Care: When the Pediatrician Became the Expert in Child Health," in Alexandra Minna Stern and Howard Markel, eds. *Formative Years: Children's Health in the United States, 1880–2000* (University of Michigan Press, 2002) pp. 91–120; *Mother and Baby* (Stanley Parker Publishing Company, ca. 1928) p. 29; and Box 29, Macy's Scrapbooks, 1929–1930, *Margaret Fishback Papers, 1863–1978 and undated, bulk 1920–1973*, HART.

6 *Our Baby Book* (Gerlach-Barklow Company, not after 1932) UCLA HQ779.09225 1932; Judith Walzer Leavitt, *Brought to Bed: Childbearing in America 1750 to 1950* (Oxford University Press, 1986) p. 269; and Mother's Aid of the Chicago Lying-In Hospital, *Our Baby's First Seven Years: A Baby Record Book Including Scientific Charts Which Will Prove of Practical Service to the Mother and Growing Child* (University of Chicago, 1928).

7 *Congratulations: A Magazine for Mothers*, 1 (1937) UCLA HQ 779.c7492; and *A Record of Baby's First Two Years* (Libby, McNeil & Libby, not before 1936) UCLA HQ779.R3105 1936.

8 Edith Truman Woolf, *Little Baby's Big Days* (C.R. Gibson, ca. 1916) UCLA HQ779 W913L 1916b copy 2; Thomas E. Cone Jr., *History of American Pediatrics* (Little, Brown, & Company, 1979) p. 220; *Baby's Health: A Practical Handbook for the Young Mother*, 6th edn. (Merval Corporation, ca. 1916) UCLA HQ779 B1158 1916; and Maida Herman Solomon, Oral Memoir, vol. I, William E. Weiner Oral History, Library of the American Jewish Committee, SLRI.

9 *Baby's Health*; and *American Baby Book: Health Record* (Public Health Service, 1921) UCLA HQ779 A512 1921.

10 *Baby's Book* (Metropolitan Life Insurance Company, 1900), MLIC; Elizabeth A. Toon, "Managing the Conduct of Individual Life: Public Health Education and American Public Health, 1910–1940" (PhD dissertation, University of Pennsylvania, 1998); Diane Hamilton, "The Cost of Caring: The Metropolitan Life Insurance Company's Visiting Nurse Service, 1909–1953," *Bulletin of the History of Medicine* 63 (1989): 414–34; *Case Studies of the Unemployed*, Case

78 p. 204; and Herman N. Bundesen, *Our Babies* (Prudential Life Insurance Company, 1928).

11 Rima D. Apple, *Mothers and Medicine: A Social History of Infant Feeding, 1890–1950* (University of Wisconsin Press, 1987); Harvey Levenstein, " 'Best for Babies' or 'Preventable Infanticide'? The Controversy over Artificial Feeding of Infants in America, 1880–1920," *Journal of American History* 70 (1983): 75–94; and *Care of the Mother and Baby's Welfare: Proper Care and Feeding* (Borden Company, 1929) UCLA WS 113 C183 1929.

12 *Our Baby's Book* (New York, 1914) UCLA HQ779.W8720 1914.

13 Nettie Johnson Story, Field Nurse Monthly Report, Indian Field Service, Department of the Interior, September, 1932, RG 75, NARA; and Ida L. Moore [A Day at Mary Rumbley's House, October 31, 1938] Folder 674, Federal Writers Project Papers, #3709, http://dc.lib.unc.edu/cdm/ref/collection/03709/id/593.

14 Letter from Mrs. Parks, March 3, 1916, Box 27, folder 4-4-3-2-1, USCB Central File, RG 102, NARA II; Letter to Mrs. Fred Maas, March 1939, Box 755, Folder 4-8-1-1, USCB Central File 1937–1940, RG 102, NARA II; Letter to Mrs. Helen J. Leone, November 15, 1938, Box 755, Folder 4-8-1-0, USCB Central File 1937–1940, RG 102, NARA II; Amy Lathrop, "Pioneer Remedies from Kansas," *Western Folklore* 20 (1961): 4; and Vance Randolph, *Ozark Superstitions* [reprint] (Columbia University Press, 1947) p. 210.

15 Lulu Hunt Peters, *Diet for Children (and Adults) and the Kalorie Kids* (Dodd, Mead & Company, 1924) pp. 86–102; and Amy Bentley, *Inventing Baby Food: Taste, Health, and the Industrialization of the American Diet* (University of California Press, 2014).

16 Meta Morris Grimball, *Baby's Year Book: Golden Days in a Baby's Life to Be Remembered* (S.I., not after 1921) UCLA HQ779.G861byb 1921; Archibald B. Roosevelt Family Papers, 1906–1978, Theodore Roosevelt Collection, HI HU; and Richard Osborn Cummings, *The American and His Food: A History of Food Habits in the United States* (University of Chicago Press, 1940).

17 Mrs. Max West, *Infant Care* (GPO, 1914) p. 49; and Letter to Mrs. E. M. Leomig, November 24, 1914, Box 26, Folder 4-4-4-1-3, USCB Central File 1914–1920, RG 102, NARA II.

18 Randolph, *Ozark Superstitions*, p. 210.

19 Wisconsin State Board of Health, "Save Your Baby," Madison Wisc. State Board of Health, n.d. Box 780, Item 114304, NYAM; and H. L. K. Shaw, "How to Save the Babies – It Is Not the Babies Born but the Babies Saved that Count, Suggestions to Mothers from the New York State Department of Health, Eugene H. Porter, Commissioner," in Appendix, US Children's Bureau, *Baby-Saving Campaigns* (GPO, 1914) p. 52; Edith Truman Woolf, *Little*

Baby's Big Days (C.R. Gibson & Company, 1916) UCLA HQ779 W913L 1916b copy 1; Francis Sage Bradley and Margaretta A. Williamson, *Rural Children in Selected Counties of North Carolina*, Rural Child Welfare Series No. 2 (GPO, 1919) pp. 39, 75; and Katherine Leonard Turner, *How the Other Half Ate: A History of Working Class Meals at the Turn of the Century* (University of California Press, 2014).

20 Emma B. Miles, *The Spirit of the Mountains* (James Pott & Company 1905) p. 23; Michael M. Davis Jr., *Immigrant Health in the Community*, reprint, originally published 1921 (Patterson Smith, 1971) p. 249; and Robert Morse Woodbury, *Causal Factors in Infant Mortality: A Statistical Study Based on Investigations in Eight Cities*, US Children's Bureau Publication No. 142 (GPO, 1925) p. 1.

21 Emma Duke, *Results of a Field Study in Johnstown, PA. Based on Births in One Calendar Year*, US Children's Bureau, Infant Mortality Series No. 3 (GPO, 1915) p. 81; Dominic A. Pacyga, *Polish Immigrants and Industrial Chicago: Workers on the South Side, 1880–1922* (Ohio State University Press, 1991) p. 74; Helen M. Dart, *Maternity and Child Care in Selected Rural Areas of Mississippi*, Rural Child Welfare Series No. 5, Bureau Publication No. 88 (GPO, 1921) p. 43; and Glenn Steele, *Maternity and Infant Care in a Mountain County in Georgia*, Bureau Publication No. 120 (1923) pp. 25–27.

22 Jessica Helfand, *Scrapbooks: An American History* (Yale University Press, 2008) p. 135; and *Our Baby: A Record* (John Wanamaker, 1916) UCLA HQ 779.09215 1916.

23 Elizabeth Robinson Scovil, *How to Bring Up a Baby: A Handbook for Mothers* (Proctor and Gamble, 1906) UCLA HQ 779 S432h 1906; and "The baby the stork left 'four flights up,'" *American Journal of Nursing* (1929), http://library.duke.edu/digitalcollections/adaccess_BH0804/.

24 Cary Eggleston, "Simple Appliance for Training Infants to Stool," *JAMA* 70 (1918): 156; Historical Census of Housing Tables, US Census Bureau, www.census.gov/hhes/www/housing/census/historic/sewage.html; and *My Baby's Book* (Brown & Bigelow, 1939) UCLA HQ779.M9945 1939.

25 Louise Zabriskie, *Mother and Baby Care in Pictures*, 2nd edn. (J.B. Lippincott, 1941); and *Army GI, Pacifist CO: The World War II Letters of Frank Dietrich and Albert Dietrich*, Scott H. Bennett, ed. (Fordham University Press, 2005).

26 Alfred F. Hess, "Newer Aspects of Some Nutritional Disorders," *JAMA* 76 (1921): 693–700; Martha May Eliot, "The Control of Rickets," *JAMA* 85 (1926): 565–63. See also "Martha May Eliot," *MMWR* 48 (1999): 851; www.cdc.gov/mmwr/preview/mmwrhtml/mm4838a2bx1.htm; Martha M. Eliot, "The Effect of Tropical Sunlight on the Development of Bones in Children in Puerto Rico," US Children's Bureau Publication No. 217 (GPO, 1933); and Martha M. Eliot, "A Demonstration of the Community Control of

Rickets," Proceedings of the Third Annual Conference of State Directors in Charge of the Local Administration of the Maternity and Infancy Act, Bureau Publication No. 157 (GPO, 1926) pp. 72–79.

27 US Children's Bureau, *Infant Care* (GPO, 1929) p. 78; and "Sunlight for Babies," US Children's Bureau, Folder No. 5, 1931.

28 "Diary by a Mother for a Baby Boy in Colorado, 1930–1931," UCLA Ms. Coll. 501.017; Ruth A. Guy, "The History of Cod Liver Oil as a Remedy," *Am J. Dis. Ch.* 26 (1923): 112–16; and Kumaravel Rajakumar, "Vitamin D, Cod-Liver Oil, Sunlight, and Rickets: A Historical Perspective," *Pediatrics* 112 (2003): e132–35, http://pediatrics.aappublications.org/content/112/2/e132.full.

29 Rima D. Apple, *Vitamania: Vitamins in American Culture* (Rutgers University Press, 1996) p. 27. Reports of Bureau of Indian Affairs nurses distributing cod liver oil can be found in Records of the Bureau of Indian Affairs, Records of the Health Division, 75.14.4 NARA I.

30 "Interview with Mrs. B. March 16, 1939," American Life Histories: Manuscripts from the Federal Writer's Project, 1936–40, American Memory Collection, LOC, www.loc.gov/item/wpalh000301/; "Interview with C. M. Deal, Jr., September 1, 1939," American Life Histories: Manuscripts from the Federal Writer's Project 1936–40, American Memory Collection, LOC, www.loc.gov/item/wpalh001785/; and "Interview with Irene Jackson," 1939, American Life Histories, Folklore Project Life Histories, 1936–39, LOC, www.loc.gov/item/wpalh000372/.

31 Metropolitan Life Insurance Company, "Sunlight the Health Giver," 1928 Box 52, Welfare Division Pamphlets, MLIC; Clair Morton, *The Perfect Baby* (Vanguard Press, 1929); "Keeping the Well Baby Well," US Children's Bureau, Folder No. 9 (revised) (GPO, 1928); "Sunlight for Babies," US Children's Bureau, Folder No. 5, 1931; Lauren Piro, "The Intriguing History of 1930s Baby Cages," *Good Housekeeping*, www.goodhousekeeping.com/life/news/a33058/hanging-baby-cages/.

32 Letter to Katherine Lenroot, August 15, 1938, Box 750 Folder 4-8-1-3-2; USCB Central File 1937–40 RG 102 NARA II; Letter to Mrs. C. Lekowski, August 17, 1938, Box 756 Folder 4-8-1-3-2; USCB Central File 1937–40, RG 102, NARA II; and on sunlamps, cod liver oil, and requests for endorsements, see Box 271, folders 4-5-3-2, and 4-5-8-2-5 to 4-6-3-3, USCB Central File 1925–28, RG 102 NARA II.

33 Robert S. Lynd and Helen Merrell Lynd, *Middletown: A Study in American Culture* (Harcourt, Brace & World, Inc., 1929) pp. 437–41; Robert S. Lynd and Helen Merrell Lynd, *Middletown in Transition: A Study in Cultural Conflicts* (Harcourt, Brace & World, 1937) pp. 393, 398.

34 James West, *Plainville, U.S.A.* (Columbia University Press, 1945); and Art Gallaher Jr., *Plainville Fifteen Years Later* (Columbia University Press, 1961).

35 West, *Plainville, U.S.A.*, pp. 171–76.

36 Gallaher Jr., *Plainville Fifteen Years Later*, pp. 118–21, 146–47.

6 HELPING BABY CITIZENS

1 Harry Middleton Hyatt, *Folk-Lore from Adams County Illinois*, 2nd edn. rev. (Memoirs of the Alma Egan Hyatt Foundation, 1965) pp. 218–19; Vance Randolph, *Ozark Superstitions, reprint edn.* (Dover Publications, 1964) pp. 97–98; and [Mrs. Mac Mabe] Folklore Project Life Histories, 1936–39, US Works Project Administration, Federal Writers Project, LOC, www.loc.gov/item/wpalh001750/ (accessed June 15, 2015).

2 Margaret Jarman Hagood, *Mothers of the South: Portraiture of White Tenant Farm Women*, new edn. (University of Virginia Press, 1996) pp. 128–29.

3 Viola I. Paradise, *Maternity Care and the Welfare of Young Children in a Homesteading County in Montana*, Rural Child Welfare Series No. 3, US Children's Bureau Publication No. 34 (GPO, 1919) p. 73.

4 Alice Goldstein, Susan Cotts Watkins, and Ann Rosen Spector, "Childhood Health-Care Practices among Italians and Jews in the United States, 1910–1940," *Health Transitions Review* 4 (1994): 45–61.

5 Jan Harold Brunvand, *The Study of American Folklore*, 4th edn. (W.W. Norton & Company, 1989); see, for example, Alan Dundes, *The Meaning of Folklore: The Analytical Essays of Alan Dundes*, Simon J. Bronner, ed. (Utah State University Press, 2007).

6 James Harvey Young, *The Toadstool Millionaires: A Social History of Patent Medicines in America before Federal Regulation* (Princeton University Press, 1961); James Harvey Young, *The Medical Messiahs: A Social History of Health Quackery in Twentieth-Century America* (Princeton University Press, 1967).

7 Letter from Mrs. C. L. Boehme, July 7, 1917; Letter to Mrs. C. L. Boehme, July 11, 1917; Letter from Mrs. Charles A. Hill, April 1, 1916; Letter to Mrs. Charles A. Hill, May 6, 1916, USCB Central File 1914–20, RG 102, Box 26, NARA II; Anderson Aldrich and Mary M. Aldrich, *Babies Are Human Beings: An Interpretation of Growth* (Macmillan Company, 1938) p. 85.

8 James Harvey Young, "'Even to a Suckling Infant': Nostrums and Children," *Transactions and Studies of the College of Physicians of Philadelphia* Ser. 5 1 (1979): 5–32.

9 American Medical Association, *Nostrums and Quackery: Articles on the Nostrum Evil and Quackery Reprinted* (American Medical Association, 1912); and Glenn Steele, "Maternity and Infant Care in a Mountain County in Georgia," US Children's Bureau Publication No. 120 (GPO, 1923) pp. 35–37.

10 "How to Organize a Better Babies Health Exhibit" (Crowell Publishing Company, 1914) comp. by the Better Babies Bureau, *Woman's Home Companion*, p. 6. Box 783, Item 116557, NYAM; "Soothing Syrup Kills Twins," *New York Times*, April 2, 1908, p. 1.

11 Chicago Department of Health, "What Must We Do to Be Saved: The Slaughter of Little Babies in the City of Chicago Amounts to 6000 Yearly, at Least 3500 of these Deaths are Avoidable, Education for Prevention" (Chicago Department of Health, 1920) p. 8, Box 264, Item 114205, NYAM; and *Growing Up* (White Publishing Company, between 1923 and 1930) UCLA HQ779.G884 1923.

12 Elmer L. Smith and John Stewart, "The Mill as a Preventive and Cure of Whooping Cough," *Journal of American Folklore* 77 (1964): 76–77; Thomas E. Cone Jr., *History of American Pediatrics* (Little Brown & Company, 1979) p. 175; T. J. Farr, "Tennessee Folk Beliefs Concerning Children," *Journal of American Folklore* 52 (1939): 115; Wayland D. Hand, ed. *North Carolina Folklore* vol. 6 (Duke University Press, 1961) p. 67; and Jeffrey P. Baker, "Immunization and the American Way: 4 Childhood Vaccines," *American Journal of Public Health* 90 (2000): 201–02.

13 Anthony Cavender, *Folk Medicine in Southern Appalachia* (University of North Carolina Press, 2003) p. 135. See, for example, Walter Williamson, *Diseases of Females and Children and Their Homeopathic Treatment...* (Rademacher and Sheek, 1854) pp. 206–07; J. H. Pulte, *Homeopathic Domestic Physician: Containing the Treatment of Diseases...* (W. B. Smith & Company, 1863) p. 358; Willis P. King, *Stories of a Country Doctor* (Hummel & Parmele, 1891) pp. 137–38; Vance Randolph, *Ozark Superstitions* (Columbia University Press, 1947) p. 119; Edwin Miller Fogel, *Beliefs and Superstitions of the Pennsylvania Germans* (American Germanica Press, 1915) p. 227; Steele, "Maternity and Infant Care in a Mountain County in Georgia," p. 40.

14 Amy Lathrop, "Pioneer Remedies from Western Kansas," *Kansas Folklore* 30 (1961): 1–22.

15 King, *Stories*, pp. 150, 153; Leonard Keene Hirshberg, "How Village Mothers and Babies May Be Saved," *The Farmer's Wife* 16 (June 1913): p. 16.

16 Susan Smith, *Sick and Tired of Being Sick and Tired: Black Women's Health Activism in America, 1890–1950* (University of Pennsylvania Press, 1995); Karen Kruse Thomas, "'Law unto Themselves': Black Women as Patients and Practitioners in North Carolina's Campaign to Reduce Maternal and Infant Mortality, 1935–1953," *Nursing History Review* 12 (2004): 47–66; Susan Smith, *Japanese American Midwives: Culture, Community and Health Politics, 1880–1950* (University of Illinois Press, 2005); Eugene R. Declercq, "The Nature and Style of Practice of Immigrant Midwives in Early Twentieth

Century Massachusetts," *Journal of Social History* 19 (1985): 113–29; Charlotte Borst, *Catching Babies: The Professionalization of Childbirth 1880–1920* (Harvard University Press, 1995); Lyle Saunders, *Cultural Difference and Medical Care: The Case of the Spanish-Speaking People of the Southwest* (Russell Sage Foundation, 1954) pp. 201–02; Judith Walzer Leavitt, *Brought to Bed: Childbirth in America, 1750 to 1950* (Oxford University Press, 1968) p. 267.

17 Molly Ladd-Taylor, " 'Grannies' and 'Spinsters': Midwife Education under the Sheppard-Towner Act," *Journal of Social History* 22 (1988): 255–75; Margaret Charles Smith and Linda Janet Holmes, *Listen to Me Good: The Life Story of an Alabama Midwife* (Ohio State University Press, 1996) p. 42; Frances Sage Bradley and Margaretta A. Williamson, *Rural Children in Selected Counties of North Carolina*, Rural Child Welfare Series No. 2; US Children's Bureau Publication No. 33 (GPO, 1918) pp. 40–41, 78–79.

18 Office of Indian Affairs, "Indian Babies: How to Keep Them Well" (GPO, 1916); Bureau of Indian Affairs, RG 75, Field Nurse Monthly Report, Elko, Nevada, July 1932, NARA; Bureau of Indian Affairs, RG 75, Field Nurse Monthly Report, Warm Springs, Oregon, September 1931, NARA; Bureau of Indian Affairs, RG 75, Red Lake Reservation, Minnesota, November 1932, NARA; Jeffrey Allen Smith, "Indian Children and Nurses: Native American Health and Field Nurses in Southern California, 1928–1948," *Native Studies Review* 15 (2004): 21–35; Emily K. Abel, *Hearths of Wisdom: American Women Caring for Kin, 1850–1940* (Harvard University Press, 2000) pp. 192–99.

19 Hazel A. Hendricks, *Survey of Health and Social Needs of Indian Children*, US Children's Bureau (GPO, 1937) p. 8.

20 R. Kuar, B. Bharti, and S. K. Saini, "A Randomized Controlled Trial of Burping for the Prevention of Colic and Regurgitation in Healthy Infants," *Child Care, Health & Development* 41 (2015): 52–56.

21 Ruth Williams Thompson, *Training My Babies* (Richard G. Badger Publishing, 1929).

22 I. A. Newby, *Plain Folk in the New South: Social Change and Cultural Persistence, 1880–1915*, reprint (Louisiana State University Press, 1989) pp. 298–99; Hagood, *Mothers of the South*, p. 139.

23 T. J. Farr, "Tennessee Folk Beliefs Concerning Children," *Journal of American Folklore* 52 (1939): 113; *The Frank C. Brown Collection of North Carolina Folklore*, Wayland D. Hand, ed., vol. 6 (Duke University Press, 1961) p. 49; Ralph Oakley Clock, *Our Baby* (D. Appleton & Company, 1912) pp. 126–28.

24 Letter from Mrs. Elmer Caldwell, October 1915; US Children's Bureau, Central File, 1914–20, RG 102, Box 26, Folder 4-4-4-1-3, NARA II; Samuel J. Crumbine, *Frontier Doctor* (Dorrance Company, 1948) p. 61; Diary by a mother for a baby boy in Colorado, 1930–31, UCLA Ms. Coll. No. 501.017.

25 Young, *The Toadstool Millionaires*, pp. 183–84; *Fletcher's Castoria Baby Book* (Centaur Company, not after 1924) UCLA HQ779.F612 1924; and *Teethina Baby Book* (C. J. Moffett Company, 1912) UCLA WS 113.T258 1912b.

26 Henry Wilkins, *The Family Adviser: Greatly Enlarged and Amended...* (B. Waugh and T. Mason, 1833) p. 452; Letter from Mrs. Diana Lemery, April 11, 1930 RG 102 US Children's Bureau 1929–32, Box 382, Folder 4-8-5, NARA.

27 Malvin E. Ring, "Is 'Teething' a Disease? Mixed Feelings of 130 Years Ago," *Bulletin of the History of Dentistry* 42 (1944): 43–44; L. Emmet Holt, *The Care and Feeding of Children: A Catechism for the Use of Mothers and Nurses* (D. Appleton and Company, 1894) p. 38; Baby Book of Ruth Norton Cleaveland, UCLA, Ms. Coll. 501.024; and *Our Baby* (s.n., not after 1919) UCLA HQ779. O9211 1919.

28 Children's Bureau, *Infant Care* (GPO, 1914) p. 54; Interview with John Belks and Martha Payne, 1938, Federal Writers' Project, Life Histories: Manuscripts from the Federal Writers' Project, 1936 to 1940," American Memory Collection, www.loc.gov/resource/wpalh2.28100116/#seq-6; Children's Bureau, *Infant Care* (GPO, 1929) p. 36.

29 Hilda Roberts, "Louisiana Superstitions," *Journal of American Folklore* 40 (1927): 151; T. J. Farr, "Riddles and Superstitions of Middle Tennessee," *Journal of American Folklore* 48 (1935): 327; Austin E. Fife, "Pioneer Mormon Remedies," *Western Folklore* 16 (1957): 156; Edwin Miller Fogel, *Beliefs and Superstitions of the Pennsylvania Germans* (American Germanica Press, 1915) pp. 310, 315; King, *Stories of a Country Doctor*, p. 142.

30 A. W. Long "Mountain Town," p. 9; Folklore Project, Life Histories, 1936–39 Federal Writers' Project; www.loc.gov/item/wpalh001811; Letter from Mrs. Henry A. Braswell, August 5, 1919; Letter to Mrs. Henry A. Braswell, August 8, 1919, USCB Central File 1914–20, RG 102, Box 27, 1914–20, Folder 4-4-4-3-3, NARA II.

31 I. S. Falk, "Fundamental Facts on the Costs of Medical Care," *Milbank Memorial Fund Quarterly Bulletin* 11 (1933): 142–43; I. S. Falk, C. Rufus Rorem, and Martha D. Ring, *The Costs of Medical Care: A Summary of Investigations on the Economic Aspects of the Prevention and Care of Illness*, reprint edn. (Arno Press and the *New York Times*, 1972) pp. 29, 61, 288.

32 Helen M. Dart, *Maternity and Child Care in Selected Rural Areas of Mississippi*, Rural Child Welfare Series No. 5, US Children's Bureau Publication No. 88 (GPO, 1921) p. 43.

33 Brian Gratton and Myron P. Gutmann, "Hispanics in the United States, 1850–1900," *Historical Methods* 33 (2000): 137–53; Arthur J. Rubel, *Across the Tracks, Mexican-Americans in a Texas City* (University of Texas Press, 1966) pp. 163, 222.

34 Lyle Saunders, *Cultural Difference and Medical Care* (Russell Sage Foundation, 1954).

35 Margaret Clark, *Health in the Mexican American Culture* (University of California Press, 1959) pp. 162–217; Josephine Elizabeth Baca, "Some Health Beliefs of the Spanish Speaking," *American Journal of Nursing* 69 (1969): 2172–76. Other studies that make the same points include Lorraine V. Klerman, Jane G. Jones, and Mona C. Hull, "Puerto Ricans in a Small U.S. City," *Public Health Reports* 81 (1966): 369–76; Isham B. Jones, *The Puerto Rican in New Jersey: His Present Status* (New Jersey State Department of Education, 1965) pp. 26–27.

36 Cervando Martinez and Harry W. Martin, "Folk Diseases among Urban Mexican-Americans," *JAMA* 196 (1966): 147–50.

7 THE INNER LIVES OF BABIES

1 Maternity Center Association, Folder 7, Box 19, and "A Report of 'The First Year of Life,' an Exhibit at the New York World's Fair, 1939, Sponsored by the Maternity Center Association, Karo, Gerber Products Company," and Maternity Center Association, Box 94, CUHSL; "Man and His Health: A Guide to Medical and Public Health Exhibits at the New York World's Fair, 1939, Together with Information on the Conservation of Health and the Preservation of Life" (Expositions Publications Inc., 1939); Folders 24 and 25, Box 565 and Box 885, and Folders 1 and 17, Box 890, New York World's Fair 1939 and 1940 Incorporated Records, 1935–45, MANYPL; and "'Babies' Race' Ends in Recriminations," *New York Times*, July 22, 1940, p. 15.

2 A. J. Liebling, "A Patron of the Preemies," *New Yorker*, June 3, 1939, pp. 20–24.

3 Meyer Berger, "At the Fair," *New York Times*, June 5, 1940, p. 31; Folders 1, 2, 3, Box 547, and Folder 10, Box 688, New York World's Fair 1939 and 1940 Incorporated Records, 1935–45, MANYPL; William A. Sliverman, "Incubator-Baby Side Shows," *Pediatrics* 64 (1979): 127–41, www.neonatology.org/ classics/silverman/silverman1.html; http://www.neonatology.org/.

4 "Dionne Quintuplets," www.thecanadianencyclopedia.ca/en/article/dionne-quintuplets/; Advertisement, *Women's Home Companion*, 1937, http://library .duke.edu/digitalcollections/adaccess_BH1265/; Allan Roy Dafoe, *Through Baby's First Years* (Brown & Bigelow, 1934) UCLA HQ779.D124b 1934; "This Week Magazine," *Chicago Daily News* December 27, 1947, pp. 4–5; Jean Komaiko, "Her Baby Was Premature," *Chicago Tribune Magazine*, September 5, 1954.

5 Martin Couney Folder, 1939–40, Box 21, Arnold Gesell Papers, Manuscript Division, LOC; Silverman, "Incubator Baby Side-Shows," David Hoogland Noon, "The Evolution of Beasts and Babies: Recapitulation, Instinct, and the Early Discourse on Child Development," *Journal of the History of the*

Behavioral Sciences 41 (2005): 367–86; Milton J. E. Senn et al., "Insights on the Child Development Movement in the United States," *Monographs of the Society for Research in Child Development* 40 (1975): 1–107; Esther Thelen and Karen E. Adolph, "Arnold L. Gesell: The Paradox of Nature and Nurture," *Developmental Psychology* 28 (1992): 368–80.

6 John E. Anderson, "Child Development: An Historical Perspective," *Society for the Research in Child Development* 27 (1956): 181–96; Michael Lewis and Alan Slater, "A Brief History of Infancy Research," in Alan Slater and Michael Lewis, eds. *Introduction to Infant Development,* 2nd edn. Rev. (Oxford University Press, 2007) pp. 3–17; Julia Wrigley, "Do Young Children Need Intellectual Stimulation? Experts' Advice to Parents, 1900–1985," *History of Education Quarterly* 29 (1989): 41–75; Nancy Bayley, "Research in Child Development: A Longitudinal Perspective," *Merrill-Palmer Quarterly of Behavior and Development* 11 (1965): 183–208.

7 Dennis Thompson, John D. Hogan, and Philip M. Clark, *Developmental Psychology in Historical Perspective* (Wiley-Blackwell, 2012); Anderson, "Child Development"; and Senn et al., "Insights on the Child Development Movement."

8 Robert T. Keegan and Howard E. Gruber, "Charles Darwin's Unpublished 'Diary of an Infant': An Early Phase in His Psychological Work," in George Eckardt, Wolfgang G. Bringmann, and Lothar Sprung, eds. *Contributions to a History of Developmental Psychology* (Mouton Publishers, 1982) pp. 127–45. James Mark Baldwin, *Mental Development in the Child and the Race, Methods and Processes,* 3rd edn. rev. 1894. Reprints of Economic Classics (New York, 1968).

9 Dorothy Ross, *G. Stanley Hall: The Psychologist as Prophet* (University of Chicago Press, 1972) pp. 279–340; Molly Ladd-Taylor, *Mother-Work: Women, Child Welfare, and the State, 1890–1930* (University of Illinois Press, 1994) pp. 43–73; Jeanne Brooks-Gunn and Anna Duncan Johnson, "G. Stanley Hall's Contribution to Science Practice and Policy: The Child Study, Parent Education, and Child Welfare Movements," *History of Psychology* 9 (2006): 247–68; William O. Krohn, "The Child Study Monthly," *Child Study Monthly* 1 (1895): 1; Nancy Schrom Dye and Daniel Blake Smith, "Mother Love and Infant Death, 1750–1920," *Journal of American History* 73 (1986): 329–53; and Evelyn Lincoln Coolidge, "The Young Mothers' Registry," *Ladies Home Journal* (1914): 40.

10 Anita Parkhust Wilcox Papers, 1892–1984, Box 1, Unpublished autobiography "One Woman" with hand-edited notes, p. 94, SLRI; Mrs. Winfield S. Hall, "The First 500 Days of a Child's Life," *Child Study Monthly* 2 (1896): 458.

11 Millicent W. Shinn, *The Biography of A Baby* (Houghton Mifflin, 1900); H. Roger Grant, "Viola Olerich, 'The Famous Baby Scholar': An Experiment in Education," *The Palimpsest* 56 (1975): 88–95.

12 Grace Hall Hemingway, "A Record of Ernest Miller Hemingway's Baby Days, Birth to 23 months old," Ernest Hemingway Collection, JFKL, www.jfklibrary .org/Research/The-Ernest-Hemingway-Collection/Hemingway-News/ Hemingway-Scrapbooks.aspx; Frederick Lewis Allen papers, Box 26, Folder, Baby Journals, LOC.

13 *The Babyhood Journal: A Record of Baby's Doings from the Day of Its Birth* (Contemporary Publishing Company, 1899) UCLA HQ779.B11384 1899 copy 2.

14 Bonnibel Butler, *The Baby's Record of Mental and Physical Growth and His Horoscope* (M.A. Donohue & Company, ca. 1912) UCLA HQ779.B985ba 1912.

15 A. O. Kaplan, *The New Baby's Biography* (Brentano's, 1908) UCLA HQ779. K14n 1908 copy 1; Harry Middleton Hyatt, *Folk-Lore from Adams County, Illinois*, 2nd edn. Rev. (Memoirs of the Alma Egan Hyatt Foundation, 1965) p. 144; Wayland D. Hand, " 'That the Child May Rise in the World': A Folk Belief and Custom of the Nursery," *Transactions and Studies of the College of Physicians of Philadelphia* Ser 4, 42 (1974): 77–80.

16 *Folk-Lore from Maryland*, collected by Annie Weston Whitney and Caroline Canfield Bullock (American Folk-Lore Society, 1925) p. 7; Adah Louise Sutton, *Dear Baby: A Chronicle of Baby's First Year* (Saalfield Publishing Company, 1907) UCLA HQ779.S967b 1907 copy 2; Adah Louise Sutton, *Dear Baby: A Chronicle of Baby's First Year* (Saalfield Publishing Company, 1907) UCLA HQ779.S967b 1907.

17 *The Frank C. Brown Collection of North Carolina Folklore*, Wayland D. Hand, ed. (Duke University Press, 1961) p. 35. William E. Koch, *Folklore from Kansas: Customs, Beliefs, and Superstitions* (Regents Press of Kansas, 1980) p. 53; Maud Humphrey, *Baby's Record* (Frederick A. Stokes, 1898) UCLA HQ779. H926b 1898; Christine Goldberg, "Choosing Their Futures: A Custom for Babies," *Western Folklore* 53 (1994): 178–90.

18 Frederick Bridges, *Phrenology Made Practical and Popularly Explained* (Sampson Low, Son & Company, 1857); A. O. Kaplan, *Baby's Biography* (Brentano's, 1891) UCLA HQ779.K14b 1891.

19 Bonnibel Butler, *The Baby's Record of Mental and Physical Growth and Her Horoscope* (M.A. Donohue Company, 1913) UCLA HQ779.B985ba 1913; James R. Lewis, *The Astrology Book: The Encyclopedia of Heavenly Influences* (Visible Ink Press, 2003) p. 310.

20 Children's Bureau, *Child Care and Child Welfare: Outlines for Study* Bulletin No. 65, Home Economics Series No. 5 (GPO, 1921); "Step by Step Character Leads to Success," *Parents' Magazine* 4 (1929): 58; Duke Ad Access, http://library .duke.edu/digitalcollections/sizes/protfam_prfad02044/; Steven Scholssman, "Perils of Popularization: The Founding of 'Parents' Magazine,' " *Monographs of the Society for Research in Child Development* 50 (1985): 65–77.

21 Ben Harris, " 'Give Me a Dozen Healthy Infants … John B. Watson's Popular Advice on Childrearing, Women, and the Family," in Meriam Lewin ed., *In the Shadow of the Past: Psychology Portrays the Sexes* (Columbia University Press, 1984) pp. 126–53; Kerry W. Buckley, *Mechanical Man: John Broadus Watson and the Beginnings of Behaviorism* (Guilford Press, 1989); John B. Watson, *Behaviorism* (W.W. Norton & Company, 1924); John B. Watson, *Psychological Care of Infant and Child* (W.W. Norton & Company, 1928); Senn, "Insights on the Child Development Movement," p. 29.

22 *Baby's Book* (S. S. Kresge Company, ca. 1939) UCLA HQ779.B115 1939; William E. Harris, "Baby Record Books," *Publishers Weekly* 119 (April 11, 1931): 1916–18.

23 Journal of Frances Gunther, Carton 1, Folder 5 Frances (Fineman) Gunther papers, SLRI; Fanny Y. Cory, *Our Baby Book* (Indianapolis, IN, 1907) UCLA HQ779.C833o 1907; Josephine Bruce, *A History of the Doings and Sayings of Our Baby* (New York, 1908) UCLA HQ 779.B887h 1908; Josephine Wheeler Weage, illust., *All about Me: Baby's Record* (Saalfield Publishing Company, ca. 1918) UCLA HQ779.A416 1918b; and Thompson et al., *Developmental Psychology*, pp. 177–78.

24 Box 290, Case Files, Community Service Society Archives 1842–1995, CUA.

25 John E. Anderson and Florence L. Goodenough, *Your Child Year by Year*, 4th edn. (Keep-Worthy Books, 1935).

26 Elizabeth B. Hurlock, *Modern Ways with Babies* (J. B. Lippincott, 1937) p. 7; Elizabeth B. Hurlock, *Baby's Early Years* (C.R. Gibson & Company, ca. 1952) UCLA HQ779.H965b 1952.

27 Elizabeth B. Hurlock, *Fashions for Babies* (F. W. Woolworth Company, 1949).

28 South Dakota State Board of Health, "The Mother's Book: Intelligent Mothers, Healthy Babies, Greater South Dakota" (Sentinel Press, n.d.) Box 607 Item 114949; NYAM; Better Babies Bureau, Women's Home Companion, "Hints to Mothers Who Want Better Babies (Women's Home Companion, 191?) p. 6 Box 783, Item 127992, NYAM; *Memories of Baby's Days* (C. R. Gibson & Company 1923) UCLA HQ 779.M533 1923; Melcena Denny Burns, *Book of Baby Mine* (Baby Mine Company, 1930) p. 50.

29 Babies' Milk Fund Association of Louisville, "The Care of Babies in Hot Weather," (Louisville, KY, 1908) Box 92, Item 116016, NYAM; Jessie Alma Pierson, *Babyhood Days* (Barse & Hopkins, ca.1915) UCLA HQ779.P624b 1915.

30 *Baby* (Reilly & Lee Company, 1914) UCLA HQ779.B112 1914b; Josephine Wheeler Weage, illus., *All about Me: Baby's Record* (Saalfield Publishing Company, ca. 1918) UCLA HQ779.A416 1918 copy 2.

31 Wrigley, "Do Young Children Need Intellectual Stimulation?"; Celia B. Stendler, "Psychologic Aspects of Pediatrics: Sixty Years of Child Training

Practices," *Journal of Pediatrics* 36 (1950): 122–34; Martha Wolfenstein, "Trends in Infant Care," *American Journal of Orthopsychiatry* 23 (1953): 120–30; Michael Gordon, "Infant Care Revisted," *Journal of Marriage and the Family* 30 (1968): 57–83; Jay Mechling, "Advice to Historians on Advice to Mothers," *Journal of Social History* 9 (1975): 44–63.

32 E. B. Kirkwood, "Baby with Forty Mothers: University Course in Home Making," *Ladies Home Journal* 37 (1920): 173–74; Jessaca B. Leinaweaver, "Practice Mothers," *Signs* 38 (2013): 405–30; Megan Elias, "'Model Mamas': The Domestic Partnership of Home Economics Pioneers Flora Rose and Martha van Rensselaer," *Journal of the History of Sexuality* 15 (2006): 65–88; http://rmc.library.cornell.edu/homeEc/cases/apartments.html; "Baby with 12 Mothers," *Look* 18 (May 18, 1954): 71–74.

33 Thompson, et al., *Developmental Psychology*, pp. 149–50; Harriet L. Rheingold and Nancy Bayley, "The Later Effects of an Experimental Modification in Mothering," *Child Development* 30 (1959): 363–72; Harold M. Skeels, "Adult Status of Children with Contrasting Early Life Experiences: A Follow-Up Study," *Monographs of the Society for Research in Child Development* 31 (1966): 1–65.

34 Arnold Gesell, "The Yale Clinic of Child Development," *Childhood Education* 8 (1932): 468–69; Walter R. Miles, "Arnold Lucius Gesell," Biographical Memoir (National Academy of Sciences, 1964). Gesell's books included *Infancy in Human Growth* (1928), *Infant Behavior* (1934), *The Psychology of Early Growth, Including Norms of Infant Behavior and a Method of Genetic Analysis* (1938), *The First Five Years of Life: A Guide to the Study of the Preschool Child from the Yale Clinic of Child Development* (1940), and *Infant and Child in the Culture of Today: The Guidance of Development in Home and Nursery School* (1943).

35 Arnold Gesell, "Science Service Radio Talks: How Science Studies the Child," *Scientific Monthly* 34 (1932): 265–67; Arnold Gesell, director, *Life Begins* (Yale Films of Child Development, 1934).

36 Folder, Inquiries 1938–40, Box 121 Arnold Gesell papers, LOC; F. B. Modell, *New Yorker*, August 11, 1956, p. 28.

37 Steven L. Schlossman, "Philanthropy and the Gospel of Child Development," *History of Education Quarterly* 21 (1981): 275–99.

38 Mary M. Shirley, *The First Two Years: A Study of Twenty Five Babies*, vol. II *Intellectual Development* (1933) reprint edn. (Greenwood Press, 1973).

39 Albert P. Weiss, "The Measurement of Infant Behavior," *Psychological Review* 36 (1929): 465–66; Margaret Grey Blanton, "The Behavior of the Human Infant during the First Thirty Days of Life," *Psychological Review* 24 (1917): 472; Dorothy Rose Disher et al., *Studies in Infant Behavior*, F. C. Dockery, ed. (Ohio State University Press, 1934); Alice Boardman Smuts et al., *Science in the Service of Children, 1893–1935* (Yale University Press, 2006); Mary C. Gatewood and

Albert P. Weiss, "Race and Sex Differences in Newborn Infants," *Pedagogical Seminary and Journal of Genetic Psychology* 38 (1930): 31–48.

40 Bernadine Courtwright Barr, "Spare Children, 1900–1945: Inmates of Orphanages as Subjects of Research in Medicine and in the Social Sciences in America," PhD diss. Stanford University, 1992; Susan E. Lederer, *Subjected to Science: Human Experimentation in America before the Second World War* (Johns Hopkins University Press, 1995); Henry K. Beecher, "Ethics and Clinical Research," *New England Journal of Medicine* 274 (1966): 1354–60.

41 John E. Anderson, *Experience and Behavior in Early Childhood and the Adjustment of the Same Persons as Adults* (Minneapolis Institute of Child Development, 1963); Arnold Gesell et al., *Biographies of Child Development: The Mental Growth Careers of Eighty-Four Infants and Children,* reprint (Arno, 1975) pp. 3–5, 118, 20.

42 Sara Lee Silberman, "Pioneering in Family-Centered Maternity and Infant Care: Edith B. Jackson and the Yale Rooming-in Research Project," *Bulletin of the History of Medicine* 64 (1990): 262–87.

43 Josephine H. Kenyon, "How to Keep a Baby's Record," *Good Housekeeping* 111 (1940): 128; Josephine Kenyon, *Healthy Babies Are Happy Babies: A Complete Handbook for Modern Mothers* (Little, Brown & Company, 1943).

44 Ellen Herman, *The Romance of American Psychology: Political Culture in the Age of Experts* (University of California Press, 1995); Edward A. Richards, ed. *Proceedings of the Midcentury White House Conference on Children and Youth* (Health Publications Institute, Inc., 1950).

45 Thomas Maier, *Dr. Spock: An American Life* (Harcourt, Brace & Company, 1998) pp. 3–10; Ann Hulbert, *Raising America: Experts, Parents, and a Century of Advice about Children* (Alfred A. Knopf, 2003).

8 BABIES' CHANGING TIMES

1 *Congratulations: A Magazine for Mothers* 6 (1942) UCLA HQ 779.C7492 v. 7 no 1; "... beyond the call of duty...," *Chicago Daily News* 1944 Aluminum Company of America, Duke Ad Access, http://library.duke.edu/digitalcollections/adaccess_W0372/; Jessie Alma Pierson, *Babyhood Days* (Barse & Hopkins, ca. 1915) UCLA HQ779.P624 copy 3; Kiku Adatto, "Saving for Democracy; Thrift Sacrifice and the World War II Bond Campaigns," in Joshua J. Yates and James Davison Hunter, eds. *Thrift and Thriving in America: Capitalism and Moral Order from the Puritans to the Present* (Oxford University Press, 2011) pp. 380–414.

2 *Congratulations* 6 (1942); and Faith M. Williams, "The Standard of Living in Wartime," *Annals of the American Academy of Political and Social Science* 229 (1943): 117–27.

3 Morleen Getz Rouse, "Daytime Radio Programming for the Homemaker, 1926–1956," *Journal of Popular Culture* 12 (1978): 315–27; and *Book of Baby Mine* (Grand Rapids, MI, 1935) UCLA HQ779.B724 1935 copy 2.

4 Williams, "Standard of Living in Wartime"; Elizabeth Temkin, "Driving Through: Postpartum Care during World War II," *AJPH* 89 (1999): 587–95; Lizabeth Cohen, *A Consumer's Republic: The Politics of Mass Consumption in Postwar America* (Vintage Books, 2004); David Steigerwald, "All Hail the Republic of Choice: Consumer History as Contemporary Thought," *Journal of American History* (2006): 385–403.

5 Box 287, Case Files, Community Service Society 1842–1995, CUA.

6 *Your Baby* (Pet Milk Company, 1943) UCLA WS113 Y803 1943; Marquis W. Childs, *This Is Your War* (Little, Brown & Company, 1942) p. 22; Joanne Lamb Hayes, *Grandma's Wartime Kitchen: World War II and the Way We Cooked* (New York: St. Martin's Press, 2000) p. 4; US Bureau of Labor Statistics, *How American Buying Habits Are Changing* (1959) reprint (Greenwood Press, 1969) p. 100; Richard Osborn Cummings, *The American and His Food: A History of Food Habits in the United States* (University of Chicago Press, 1940) p. 173; Ronald R. Kline, *Consumers in the Country: Technology and Social Change in Rural America* (Johns Hopkins University Press, 2000) p. 201.

7 Dorothy V. Whipple, *Our American Babies: The Art of Baby Care* (M. Barrows & Company, 1944) pp. 8–11; Amy Bentley, *Eating for Victory: Food Rationing and the Politics of Domesticity* (University of Illinois Press, 1998).

8 Letter to Miss Dorothy Stote, Editor, *Infant's & Children's Wear Review,* June 14, 1943 Folder 4-8-4-0, Box I06, USCB Central File, 1941–44, RG 102 NARA II; *The Life Journal of [blank line] Presented by [blank line] on [blank line]* (Richard C. Krueger, Inc. ca. 1941) UCLA HQ779.L719 1941.

9 Box 105, USCB Central File 1941–44 RG 102 NARA II; Letter to the Children's Bureau, Folder 4-8-1-3-2, Box 106, USCB Central File 1941–44, RG 102, USCB, NARA II.

10 Rouse, "Daytime Radio"; "Baby Institute" Folder, Box 8, Papers of Maxwell Gitelson, LOC; "The Blue Network Today: A Memorandum on Its first Independent Year, and Its Present Position in the American System of Broadcasting" (Blue Network Company, 1943) pp. 7–8.

11 "Heinz Test," *Broadcasting* 24 (March 29, 1943): 10; http://american radiohistory.com/Archive-BC/BC-1943/1943-03-29-BC.pdf; *Your Baby's Diary and Calendar* (H. J. Heinz, 1945) UCLA HQ770.H805 1945; "Pied Piper," *New Yorker* (February 13, 1954): 24.

12 "Business World," *New York Times,* June 13, 1941, p. 28; and *General Maximum Price Regulations* (Office of Price Administration, 1942) p. 16.

13 Shigeko Sese Uno, http://archive.densho.org/Resource/popuptext.aspx?v=s&i=denshovh-ushigeko-01-0015&t=Shigeko+Sese+Uno+Segment+15+Transcript; Ruth Y. Okimoto, http://archive.densho.org/Resource/popuptext.aspx?v=s&i=denshovh-oruth-01-0010&t=Ruth+Y.+Okimoto+Interview+Segment+10+TranscriptInterview; Fumiko Hayashida, http://archive.densho.org/Resource/popuptext.aspx?v=s&i=denshovh-hfumiko-01-0025&t=Fumiko+Hayashida+Segment+25+Transcript; Louis Fiset, "Public Health in World War II Assembly Centers for Japanese Americans," *Bulletin of the History of Medicine* 73 (1999): 565–84; Louis Fiset, *Camp Harmony: Seattle's Japanese Americans and the Puyallup Assembly Center* (University of Illinois Press, 2009); Susan L. Smith, "Women Health Workers and the Color Line in the Japanese American 'Relocation Centers' of World War II," *Bulletin of the History of Medicine* 73 (1999): 585–601.

14 "450 Baby Formula Prepared Daily," *Daily Tulean Dispatch*, August 7, 1942, p. 2, http://archive.densho.org/Resource/popupenlarged.aspx?i=denshopd-i65-00014; "Baby Formula," *Tulare News*, August 8, 1942, pp. 1, 4, http://archive.densho.org/Resource/popupenlarged.aspx?i=denshopd-i197-00028; "Babies Fed Scientifically," *Fresno Grapevine*, June 6, 1942, p. 3, http://archive.densho.org/Resource/popupenlarged.aspx?i=denshopd-i190-00005; Japanese American Relocation Project, Box 43 File 5, UCLA Special Collections; Aiko Herzig, Interview Segment 10, http://archive.densho.org/Resource/popuptext.aspx?v=s&i=denshovh-haiko-02-0010&t=Aiko+Herzig+Interview+Segment+10+Transcript.

15 "Baby Clinic to Be at Hospital," *Rohwer Outpost*, October 25, 1944, p. 3; "Life Begins," *Rohwer Outpost*, July 5, 1944, http://archive.densho.org/Resource/popupenlarged.aspx?i=denshopd-i143-00181; "Six New Babies over Week-End," *Manzanar Free Press*, August 10, 1942, p. 1, http://archive.densho.org/Resource/popupenlarged.aspx?i=denshopd-i125-00045; "Center Wide Baby Show Slated for Next Week," *Heart Mountain Sentinel*, November 18, 1944, p. 3, http://archive.densho.org/Resource/popupenlarged.aspx?i=denshopd-i97-00207; Gwenn M. Jensen, "System Failure: Health Care Deficiencies in the Japanese American Detention Centers," *Bulletin of the History of Medicine* 73 (1999): 602–28.

16 US Department of Labor, *Administrative Politics, Emergency Maternity and Infant Care Program, EMIC Information Circular No. 1, December 1943* (GPO, 1943); Child Welfare League of America, "The Impact of War on Children's Services" (Child Welfare League of America, 1943); Karen Kruse Thomas, "'Law unto Themselves': Black Women as Patients and Practitioners in North Carolina's Campaign to Reduce Maternal and Infant Mortality," *Nursing History Review* 12 (2004): 47–66.

17 Stuart W. Adler, "Medical Care for Dependents of Men in Military Service," *American Journal of Public Health* 33 (1943): 645–50; "Corporal Kelly and His Son: The Emergency Maternity and Infant Care Program," *American Journal of Nursing* 44 (1944): 366–70; Martha M. Eliot, "Experience with the Administration of a Medical Care Program for Wives and Infants of Enlisted Men," *American Journal of Public Health* 34 (1944): 34–39; Nathan Sinai and Odin W. Anderson, *EMIC (Emergency Maternity and Infant Care): A Study of Administrative Experience*, Bureau of Public Health Economics, Research Series No. 3, (School of Public Health, University of Michigan, 1948); *The Emergency Maternity and Infant Care Program*, rev. edn. (GPO, 1945); Oral History of Katherine Bain, MD, December 12, 1996, American Academy of Pediatrics, www.aap.org/en-us/about-the-aap/Pediatric-History-Center/Documents/Bain.pdf; Barbara Starfield, "Motherhood and Apple Pie: The Effectiveness of Medical Care for Children," *Milbank Memorial Fund Quarterly* 63 (1985): 523–46.

18 John I. Robinson, "The Dependents' Medical Care Program," *American Journal of Public Health* 47 (1957): 1552–55.

19 Susan E. Riley, "Caring for Rosie's Children: Federal Child Care Policies in the World War II Era," *Polity* 26 (1994): 655–75; James L. Hymes Jr., "The Kaiser Child Service Centers – 50 Years Later, Some Memories and Lessons," *Journal of Education*, 177 (1995): 23–38; Hearing before the Committee on Education and Labor, US Senate, 78th Congress, 1st. Sess, "Wartime Care and Protection of Children," June 8, 1943.

20 Jane Lynott Carroll, "Raising a Baby on Shifts," *Parent's Magazine* 18 (1943): 18, 20, 77–78.

21 Hermien D. Nusbaum, *Our Baby's First Seven Years*, new and rev. edn. (Mothers' Aid of the Chicago Lying-In Hospital, 1943) UCLA HQ779 O928 1943, copy 2; May Farini, *Baby's Days and Baby's Ways* (C. R. Gibson & Company, ca. 1943) UCLA HQ779.F227b 1943; Lawrence L. Foley and Chas. D. McMillin, *Log-o'-Life* (Mc-Millin Foley Publishing Company, ca. 1939) UCLA HQ779 L831 1939; Frances Brundage, *Our Baby* (Raphael Tuck & Sons, not after 1914) UCLA HQ779.B894o 1914.

22 "CDC on Infant and Maternal Mortality in the United States: 1900–1999," *Population and Development Review* 25 (1999): 821–26; Price V. Fishback and Michael R. Haines, "The Impact of the New Deal on Black and White Infant Mortality in the South," *Explorations in Economic History* 38 (2001): 93–122; Baby Book of Leslie Anne Hoag/Hope Ms. Coll 501.028 UCLA.

23 Elizabeth Carpenter Tandy, "The Health Situation of Negro Mothers and Babies in the United States" (GPO, 1940); "The End of EMIC," *Social*

Service Review 21 (1947): 402–03; Price V. Fishback and Michael R. Haines, "The Impact of the New Deal on Black and White Infant Mortality in the South," *Explorations in Economic History* 38 (2001): 93–22; Gopal K. Singh and Stella M. Yu, "Infant Mortality in the United States: Trends, Differentials, and Projections, 1950 through 2010," *American Journal of Public Health* 85 (1995): 957–64; Edward H. Beardsley, *A History of Neglect; Health Care for Blacks and Mill Workers in the Twentieth-Century South* (University of Tennessee Press, 1987); Carolyn Leonard Carson, "And the Results Showed Promise ... Physicians, Childbirth, and Southern Black Migrant Women, 1916–1930: Pittsburgh as Case Study," *Journal of American Ethnic History* 14 (1994): 31–64; Ellen J. Stekert, "Focus for Conflict: Southern Mountain Medical Beliefs in Detroit," *Journal of American Folklore* 83 (1970): 115–47.

24 "Table Ab40-51 Crude Birth Rate and General Fertility Rate by Race: 1800–1998," *Historical Statistics of the United States,* Millennial Edition, online; Central Intelligence Agency, World Fact Book, www.cia.gov/library/publications/the-world-factbook/rankorder/2054rank.html; Fielding Ogburn, "War, Babies, and the Future," (Public Affairs Committee, Inc., 1943) p. 4, Box 585, Item 131714, NYAM; Victor Lebow, "The Nature of Postwar Retail Competition," *Journal of Marketing* 9 (1944): 11–18; Ray E. Baber, "Marriage and Family after the War," *Annals of the American Academy of Political and Social Science* 229 (1943) 164–75; Lizabeth Cohen, *A Consumer's Republic: The Politics of Mass Consumption in Postwar America* (Alfred A. Knopf, 2003).

25 Lois Meek Stolz, "The Effect of Mobilization and War on Children," in Edward A. Richards, ed. *Proceedings of the Midcentury White House Conference on Children and Youth* (Health Publications Institute, 1950) pp. 111–22; Aileen Hogan, "Bomb Born Babies," *Public Health Nursing* 43 (1951): 383–85.

26 Letter, August 27, 1961; Box Public Correspondence, August 1960–February 1962, Benjamin Spock Papers, SYR; Letter, January 10, 1962, Box Public Correspondence, August 1960–February 1962, Benjamin Spock Papers, SYR.

27 Angela N. H. Creager, "Radiation, Cancer, and Mutation in the Atomic Age, *Historical Studies in the Natural Sciences* 45 (2015): 14–48; Allan M. Winkler, "The 'Atom' and American Life," *The History Teacher* 26 (1993): 317–37; "St. Louis Baby Teeth Survey, 1959–1970," http://beckerexhibits.wustl.edu/dental/articles/babytooth.html; Paul Boyer, *By the Bomb's Early Light: American Thought and Culture at the Dawn of the Atomic Age* (Pantheon, 1985); Letter, May 12, 1962, Box Public Correspondence March 1962–May 1963, Benjamin Spock Papers, SYR.

28 Letter, November 12, 1960, Box Public Correspondence, August 1960–February 1962, Benjamin Spock Papers, SYR.

29 Urie Bronfenbrenner, "The Changing American Child – A Speculative Analysis," *Merrill-Palmer Quarterly of Behavior and Development* 7 (1961): 73–84; Michael Zuckerman, "Dr. Spock: The Confidence Man," in Charles E. Rosenberg, ed. *The Family in History* (University of Pennsylvania Press, 1975) pp. 179–207.

30 C. Anderson Aldrich and Mary M. Aldrich, *Babies Are Human Beings: An Interpretation of Growth* (Macmillan, 1941) p. 102; Benjamin Spock, "C. Anderson Aldrich" [obituary], *Psychosomatic Medicine* 11 (1949): 249; Stella B. Applebaum, *Baby: A Mother's Manual* (Ziff-Davis, 1946) p. 72.

31 Alan Petigny, *The Permissive Society, America, 1941–1965* (Cambridge University Press, 2009); Ellen Herman, *The Romance of American Psychology: Political Culture in the Age of Experts* (University of California Press, 1995); William Graebner, "The Unstable World of Benjamin Spock: Social Engineering in a Democratic Culture, 1917–1950," *Journal of American History* 67 (1980): 612–29.

32 Emily Post, *Children Are People and Ideal Parents Are Comrades* (Funk and Wagnalls Company, 1940) pp. 6–7; Allan Roy Defoe, *How to Raise Your Baby* (Bartholomew House, 1942) p. 20; *Baby's First Years* (Brown & Bigelow, 1939) UCLA HQ 779. B11577 1939 copy 2; Josephine Hemenway Kenyon, *Healthy Babies Are Happy Babies*, 3rd edn. Rev. (Little, Brown, & Company, 1943) p. vii.

33 Ruth Schwartz Cowen, *More Work for Mother: The Irony of Household Technology from the Open Hearth to the Microwave* (Basic Books, 1985); Nancy Pottishman Weiss, "Mother, the Invention of Necessity: Dr. Benjamin Spock's B and Child Care," *American Quarterly* 29 (1977): 519–46; Rima D. Apple, *Perfect Motherhood: Science and Childrearing in America* (Rutgers University Press, 2006).

9 BABY BOOM BABIES

1 Clair Brown, *American Standards of Living, 1918–1988* (Blackwell, 1994) pp. 187–267; "No, Your Post-war Admiral Radio Won't Bathe the Baby," *Colliers*, 1944, Ad Access Duke, http://library.duke.edu/digitalcollections/adaccess_R0062.

2 "There's Nothing Like It on Earth for Traveling with a Baby!" *Good Housekeeping*, 1949, Ad Access, http://library.duke.edu/digitalcollections/adaccess_T0350/.

3 US Department of Health Education and Welfare, *Vital Statistics of the United States 1965* vol. 1 Natality, (1967) Table I-24, www.nber.org/vital-stats-books/nat65_1.CV.pdf; Lawrence J. Clark et al., "The Impact of Hill-Burton: An Analysis of Hospital Bed and Physician Distribution in the United States, 1950–1970," *Medical Care* 18 (1980): 532–50; Max D. Bennett, "Influence of

Health Insurance on Patterns of Care: Maternity Hospitalization," *Inquiry* 12 (1975): 59–66; The Nursery Kit (ca. 1955) UCLA Ms. coll. No. 502.013.

4 Arlene M. Butz et al., "Newborn Identification, Compliance with AAP Guidelines for Perinatal Care," *Clinical Pediatrics* 32 (1993): 111–13; *Better Homes & Gardens Baby Book* (Meredith Publishing Company, 1947) UCLA HQ779.B565b 1947; *Baby's Own* (Wise Remembrance Company, 1952) UCLA HQ779.B118 1952.

5 Janet Laura Scott, *Our Baby's Book: From Birth to Seven Years* (C. R. Gibson & Company, 1948) UCLA HQ779.S429ba 1948; Ruth Caroline Eger, *Baby's Own Story: The First Five Years* (s.l., ca. 1939) UCLA HQ779.E29b 1939; Baby book of Sally Ann Griffith, in author's possession; *Congratulations: A Magazine for Mothers* 16 (April 1952): 22. UCLA HQ779.C7492.

6 CDC Vaccines and Immunizations, www.cdc.gov/vaccines/pubs/pinkbook/ meas.html; Walter A. Orenstein, Mark J. Papania, and Melinda E. Wharton, "Measles Elimination in the United States," *Journal of Infectious Diseases* 189 (2004) Suppl. 1, S1–S3; David M. Oshinsky, *Polio: An American Story* (Oxford University Press, 2006); Paul Starr, *The Social Transformation of American Medicine* (Basic Books, 1982); and Jeffrey P. Baker, "Immunization and the American Way: 4 Childhood Vaccines," *American Journal of Public Health* 90 (2000): 199–207.

7 Benjamin Spock, *Common Sense Book of Baby and Child Care* (Duell, Sloan & Pearce, 1946) pp. 187–92; Letter February 1961 and reply February 1961, Box, Public Correspondence, August 1960–February 1962, Benjamin Spock papers, SYR; Jeffrey P. Baker and Samuel Katz, "Childhood Vaccine Development: An Overview," *Pediatric Research* 55 (2004): 347–56; Dorothy Martin, *Baby Days* (C. R. Gibson & Company, 1954) HQ779.B1134 1954.

8 *Our Baby's Album* (s.l., ca. 1950) UCLA HQ779.O9214 1950; *Life with Baby* (Glendale Knitting Corporation, ca. 1946) UCLA HQ779.L722 1946; *Our Baby's Book* (s.l., ca. 1951) UCLA HQ779.O914 1951.

9 Amy Bentley, *Inventing Baby Food: Taste, Health, and the Industrialization of the American Diet* (University of California Press, 2014) p. 58 and passim; Lynn Welner, "Baby Food," in Andrew F. Smith, ed., *Oxford Encyclopedia of Food and Drink in America* (Oxford University Press, 2004) online edition www .oxfordreference.com/view/10.1093/acref 97801951; and www.trademarkia .com/babies-are-our-business–our-only-business-72017273.html.

10 *Foods for Baby, Vegetables, Fruits, Cereals, Soups, and Mealtime Psychology* (Gerber Products Company, 1939) UCLA W6.C697 v.29 box 2 no. 9 1939.

11 US Department of Health, Education and Welfare, *Infant Care*, Children's Bureau Publication No. 8 (GPO, 1955) p. 21; "No One Eats Better Than the Baby," *Look* 18 (May 4, 1951): 96–97.

12 Folder, Beech-Nut 1962–64, Box 132 Consumer Magazine Baby Food, D'Arcy
Masius Benton & Bowles Archives, 1929–95, HART; "Quadruplets, Boy and 3
Girls, Are Born to Rego Park Couple," *New York Times*, October 24, 1963, p. 35.

13 Jane Nickerson, "News of Food," *New York Times*, August 27, 1947, p. 26;
Box 63, Folder "General Foods – Birds Eye" 1960–61, "Frozen Instant Baby
Food" incl. Newspaper, HART; Box 61, Folder 11; Business Promotion, Baby
Food Companies, 1970–74, Raymond Loewy Papers, LOC; http://education
.ssc.nasa.gov/fft_halloffame.asp; and www.gerber.com/why-gerber/our-
history-and-heritage.

14 John E. Anderson and Florence L. Goodenough, *Your Child Year by Year: A
Developmental Record and Guide from Birth to the 16th Year*, 8th edn. (Keep-
Worthy Books, Inc., 1945) UCLA HQ779.A54m 1945; *Better Homes & Gardens
Baby Book: A Handbook for Mothers from Prenatal Care to the Child's Sixth Year*
(Better Homes & Gardens Child Care and Training Department, 1946)
UCLA HQ779.B565b 1946; Review of "Our Baby's First Seven Years," *Time*
71 (February 28, 1958) p. 40; *Our Baby's First Seven Years: A Baby Record Book
Including Scientific Charts Which Will Prove of Practical Service to the Mother and
Growing Child*, new edn. (Mother's Aid of the Chicago Lying-In Hospital,
1956) UCLA HQ779.0928 1956; Peter N. Stearns, Perrin Rowland, and Lori
Giarnella, "Children's Sleep: Sketching Historical Change," *Journal of Social
History* 30 (1996): 345–66.

15 Lawrence L. Foley, *Log-o'-life* (Cleveland, OH, 1939) UCLA HQ 779.L831
1939 copy 3.

16 Hermien D. Nusbaum, *Our Baby's First Seven Years*, rev. edn. (University of
Chicago, 1938) UCLA HQ779.0928 1928; Hermien D. Nusbaum, *Our Baby's
First Seven Years*, new and rev. edn. (University of Chicago, 1941) UCLA
HQ779.0928 1941; *Your Baby's Diary and Calendar* (H. J. Heinz Company,
1948) UCLA HQ779.Y805 1948.

17 Baby book of James Walton, copy in author's possession.

18 Edward A. Richards, ed. *Proceedings of the Midcentury White House Conference
on Children and Youth* (Health Publications Institute, Inc., 1950); Hermien
D. Nusbaum, *Our Baby's First Seven Years*, rev. edn. (University of Chicago,
1938) UCLA HQ779.0928 1928; Joseph Shapiro baby book, in author's
possession.

19 Henry H. Goddard, "Wanted: A Child to Adopt," *Survey* 27 (1911): 1003–09;
Viviana A. Zelizer, "From Baby Farms to Baby M," *Society* 25 (1988): 23–28;
Ellen Herman, *Kinship by Design: A History of Adoption in the Modern United
States* (University of Chicago Press, 2008); Arnold Gesell, "Psychoclinical
Guidance in Child Adoption," US Children's Bureau, *Foster Home Care for
Dependent Children* (GPO, 1926) p. 204.

20 Letter, April 20, 1933, Folder, Clinical Case Inquires, 1929–35, Box 59, Arnold Gesell papers, LOC; Letter, March 11, 1940, Adoption Folder, Box 45 Arnold Gesell Papers, LOC; and Theresa R. Richardson, *The Century of the Child: The Mental Hygiene Movement and Social Policy in the United States and Canada* (State University of New York Press, 1989) p. 135.

21 Vernon Pope, "Yale University's Clinic of Child Development Shows How a Baby's Mind Grows," *Saturday Evening Post* 215 (May 15, 1943): 20–21, 74–75; and Anonymous, "We Adopt a Child," *Atlantic Monthly* 165 (1940): 316–23.

22 Children's Bureau, *Adoption Laws in the United States: A Summary of the Development of Adoption Legislation and Significant Features of Adoption Statutes, with the Text of Selected Laws*, Publication No. 148 (GPO); Ellen Herman, "The Paradoxical Rationalization of Modern Adoption," *Journal of Social History* 36 (2002): 339–85.

23 Arnold Gesell, *Infancy and Human Growth* (Macmillan Company, 1928) p. 385; E. Wayne Carp and Anna Leon-Guerro, "When in Doubt, Count: World War II as a Watershed in the History of Adoption," in E. Wayne Carp, ed. *Adoption in America* (University of Michigan Press, 2002) pp. 181–217; Frances Lockridge, *Adopting a Child* (Greenberg, 1947) pp. 12, 91; Herman, *Kinship by Design*; Ellen Herman, "Families Made by Science; Arnold Gesell and the Technologies of Modern Child Adoption," *Isis* 92 (2001): 684–715; Herman, "Paradoxical Rationalization of Modern Adoption."

24 Spock, *Common Sense Book of Baby and Child Care*, pp. 503–05.

25 Frances Lockridge, *Adopting a Child* (Reader Service, 1948) p. 16.

26 Eleana J. Kim, *Adopted Territory; Transnational Korean Adoptees and the Politics of Belonging* (Duke University Press, 2010).

27 Letter, October 22, 1962, Box 11, Jolane Baumgarten Solomon Papers, SLRI.

28 "Chicago Foundlings Home Report July 1942," Box 278 Welfare Council of Metropolitan Chicago Archives, 1914–78, CHM; William Robert Johnston, "Historical Statistics on Adoption in the United States, Plus Statistics on Child Population and Welfare," www.johnstonarchive.net/policy/adoptionstats.html.

29 Regina G. Kunzel, *Fallen Women, Problem Girls: Unmarried Mothers and the Professionalization of Social Work, 1890–1945* (Yale University Press, 1993).

30 "Juvenile Delinquency (Interstate Adoption Practices)." Hearings before the Subcommittee to Investigate Juvenile Delinquency of the Committee on the Judiciary, Eighty-Fourth Congress, November 14 and 15, 1955 (Washington, DC, 1956) [hereafter Interstate Adoption Practices, November 1955] p. 257.

31 Paula F. Pfeffer, "Homeless Children, Childless Homes," *Chicago History* (1987): 51–65; "Black Market Babies Now Cost $2,500 in Brooklyn, Doctor Says," *New York Times*, June 8, 1947, p. 1; "'Baby Market' Charged," *New York*

Times, September 13, 1950; "'Baby Market' Charged: Memphis Foundling 'Sales' Estimated at $1,000,000," *New York Times,* September 13, 1950, p. 23; Linda Tollett Austin, *Babies for Sale: The Tennessee Children's Home Adoption Scandal* (Praeger, 1993); "4 Doctors among 9 Indicted Here in a $500,00 Baby Black Market," *New York Times,* November 2, 1951, p. 1; Elizabeth Toomey, "Baby Black Market with Disregard to Boundary Flourishes as Price Varies from $3500 to Medic Fee," *Times-News,* January 23, 1954, p. 3.

32 Milton MacKaye, "The Cradle," *Saturday Evening Post,* April 9, 1938, pp. 12–13, 95–100; Katherine F. Lenroot to Eleanor Roosevelt, March 4, 1944, Children's Bureau Papers, Box 169 Folder 7-3-3-4 Adoption History Project, http://pages.uoregon.edu/adoption/archive/LenroottoERltr.htm

33 Interstate Adoption Practices, July, 1955, p. 3.

34 Interstate Adoption Practices, July 1955, pp. 82–88.

35 "Senate Opens Study into Baby-Selling," *New York Times,* June 17, 1965, p. 29.

36 Kraft Television Theater, "Babies for Sale," NBC Television: directed by Alan Anderson, July 18, 1956.

37 "8 Seized in Baby-Selling Ring; Million-Dollar Racket Charged," *New York Times,* September 25, 1959, p. 12; and "Family Income in the United States: 1955," *Current Population Reports* Series P-60, No. 24 (Washington, DC, 1957) p. 1, www2.census.gov/prod2/popscan/p60-024.pdf.

38 Lockridge, *Adopting a Child,* p. 16; Marian A. McLeod, *All about You: An Adopted Child's Memory Book* (C.R. Gibson & Company, 1959).

39 Carp and Leon-Guerro, "When in Doubt, Count"; Brian Paul Gill, "Adoption Agencies and the Search for the Ideal Family," in *Adoption in America,* pp. 181–217; Ronald Kotulak, "'You Keep Baby,' Mothers Tell Hospital," *Chicago Tribune,* April 12, 1964.

40 Letter from Catherine Strunk Amatruda, July 29, 1935, Folder Clinical Cases 1929–35, Box 59, Arnold Gesell Papers, LOC.

41 Elizabeth L. Brennan, "A Matter of Difference: A Contextual Perspective on the History of Children with Mental Retardation in the United States," in Philip L. Safford and Elizabeth J. Safford, eds. *Children with Disabilities in America: A Historical Handbook and Guide* (Greenwood Press, 2006) pp. 65–86. Spock, *Common Sense Book of Baby and Child Care,* pp. 502–03; Letter, May 1961, Box Public Correspondence, August 1960–February 1962, Spock Papers; Letter, July 1, 1963, Box Public Correspondence, March 1962–May 1963, Spock Papers, SYR; Rima D. Apple, *Perfect Motherhood: Science and Childrearing in America* (Rutgers University Press, 2006) p. 131.

42 Leslie J. Reagan, *Dangerous Pregnancies: Mothers, Disabilities, and Abortion in Modern America* (University of California Press, 2010).

CODA

1 "Achievements in Public Health, 1900–1999: Healthier Mothers and Babies," www.cdc.gov/mmwr/preview/mmwrhtml/mm4838a2.htm.

2 Myron E. Wegman, "Infant Mortality in the 20th Century, Dramatic But Univen Progress," *Journal of Nutrition* 131 (2001): 4015–85; and Marian F. MacDorman, T. J. Matthews, Ashna D. Mohangoo, and Jennifer Zeitlin, "International Comparisons of Infant Mortality and Related Factors: United States and Europe, 2010," *National Vital Statistics Report* 63 (2014), www.cdc .gov/nchs/data/nvsr/nvsr63/nvsr63_05.pdf.

3 Bernadette D. Proctor, Jessica L. Semega, Melissa A. Kollar, "Income and Poverty in the United States: 2015," US Census Bureau, www.census.gov/ library/publications/2016/demo/p60-256.html; "What Is 'Deep Poverty?'" Center for Poverty Research, University of California, Davis, www.census.gov/ library/publications/2016/demo/p60-256.html; Eduardo Porter, "Giving Every Child a Monthly Check for an Even Start," October 18, 2016, *New York Times*, www.nytimes.com/2016/10/19/business/economy/giving-every-child-a-monthly-check-for-an-even-start.html; and Mercedes Ekono, Yang Jiang, and Sheila Smith, "Young Children in Deep Poverty," National Center for Children in Poverty, Columbia University, Mailman School of Public Health, January 2016, www.cdc.gov/mmwr/preview/mmwrhtml/mm4838a2.htm.

4 Dave Gilson, "Politicians Kissing Babies: A Short History," *Mother Jones*, January 17, 2012, www.motherjones.com/media/2012/01/politicians-kissing-babies-brief-history.

INDEX